CONTEMPORARY WOMEN NOVELISTS

A COLLECTION OF CRITICAL ESSAYS

Edited by
Patricia Meyer Spacks

Prentice-Hall, Inc.   A SPECTRUM BOOK *Englewood Cliffs, N.J.*

Library of Congress Cataloging in Publication Data
Main entry under title:

CONTEMPORARY WOMEN NOVELISTS.

(Twentieth century views) (A Spectrum Book)
Bibliography: p.
    1. English fiction — Women authors — History and
criticism — Addresses, essays, lectures.
2. American fiction — Women authors — History and
criticism — Addresses, essays, lectures.   3. English
fiction — 20th century — History and criticism —
Addresses, essays, lectures.   4. American fiction
— 20th century — History and criticism — Addresses,
essays, lectures.   5. Women in literature — Addresses,
essays, lectures.   I. Spacks, Patricia Ann Meyer.
PR116.C6   813'.03   77-4503
ISBN 0-13-171330-2
ISBN 0-13-171322-1 pbk.

813.509
C 761

10   9   8   7   6   5   4   3   2

PRENTICE-HALL INTERNATIONAL, INC., *London*
PRENTICE-HALL OF AUSTRALIA PTY. LIMITED, *Sydney*
PRENTICE-HALL OF CANADA, LTD., *Toronto*
PRENTICE-HALL OF INDIA PRIVATE LIMITED, *New Delhi*
PRENTICE-HALL OF JAPAN, INC., *Tokyo*
PRENTICE-HALL OF SOUTHEAST ASIA PTE. LTD., *Singapore*
WHITEHALL BOOKS LIMITED, *Wellington, New Zealand*

Acknowledgments

The quotation from *The Man without Qualities* by Robert Musil (London: Secker & Warburg, 1960-61), vol I, p. 130, translated by Eithne Wilkins and Ernst Kaiser, is used by kind permission of the publisher.

Quotations from *The Street* by Ann Petry are used by permission of Houghton Mifflin Company. Copyright © renewed 1974 by Ann Petry.

Quotations from *Country Place* by Ann Petry are used by permission of Houghton Mifflin Company and Russell & Volkening Inc. Copyright © renewed 1974 by Ann Petry.

Contents

Introduction

by Patricia Meyer Spacks

I

Why consider a miscellaneous assortment of recent women novelists in conjunction with one another? The enterprise needn't imply the assumption that a work can be comprehended only in relation to its author, much less the more specific view that gender determines the nature of creation. Such a collection, however, suggests commitment at least to ask questions about precisely such matters. Twentieth-century views of contemporary women novelists reflect the same dilemmas as twentieth-century views of women in general. Sociologists, psychoanalysts, anthropologists—as well as literary critics—have trouble agreeing about exactly what difference sex makes. Some critics assume that authorial sex determines narrative and ideological content; some choose to ignore even a hint of such possibility. (Compromise positions, of course, are also possible.) At either extreme, the fundamental quandary remains: is the woman novelist a special breed?

Critical discussion of women writers seems even now at a primitive stage, although women have written a large proportion of published novels ever since the genre first developed in the eighteenth century. Ford Madox Ford has an established place in literary history; his close associate Jean Rhys must be "introduced." A bibliography of current work on twentieth-century literature lists 216 items; fourteen of them concern women writers. An author like Doris Lessing, the content of whose work has immediate political relevance, receives a great deal of often doctrinaire attention; but Eudora Welty as a novelist continues almost unnoticed by critics in comparison with, for example, William Faulkner. Conceivably the relative invisibility of women writers reflects special critical difficulty in dealing with them.

Yet the tentative air of much criticism about women does not necessarily weaken it. Although the need to summarize and explain may preempt space and preclude subtle literary analysis or definitive judgment, it can contribute to a special sense of urgency. Instead of refining established dicta or carving a fretwork from familiar material, critics of women novelists, demanding attention for what has been hardly noticed, often cover expanses of new ground. Their relation to that vexed question of the author's importance to the work frequently has particular immediacy, although every resolution of the question seems to involve the critic in difficulties. Affirmation of the author's importance can lead, depending on the critic's commitments and biases, to patronizing allowances for the novelist's sex or to blanket glorification; separation of the creation from its creator, on the other hand, may simplify the problem of investigation at the cost of eliminating vital sources of aesthetic complexity. Equally perplexing related issues, familiar in other contexts, urgently plague the critic of women. What part does ideology play in fiction; must one assess the novelist's doctrine as well as her art? How do the critic's personal involvements affect his or her presentation of a text?

One may hope to achieve "objectivity" by evading such issues: concentrating on fictional technique and ignoring the author's gender. Some of the essays here included demonstrate the value of this mode. John Edward Hardy, approaching Eudora Welty with respectful attention to her use of novelistic detail, makes penetrating discriminations; Linda Kuehl shows a similar attitude toward Iris Murdoch; Malcolm Bradbury dispassionately examines Muriel Spark's conspicuous abstinence from passion. All consider the ways in which the novelist manipulates character, plot, and symbol to create her special effects, giving only peripheral importance to what she has to say—or, more accurately, suggesting how the technique *is* the saying. Extensions of this essentially formalist approach emerge in Joyce Carol Oates's review of Welty, stressing the "musicality" of a novel and trying to determine the nature of its art. Dagmar Barnouw and Frederick Karl on Lessing, despite their considerable interest in the philosophic and political implications of her fiction, insist on the vital link between subject and technique in her novels; Lessing, of course, calls emphatic attention to her own technique and its meanings in her best-known work, *The Golden Notebook,* despite its strong ideological bias.

Emphasis on technique as the foundation of critical investigation yields varying results. Kuehl, citing Murdoch's dictum that form "is the artist's consolation and ...temptation," attempts to demonstrate that the novelist's concern with form at the expense of character seriously weakens her achievement. Hardy, dealing with Welty's *Delta Wedding*, argues that "the most important thing about the novel is its formal structure," the sacrifice of character to form epitomizing Welty's special accomplishment. As the essays embodying these contradictory points of view illustrate, approaching a novel through its formal principles offers provocative possibilities. Hardy's concept of form includes more than Kuehl's. His critique begins with certain obvious aspects of subject matter in *Delta Wedding*, maintaining that only by perceiving their formal importance in the total structure can one properly assess, for example, the intricate relationships of characters within the novel. Rightly understood, the novel can and does "establish for itself the perspective in which we are to look at its features": the perspective from which we perceive the book as a constructed whole and seek the elements of its construction. The kind of "form" Hardy praises, in other words, profoundly organic, cannot be separated finally from content.

"Besides being damaged by predetermined roles and ambivalent detachment," Kuehl writes of Murdoch's characters, they "are additionally dehumanized by the mechanical parts they are forced to play." Bradbury's enthusiasm for Spark as someone in the process of becoming "a particularly distinguished novelist" focuses on her deliberate dehumanization of her characters (her work "seems finally to deny the notion of personal authenticity"), her subordination of personality to plot, her increasing stress on plot as an end in itself: "The curious inescapability of plot is her subject, and in some real sense her satisfaction." No split mars the tight structures Spark employs; she presents her work as that of an aesthetician, her aesthetics implying moral as well as artistic conviction. Bradbury implies that hers is a peculiarly twentieth-century mode, breaking definitively with the techniques of a past even as recent as that of Henry James. Spark's form does not, like Welty's, derive from the substance of her novels; it supplies that substance. Bradbury records the reverberations of this central truth.

These three essays, then, approach their subjects through technique for very different purposes. All three—and, in fact, all the essays in this collection—possess the special energy which comes from partisanship in critical debate. Hardy defends Welty against the charge of upholding anachronistic racial and social attitudes by showing how the views expressed in her novel partake in an intricately imagined form. Kuehl joins in the attack on Murdoch for subordinating realism to artifice without adequately justifying her procedure. Bradbury tries to rescue Spark from accusations of sterility by demonstrating the value of her abstinence from traditional means of gaining narrative richness and verisimilitude for the particular meaning she conveys. Hardy, in other words, claims by implication that a novelist bears no necessary responsibility for any opinion communicated in her novel and need express no view of life; Kuehl wants the novelist to convey a coherent attitude toward life and art; Bradbury maintains that a coherent view of art is identical with an attitude toward life. The incompatibility of the implied standards of course derives partly from the fact that the essays suggesting them concern three different novelists. But, conversely, critical preference for one writer over another, like distaste for a particular kind of novelistic performance, often issues from specific intellectual commitments. The novelists treated in this book appear to demand in their practice an eclectic range of critical standards. By the assumptions which make it possible to admire Spark, Welty seems an old-fashioned and irrelevant writer; conversely, Welty's power implies the possibility of standards by which Spark becomes trivial. Even the common approach through formal questions may conceal extreme critical divergence.

Such divergencies multiply with the essays. Are ideas valuable as novelistic material? Oates, praising Welty, observes that as far as she can see, the novelist's fiction contains no ideas at all. The comment implies a positive judgment. Welty functions as artist, language her medium, imagined people and happenings her raw material, to assemble a structure analogous to that of a musical composition. Its substance refers, as Oates points out, to ways of life no longer existing—if, indeed, they ever existed. The fiction has the authenticity and authority of imagination, not of reality; it speaks to our emotions through the manner of its embodiment in language. Lessing, conspicuously a novelist of ideas, praised for her ideas, also manipulates form, her critics argue, to generate emotion. But two commentators attempting to interpret and evaluate the same Lessing texts reach very different conclusions.

Karl sees the first four volumes of the *Children of Violence* series as belonging to the genre of *Bildungsroman*, with *The Four-Gated City*, the final novel in the sequence, deviating from this established pattern; Barnouw maintains that *The Four-Gated City* alone conforms to the necessities of *Bildungsroman*, its predecessors do not. In Karl's view, *The Golden Notebook* as a formal achievement embodies more ambition than *The Four-Gated City*; Barnouw reverses that judgment also. Karl sees Lessing as "resolving" the problem of relations between the sexes in an unsatisfactory way; Barnouw believes that she does not even pretend to resolve it. Both critics perceive a close connection between Lessing's central concern with the plight of women in our time and her consistent formal experimentation, but they value that experimentation differently. Both note some of the same symbols in Lessing's fiction, expressing conflicting attitudes toward the symbols. Karl compares Lessing with Anthony Powell, Joyce (to whom he sees her as linked by her ways of employing fictional form), Proust, Beckett, Kafka, and Pinter, but he values also her special affinities with the nineteenth-century novel; Barnouw compares her with Robert Musil, that dazzling exemplar of modernist sensibility, and acknowledges no ties to the literary past. Two trained critical intelligences, in short, at work on the same texts, discover opposite "facts" at every turn.

A novelist who, like Lessing, frequently implies the polar opposition of male and female creates special problems for male and female critics alike, seeming to demand partisanship about more than literary matters. Sexual politics often dominate critical discussion of novelists who present themselves vividly and unmistakably as women. Mary McCarthy, for instance: consider the conflicting reactions implied by my piece on *The Company She Keeps* and Norman Mailer's diatribe about *The Group*. Mailer's "Case Against McCarthy" castigates her in effect for not being a man, not knowing about men ("now there's a hint...that the Saints will preserve our Mary-Joan and bless her with a book that can comprehend a man"), and not recognizing her own innate inferiority to the masculine species. My case for her praises her for being a woman, for knowing about women, for rendering in subtle detail the complexities of a female point of view. The prejudices barely concealed by these two pieces of critical prose oppose one another; so, therefore (or partly therefore) do their judgments (not of the same book, specifically: but Mailer judges

the writer as well as the book, and dismisses by implication Mc-
Carthy's earlier fiction). Although such judgments may be supported by arguments referring to a novel's technical expertise,
its structural and rhetorical patternings, they rest finally on responses generated by the fiction's subject.

As Karl points out in his essay on Lessing, there has not yet
been much concerted effort to render authentically in fiction the
facts of female experience; this represents a relatively fresh area
for critical response. Moreover, the undertone of anger suf-
fusing most serious fiction by women about female life is likely
to call forth strong personal reactions which must be surmounted
or incorporated in any critical statement. Of course criticism that
is far from objective can be powerful, provocative, and full of
insight: Mailer's review, infuriating though it may be, proves the
point. Virginia Beards' account of "Margaret Drabble's bleak
pessimism regarding love, marriage, and the casual disasters
besetting the female" gains energy from its writer's obvious involvement in the female condition. But the particular kinds of
emotional involvement apparent in many of these essays also call
attention to the preliminary state of critical discourse about contemporary female novelists. We have not had time to develop
aesthetic distance on such writers. Nor is it clear how desirable
aesthetic distance would be for dealing with texts which appear
to demand directly of their readers commitments about life as
well as literature. Critical passion can readily be aroused over
the fourth book of *Gulliver's Travels;* Swift's account of
Houyhnhmns and Yahoos arouses uncomfortable recognitions
about our own lives, and the critical fervor it stimulates necessarily reflects that fact. Yet it is possible to express personal
responses to *Gulliver's Travels* through debate about the nature
of the persona, the limitations of satire, the influence of Christian
doctrine or deistic heresy or classical logic on the text. Margaret
Drabble and Mary McCarthy imply no such resources for dealing
with their uncomfortable narratives. Describing contemporary
realities in contemporary tones of voice, they involve us in dilemmas of life difficult to convert into literary cruxes. Because the
openly revealed viewpoint of women on their own realities is
both a relatively new and a particularly urgent literary concern,
it engages readers powerfully and often confusingly. If the critic
ventures forth from the comparative safety of concentration on
technique, he may find himself—even more, she may find herself

—in trouble, dealing in gender politics rather than criticism.

Many serious analysts of women's novels in fact work to rescue their subjects from any charge of feminism as though it were an accusation. Conrad's male novels have never required apology: his masculine characters, as readers readily accept, articulate the moral crises of humanity. The faintly defensive tone in which critics explain that women novelists do not care solely about women suggests that similar assumptions are not assumed to govern the reading of fiction about females. Thus Thelma Shinn, for example, opens her treatment of Ann Petry with these sentences: "Ann Petry is black; she is also a woman. Yet her novels are not limited ethnically nor sexually." Through plot summary and extensive quotation from three novels, Shinn supports her thesis that Petry concerns herself rather with the difficulties of individuals in a decadent society than with the special problems of women (or blacks). Similarly, Elgin Mellown on Jean Rhys. Pointing out the consistency with which Rhys (like Lessing) sees women as victims, men as comparatively free, Mellown does not locate this as a particularly "feminist" position: on the contrary. Although he perceives the various central characters of the Rhys novels as contributing to a view of "woman in one of her archetypal roles," he maintains that this version of "woman" in fact represents an attitude toward humanity, a means of enforcing the novelist's "single vision of a world in which free will is a myth and the individual has no power to control his destiny." The pronoun *his* underscores Mellown's refusal to allow Rhys's fiction to be read as dealing merely with women's plight.

Like Doris Lessing's apologists, Mellown calls attention to his subject's technical accomplishment, praising the "perfect fusion of content and technique" in Rhys's novels, thus denying once more the preeminent importance of her concern with her own sex as a justification for critical interest. Beards, writing about Drabble, specifies the vital place of technique in freeing novelist and critic alike from political limitation. Her remarks on Drabble's transcendence of feminism provide a useful perspective on some general problems of women's fiction. Like Mellown on Rhys, she must introduce her subject to an audience whose familiarity with the novels cannot be assumed. She uses even plot summary, however, as part of her effort to elucidate how Drabble has emerged as a creator of *fiction* rather than a promulgator of doctrine. Concentrating as she often does on the miseries of the female condition, the novelist might have readily relaxed into providing objective correlatives for the theories of Kate Millett—and indeed Beards quotes from Millett to clarify Drabble's concerns. But she also suggests the ways in which Drabble's novels avoid feminist politics: by their essential pessimism (commitment to political action implying, in Beards' view, optimistic faith in the possibility of change), by their increasingly lucid perception that the miseries of our condition involve men as well as women and do not depend on political fact alone, and by their attention to the specifically aesthetic problems of imitation and of discovering appropriate form. (Beards sees Drabble's manipulation of first-person and third-person narrative, for example, as conveying the subtleties of her psychological awareness.)

These ideas about Drabble apply also to other women novelists. As we have already seen, Shinn claims for Petry and Mellown for Rhys a comparable broadening of concern from the female to the human plight; the critics of Rhys and Lessing argue the importance of the novelist's commitment to technical inventiveness. The note of pessimism is pervasive in women's writing when it focuses on women's fate: true amelioration rarely seems conceivable. But as Beards presents these points, they imply some felt necessity to seek special justification for the woman who writes of women's condition. The group of critics here represented, whether they concentrate on form or on content, rarely suggest that women novelists have special resources because of their sex; several hint that women as subjects and as writers of fiction are widely perceived to suffer special debilities. The essays taken together imply no coherent view of what it means to be a female writer of fiction. They show that women, like men, treat many subjects, employ many techniques, fulfill many purposes by their writings; they complicate rather than resolve that difficult question we started with: whether women novelists are a special breed.

II

If critics of individual authors provide no clarity about whether women novelists share anything beyond their sex, perhaps reflection about an assortment of such novelists may lead to tentative conclusions in an area where clear answers obviously cannot exist. The eight novelists treated in this collection exemplify the eclecticism of twentieth-century fiction. Their subjects range from the difficulties of a young woman alone to the machinations of a crew of servants concerned to profit from their employers' demise; the geographical scope of their narratives extends from Harlem to Africa to Ireland to Paris; they employ meticulous realism and extravagant fantasy; they offer happy endings, sad endings, inconclusive endings; they dwell variously on character, plot, point of view, theme. By every obvious standard they demonstrate diversity. Only the accidents of sex and chronology—all have written within the second third of the twentieth century—clearly link them.

They have been chosen, in fact, partly to suggest the wide range of women novelists in our time. Their great diversity is important to emphasize, for the novels these women have written, and the critical attention they have been given, make it apparent that one can no longer believe in "female subject matter" (certain kinds of material make a work vulnerable to dismissal as a "lady novel," but "ladies" now write about everything) or a distinctive female style, plot, tone. This collection calls attention to the truth that in no simple sense does a woman novelist necessarily declare her sex by her writing.

Yet one cannot merely conclude that the matter of sex is irrelevant, however difficult its relevance may be to ascertain: our initial question remains worth pondering. In the second volume of Doris Lessing's *Children of Violence* series, *A Proper Marriage,* the protagonist, Martha Quest, seeks clarification for her problems through reading books. She approaches novels always with the conscious inquiry, "What does this say about my life?" Novels, as it turns out, say little about her life; Martha concludes "that the novelists had not caught up with life; for there was no doubt that the sort of things she or Stella or Alice talked about found no reflection in literature—or rather, it was the attitude of mind they took for granted that did not appear there, from which she deduced that women in literature were still what men, or the men-women, wished they were."

No one has done more than Lessing herself to remedy the state of affairs Martha describes; novels by other women in our time with increasing frequency and emphasis attempt to render women as they are rather than as they may be wishfully imagined. Six of the novelists here treated—Murdoch and Spark the exceptions—present female characters with special intensity and insight. And although the apparent attitudes of the novelists—toward life, toward their characters, toward the business of writing fiction—differ greatly, the women they render have surprising points of identity.

At apparent extremes, for example, are Eudora Welty, an American writer evoking the patterns of life in a beloved, stable social context, her women characters unquestioning of their lot, and Doris Lessing, an Englishwoman who lived her early life in Africa, writing of women racked by questions arising from their awareness of their condition and from the anguish of chaotic social change. In *Delta Wedding,* evoking the Mississippi Delta of the 1920s, Welty describes an intricate social structure superficially controlled by females. Although individual young women may rebel against the exigencies of their particular sexual commitments, none challenges the notion that life consists of having babies, taking care of one's men, demonstrating hospitality, exchanging gifts, dancing, playing the piano, cooking or arranging that cooking be done. By the time of *The Optimist's Daughter,* set in the 60s, existence no longer continues in so expansive and leisurely a fashion. But women still concern themselves with property, with their relationships to men, with paying visits; and the central character, a widow pursuing an independent career in the North, returns to her Southern origins at the time of her father's death with grateful acceptance of much that those origins imply. Lessing's Martha Quest, at the other extreme, rebels from childhood: against her family, the mores of her society, the expectations that govern her. Anna Wulf in *The Golden Notebook,* striving unsuccessfully to be that "free woman" she can only dimly imagine, also consistently defies conventional expectation; the middle-aged protagonist of *The Summer Before the Dark* painfully *learns* to defy: a vital lesson.

Toward the end of *Delta Wedding,* the young woman Shelley confronts, as all the other important female characters have confronted before her, the mystery of the male, embodied in a violent scene between the overseer Troy (soon to marry Shelley's sister) and two black workers. Dominated, even awed, by Troy's effective power, Shelley nonetheless concludes that it represents only a "convincing performance," that all men imitate other men, even —a thought quickly retreated from—her father, that "all men could not know any too well what they were doing." She decides that men are "no better than little children....Women, she was glad to think, did know a *little* better—though everything they knew they would have to keep to themselves…oh, forever!" What women know, the novel has demonstrated, is their hidden power, their ultimate powerlessness: they *have to* keep their knowledge hidden—precisely what Martha Quest comes to know, and Anna Wulf. Men are children: Martha looks at her husband and knows this, Anna sees the fact variously exemplified in her lovers. Women, contemplating male existence, perceive, as characters in Lessing's fiction and in Welty's, elaborate patterns of make-believe. But they can do nothing with their knowledge, if knowledge it is, except keep it hidden—"forever." Their inability to use their knowledge makes for them their painful fates.

Rhys's pathetic and often distasteful victims of their own psychology and of social arrangements, Petry's desperately striving women, McCarthy's sophisticates: all display comparable combinations of felt superior wisdom and experienced inferior power. Margaret Drabble's heroines work the pattern out in great detail. The central character of *The Waterfall*, a poet who has driven her husband to desert her in an advanced state of pregnancy, finds erotic satisfaction and artistic revivification through a sexual relationship with the owner of a garage, a man primarily interested in fast cars. Unable to take his concerns seriously, she does not even attempt to share hers with him, apparently believing that men, however limited their utility for women, are in all their inadequacy a painful necessity of female existence. The principal woman in *The Needle's Eye* has separated from her dreadful husband at the novel's beginning but is back with him at the end. He plays games, she takes life seriously; but he has effective power, she possesses only what she knows.

Women's "attitude of mind" in its current manifestations, then, provides a significant subject for these writers who, moreover, despite all their differences, depict in their female characters a surprisingly consistent attitude. (Of course I am ignoring conspicuous differences among these characters too; their essential identity survives such differences.) But what of Murdoch and Spark in this connection? Neither provides obvious solace for the real-life Martha Quest who might seek in literature some direct evidence that other women have thought and experienced like her. Neither, indeed, offers much in the way of real characterization at all, whether their subjects be male or female. The personages in their novels possess psychologies, often elaborately

expounded, but lack verisimilitude. And the lack obviously reflects novelistic purpose, not any failure of artistic competence
or will.

Murdoch and Spark both write novels of structure rather than
novels of character; the critical essays about them in this volume
emphasize exactly this fact. Their typical novelistic patterns reveal some connections to the view of the female condition conveyed more directly through the specific means of characterization
in other novels. Murdoch's novels and Spark's, dissimilar though
they too are in most respects, share a common emphasis on the
ambiguities of passivity, conveyed through structures of inter-
change between passive and active—often involving literal or
symbolic giving and taking—in which passivity turns out to contain hidden power, frequently the power of knowledge. A character's sex, in these fictions, does not determine his degree of
activity; one can only speculate how much the novelist's sex
determines her concern with particularly ambivalent forms of
power.

In Spark's *The Prime of Miss Jean Brodie,* for instance, characters group themselves in socially assigned roles traditionally
differentiated by their levels of relative authority and passivity:
schoolgirls and teacher, headmistress and staff, the nun, com-
mitted to her discipline of obedience, in contrast with those in
the outside world. The novel works by systematic violation—or
at least distortion—of conventional expectation about such roles.
The teacher who manipulates her students to serve her own
narcissistic needs is finally controlled by them; the headmistress
proves powerless against a teacher until aided by a student; the
nun exerts more effective force on others than anyone else in the
world of the book. Knowledge provides a significant resource for
the exercise of power. Miss Brodie's initial authority derives
largely from what she claims to know; Sandy's ultimate effective-
ness depends on her carefully amassed store of personal information, from which she on occasion chooses to give. Those who most
loudly proclaim their power turn out to have, in fact, the least
force in the mainly female society Spark evokes. In *Not to Disturb* she deploys a more balanced heterosexual cast. Here, too,
lines of power initially seem established by social roles: servants
and masters. Off-stage are those other important characters, the
journalists, who from one point of view exemplify ultimate power
—theirs is the money which constitutes motivation—but from

another vantage point are seen as manipulated by the servants. The servants, behaving like servants, yet mysteriously seem to control events. Their control, like Sandy's, stems from knowledge: of what is going to happen, which they do not cause, only allow, but appear nonetheless in their knowledge to ordain.

Their position thus may be thought to resemble that of the novelist—an analogy probably far from accidental, considering the emphasis in many of Spark's novels on "plot," "scenario," or "tragedy." In Murdoch's fiction, equally emphatically, crucial knowledge belongs to the author, alone cognizant of what is going to happen—a truth, of course, of all fiction, but one of which Murdoch's makes the reader peculiarly aware—and of what really *has* happened. Characters and reader exist in comparable states of tense ignorance, occasionally enlightened enough to recognize their pitiable lack of adequate comprehension. Has or has not Montague Small's dead wife *(The Sacred and Profane Love Machine)* been unfaithful? What do Blaise Gavender's wife and his mistress really want of him? Who or what is *real?* Murdoch insistently raises such questions, with their varying levels of complexity and significance, only to suggest that one must learn to exist without answers. Within the world of the novels, too, characters bestow or withhold knowledge and other valuable commodities in more or less arbitrary fashion. In *An Accidental Man,* the young American protagonist who has been given everything he wants—rich fiancée, glamorous position at Oxford, escape from the American draft and the Vietnam War—learns that he must yield all these in order to gain self-esteem. Subsidiary characters include a Buddha-like diplomat, who, losing his treasured collection of Chinese porcelain, learns that his desire to give help, experienced by recipients as a mode of aggression, must also be relinquished. The more or less mad Dorina gradually gives up virtually every source of satisfaction; when she gives up life itself, she achieves her greatest effective power. Like most of Murdoch's fiction, the novel ends in a "life-must-go-on" vein: the party which reveals sexual and social realignments sounds precisely like all previous parties; no insight derived from the patterns of painful reversal has made the slightest real difference to anyone. But the arrangement of events says to the reader, at any rate, that wisdom, impossible purposefully to transmit, must constitute its own satisfaction, and that one should not facilely assume a connection between apparent energy and effective force: victims also make things happen. The author's concealed yet oddly ostentatious control of events epitomizes the efficacy both of giving and of withholding.

The hidden potency of victimization, the concealed action of passivity, the necessity of relinquishment: such themes may determine novelistic structure as well as detail for Murdoch and Spark. The hypothesis, of course, demands much fuller investigation, involving such matters as the special relation between author and characters in both Spark's fiction and Murdoch's, the importance of giving and taking as sources of plot and of imagery, and the question of whether issues about passivity exert more determinative force on the structure of these novels than on those of fiction by contemporary male writers. Such an approach indicates a possible way of speculating about the import of authorial sex in fictional creation and of linking novels which proclaim female experience as their central subject with those ostensibly concerned with broader matters. For even a cursory survey of some of the fictions about women mentioned already suggests that they too involve patterns of passivity and deal with giving and taking both in abstract and concrete terms. *Martha Quest,* that brilliant study of adolescent rebellion, proceeds, for example, through vignettes of passivity. Martha's determination to make for herself a life different from her mother's leads her to no purposeful, self-ordained action. She exists at the disposal of others; the group of novels that relate her entire career examine her many, often superficially unaccountable, choices of mentor. To assume responsibility for herself long exceeds her capacities. Through her ways of dressing she reveals the fantasies which substitute for responsible acceptance of actuality. Making a gown for a party—a gown altogether inappropriate to the real occasion, but a vivid rendition of her dreams—constitutes the most significant self-determined act of Martha's adolescence. But even that represents an evasion: a devious means of conveying hostility toward her mother and of expressing her hopes for herself, both disguised in an act of apparent compliance to the demands of a festivity organized by others.

Mailer, in his remarks on McCarthy, hints that the woman writer's preoccupation with objects reflects the crass materialism of her sex. Martha's dress suggests an alternate way of interpreting this pervasive concern. Through things, much fiction implies, women convey their natures. Concretions serve the psyche. Destined by society to assume responsibility for the artifacts of domestic life, women invest with meaning the objects they protect. To perceive clothing as an expression of the self requires no great effort of imagination; to extend human significance to remoter objects, a more demanding exercise, seems equally characteristic of many female novelistic characters. The phenomenon may be taken to illustrate that women are less, not more, "crass" than their male counterparts, since their interest focuses not in objects but in the objects' signification. The point emerges clearly in Welty's novels, permeated with the substantial details of Southern life and with actions of giving and taking, losing and keeping and exchanging. Gifts organize crucial events in *Delta Wedding:* Ellen's garnet pin, a gift from her husband, lost and found and lost again; the night-light, preserved through the generations to be given, then broken; George's pipe, secreted by the child Laura in order to be offered as a gift; the house Marmion. The family reunion which focuses the action of *Losing Battles* is first of all an occasion for giving; the conflicts of *The Optimist's Daughter* grow largely out of disputes over who has the right to take, or keep, family possessions. Giving and keeping (preserving, not hoarding) transmit feeling; and giving contains more power than taking. Things in their private symbolisms communicate better than words for the Welty characters, reluctant to take full responsibility for their feelings. Laura's great love is expressed to her satisfaction in the act of giving George his own pipe, but the fulfillment of such expression depends partly on the fact that it need not be fully understood by giver or recipient. The necessities and the potencies of evasion—not merely, but sometimes, connected with the female fate—express themselves in these patterns of giving.

The importance of giving as a feminine resource becomes particularly apparent as opportunities to employ it diminish. In Petry's *The Street,* abundant ugly objects epitomize the degradation and limitation of the environment, but Lutie, the protagonist, can hardly express herself through objects: she owns almost nothing. She suffers from the lack of beauty in her substantial world, from the lack of emotional sustenance which the other deprivation symbolizes. Before the action of the novel begins, she has lost her husband; by the end she loses her son. All she has to give or withhold is her body. When that is demanded of her as the price for help she needs, or believes herself to need, she commits murder. Deprived of the luxuries of passivity and of giving, through which women in many novels find expressive resources, Lutie discovers not only their impossibility but also the symbolically related impossibility of getting satisfaction from an unfeeling world. Only hostile action—itself futile and self-destructive—remains to her. Informed by extreme social pessimism, the novel carefully records processes of deprivation which withdraw the possibility of giving, hence finally of being.

In Drabble's *The Needle's Eye,* the central female character, Rose Vassiliou, has inaugurated her adult life by giving away, in one grand and futile gesture, her fortune. She wants to achieve moral purity by constructive relinquishment; in fact, at the novel's end, she reaches qualified moral success only by accepting impurity and compromise, abandoning some of her cherished divestitures. *The Needle's Eye* makes clear how irrelevant is the issue of "materialism": the action, not the substance, of giving matters. More explicitly aware than many other novelists of the complexities of altruism, Drabble allows her characters to reflect about such matters as the nature of true charity. Rose, who gives eagerly and naturally, giving away her history, her money, her self, everything except her children, feels herself less "charitable" than Simon, the cold lawyer, whose givings, more theoretically motivated and far more limited than hers, derive more from will than from feeling. Her judgment in this matter, not necessarily accurate, reflects her uneasiness about her own value. Heiress to a large fortune, Rose seems far removed from Lutie, of *The Street,* whose lack of money summarizes her life's distresses. But both women, with different kinds of urgency, confront the same problem: how can, how should, a woman exert force in the world? Neither successfully resolves the dilemma: Lutie's final recourse to action is altogether destructive; Rose's final lapse into passivity, convincingly depicted as the best choice open to her, ends *The Needle's Eye* on a note of pathos.

The stress on patterns of exchange in these novels focused on women emphasizes the difficulties of female action. Mary Mc-Carthy's sophisticated Vassar graduates and Jean Rhys's sexual waifs make similar discoveries. The Rhys characters never appear to expect personal fulfillment; McCarthy's women have been educated to larger hopes. But Margaret Sargent, the young woman in *The Company She Keeps* who finds herself giving her body to a porcine man in a Pullman compartment, exemplifies the same truth as the protagonist of *Good Morning, Midnight*, who goes to bed with the unknown man in the next room as a final gesture of charity. Women in these novels who, conversely, ask to be given to, receive not bread but stones. Thus Marya, toward the end of *Quartet*, pleads with her husband, "I wanted to beg you to be good to me, to be kind to me. Because I'm so unhappy that I think I'm going to die of it....Help me!" Her husband responds, "You must think I'm Jesus Christ....How can I help you? What fools women are!" He makes a gesture, however, toward providing sexual consolation, only to be told, "That isn't what I want." The scene and the novel end with his flinging her violently against a table, leaving her unconscious on the floor. She has, perhaps, received what she really wants: punishment for her ineradicable sense of wrongness, badness, the source of much of her unhappiness. And perhaps some comparable feeling of the self's badness underlies Rose's giving, and Meg Sargent's, and Lutie's futile attempts; perhaps, indeed, it accounts for the pervasive themes of passivity—which may function as a means of averting guilt—and of giving, in novels by women, even when such novels do not present themselves as explicitly *about* women.

Such possibilities open up new reaches for investigation, emphasizing the fact that the relevant questions about women's writing are only beginning to be asked. My glancing suggestions about the substance of several novels can barely hint at the complex emphasis on patterns of taking and giving and the ways in which they summarize persistent female conflicts about action/passivity, dependence/independence. Not, of course, that such conflicts belong exclusively to females; nor do the patterns of taking and giving characterize only female novels. The special ways in which women's novels utilize them, however, demand fuller examination.

The most important function of a collection such as this must be to suggest the need and the possibility for more extended critical inquiry in an area where intelligent generalization is still painfully limited.

Margaret Drabble: Novels of a Cautious Feminist

by Virginia K. Beards

Margaret Drabble's bleak pessimism regarding love, marriage, and the casual disasters besetting the female locked into heterosexuality and a less radical life style is the focus of her first five novels, written since 1964. Published and praised in England, she seems little read in the United States, a transatlantic reader's loss since the currency of her vision is remarkable.

Bungled and achieved female self-definition is her consistent theme; her women might set out to pay homage to patriarchy's dearest forms but en route their increasing awareness of the absurdity of their sexual, social, and economic positions results in their befuddlement and defeat within the system. Only occasionally and in a limited sense do her women manage to infiltrate intellectually or economically the masculine milieu. Drabble turns to the novel to explore the various options of women today; she evidently lacks the idealism that active feminist politics demands while her awareness of human inequities needs no heightening through consciousness raising sessions. The conversion of the sexual protest into novels is what makes her interesting. The choices of artist over activist and imitation over frontal attack allow a subtlety and sensitivity that politics frequently precludes.

Margaret Drabble leisurely inspects patterns of female development and the nuances of both male oppression and sexual liberation; unlike her political counterpart who is sustained by a vision of a new order, Drabble's outlook is grim. Her conclusions are often nihilistic and suggest sexual tyranny is here to stay, a component of a deterministic universe. Neither a missionary, an idealist, nor a prophet, Drabble offers the reader practical imita-

"Margaret Drabble: Novels of a Cautious Feminist" by Virginia K. Beards. From *Critique*, 15, no. 1 (1973), 35-47. Reprinted by permission of *Critique*.

tions of the real world. The novels incisively diagnose female complaints while avoiding talky and dubious prognoses and treatment programs; rhetoric and wish-fulfillment are, mercifully, out of bounds in her work. Because the English novel has traditionally contributed to social reform through its criticism of social inequities, the enduring gains in woman's rights may as well be made by cautious and introspective artists, such as Drabble, as by the movement's activists and political theoreticians.

The inevitable problems of the mid-twentieth-century woman provide the specific plot complications in all Drabble's novels; both female and male character is revealed and developed in relation to familiar feminist issues of education, sexuality, marriage, motherhood, and economic dependence. Take education. Three ideas from theorist Kate Millett are relevant to a reading of Drabble as an artist working with a common ideology. Millett argues that the equation of knowledge with power results in the "fairly systematic ignorance patriarchy imposes on women."[1] Expanding the idea she considers the education women receive when they slip by the sexual screening processes of higher learning or when they seek refuge in a woman's college. She notes that women often pursue studies that are anachronistic; males enter scientific and technological disciplines crucial to our age while women usually genteelly commit themselves in their studies to the ideals of renaissance humanism. (What an irony, when one considers that the "liberal arts" originally referred to the studies available to a "free man"—one who was not a serf!) Millett concludes female education in the humanities "is hardly more than an extension of the 'accomplishments' they once cultivated in preparation for the marriage market" (43).

In Drabble's first novel, *A Summer Bird-Cage* (1963), Sarah comes down from Oxford with "a lovely, shiny, useless new degree," goes to Paris to tutor French girls privately—a course that one cannot imagine a male "first" following—and after a few months is relieved when her sister's imminent wedding provides an excuse to return to England. School-marming it in Paris lacks both seriousness and future to a girl who had in happier days headily opened a college essay on Hobbes with: "In the *Leviathan* Hobbes demonstrates nothing adequately except the limitations of his own studybound conception of human nature." Her return

---

[1]Kate Millett, *Sexual Politics* (London, 1971), p. 42.

to England somewhat heightens her awareness of sexual inequality yet she never frees herself enough from sexual conditioning to act on her own behalf. She becomes rather vaguely employed at the BBC "filing things" and rejects an academic career. Her explanation as to why she will not become a don indites everyone's absurd attitudes to the female out of the kitchen or bedroom:

> I used to fancy myself as one [a don]. But I'll tell you what's wrong with that. It's sex. You can't be a sexy don. It's all right for men being learned and attractive, but for a woman it's a mistake. It detracts from the essential seriousness of the business....You'd soon find yourself having to play it down instead of up if you wanted to get to the top, and when you've only got one life that seems a pity.[2]

But the choice is not easy. She lunches with academic friends of her research scientist fiancé who is currently working in America. They kindly invite her out in the spirit of "for old times' sake" yet the experience underlines for her the secondary status of the educated woman within patriarchy:

> It was a nice thought, and a nice lunch, but it made me feel curiously passé, and I felt the impulse to tell everyone that I had got a degree too, as good as any of theirs, which is always a danger signal. I resisted it....I felt as though everyone else was leading a marvellous progressive life except me, and I had been subtly left behind.
> (110)

The title of the novel comes from John Webster's lovely simile, "'Tis just like a summer bird cage in a garden, the birds that are without despair to get in, and the birds that are within despair and are in a consumption for fear they shall never get out." It indicates Drabble's artistic preoccupation: the themes of sexual conflict and domestic entrapment are developed in relation to several other "birds" as well as Sarah. Her sister, Louise, splendidly drunk and in dirty underwear, puts on an elegant white bridesdress to marry a wealthy, irascible homosexual novelist as a way out of "the secretarial course-coffee bar degradation" that London offers her. Her bizarre alternative shows the enormity of the marriage value in her upper middle-class society and, its corollary, female laziness and non-aggression. Sarah's roommate,

---

[2]Margaret Drabble, *A Summer Bird-Cage* (London: Weidenfeld and Nicolson, 1963), pp. 183-4.

Gillian, has just flown the cage by walking out on her painter-husband who demanded her services as model, domestic, and sexual partner. Drabble's clear vision of the damaged female ego is never better than in the anecdote Gillian tells about her marriage. After bitterly complaining of her boredom to her husband—she said she felt like a "still life"—he cruelly pushed canvas, paints, and brushes at her and, anticipating his triumph, gamefully ordered her to paint him. Of course, she failed; her art work was, by her own admission, like a child's. The anecdote implies much that is apropos to the sexual battle as seen by both the novelist and women's liberation activists: the woman is conditioned to accept a role, but she is unhappy being treated as an incompetent child in some things and as a capable helpmate in others. Her latent abilities, talents, and any shreds of skill in the male realm are discouraged until she becomes, in fact, truly incapacitated. As this point the egocentric male mate can breathe a sigh of relief and carry on unharrassed. To Gillian, a female of developing consciousness, her status in a marriage of this type is untenable and so, like Nora, she leaves.

Drabble's consideration of what often happens to intelligent but traditionally educated women in marriage is further developed in her later novels. *The Garrick Year* (1964) opens with a chilling scene in which Emma Evans, its central character, is literally being devoured by men. As she sits nursing her voracious infant son, she is verbally assaulted by her actor-husband who informs her that in the interest of his career they are going to move to a provincial town with a prestigious repertory theater. The move spells both physical and mental hardship. In addition to its logistics, she will have to turn down an offer in television—ironically, by a company which was going "to have another attempt at the equality of the sexes by allowing women to announce serious events as well as forthcoming programmes"—that would have got her out of her London nursery and back into life. Exhausted and aware that arguing will make her milk stop and thus her child will be badgering her all night, she sits passively listening in a classic double bind—damned if she responds to her husband and damned if she does not. A pathetic fear of loneliness, belief in family unity, plus a twisted commitment to the concept of marriage keeps Emma from wishing her husband farewell and sending him off to the provinces. Her devotion to the marriage is suspect since she has rejected him sexually and, in fact, practices sexual appeasement in finally agreeing to the provincial theater adventure. She says yes to the move in bed that night in return for his consent "to be understanding about having his hand pushed off my thighs, in view of Joseph [the baby] and my weariness."

The novel is unified by Emma's pattern of persistency in a dreary role which her culture and class have taught her is normal and satisfying. Further evidence of Drabble's preoccupation with the stultification of the educated and curious woman in marriage is that Emma studies Italian grammar or compulsively memorizes a list of the dates of events leading up to the Sicilian Vespers while nursing her child. She blandly admits later, "what charm they had for me I cannot now imagine." While her behavior in everyday life might seem refreshing or pleasingly zany, its presence in the novel forces the reader to acknowledge the lopsidedness of patriarchial arrangements. The atmosphere of subjugation and up-against-the-household-wall fills *The Garrick Year;* female passivity in the humiliating norm of helpmate behavior is the unrelenting focus. The horror of the condition is clarified in the novel as it rarely is in life.

Clara Maugham in *Jerusalem the Golden* (1967) also shows female aimlessness caused by the pressure of cultural values. She drifts into graduate school in London because she cannot face the drabness of life in her provincial town, while her friend, Clelia, finds her marginal job in an art gallery has become a baby-sitting service for its owner. The nearly catatonic Jane Gray of *The Waterfall* (1969) is a minor poet who has ceased writing with the onset of marriage. She resumes writing only after turning her sexually chauvinistic husband out and finding an erotically perfect relation with another man. Drabble always keeps her women in the traditional sex role; they love men, not one another. Jane Gray's paradoxical embracing of the so-called male oppressor in order to gain freedom is not, however, presented as an ideal solution. She is emancipated through coitus itself; Drabble insists on emphasizing the void of intellectual, social, and artistic compatibility between the couple. The novel only concedes that better sex makes Jane slightly more functional and diminishes her withdrawal symptoms. The couple's inability to find anything beyond splendid orgasm in their relation heightens her sense of isolation. She considers herself in "sexual bondage" after meeting James.

Unmarried women who operate somewhat outside patriarchal values function better in Drabble's world. With *The Millstone* (1965) she moves away from the traditional woman who stays unhappily married. Here she considers life without marriage or male dominance. The novel suggests a growth in the author's feminist consciousness, a search for alternatives. Educated Rosamund Stacey finds herself pregnant but rejects both abortion and marriage. The knowledge that she is equipped to earn her living as a scholar allows her to remain independent and have the child. She follows an achievement pattern more prevalent with males— her career progresses not in spite of the offspring but because of it. Rosamund's reaction to her dependent is "male"—needing more income she accelerates her scholarly work and is acknowledged accordingly. Conversely, a common middle-class "female" reaction to motherhood is to use it as an excuse not to succeed outside of the home or, indeed, to go out of the home at all. Significantly, Rosamund successfully defines herself in relation to values other than the male-superiority female-dependency ones of patriarchy.

While Drabble presents women who eventually free themselves from the strictures of marriage and female underachievement, sexual dis-ease is epidemic among them. In her ealier novels sexual intercourse has a variety of distressing attributes: the woman may feel physical pain or tedium, she may trade sex for real security or an imagined need, she may act rather than participate. We have much fake thrashing about and little real passion until *The Waterfall*. Because her women are ill at ease with their bodies in the novels, Drabble's use of the first-person narrative works beautifully. Properly brought up and repressed middle-class women tell their stories; their sexual reticences, silences, and strategies of avoidance result in full-drawn portraits of the class and culturally eroded female libido. For instance, the narrator of *A Summer Bird-Cage* evades describing sex altogether. Marriages fall apart, love affairs are begun, the absent fiancé is sorely missed but rarely a word from anyone says what happened in bed. While the novel is surely about marriage and sexual politics as we understand the terms today, passion does not soil its sheets. The focus is on the shifting power relations between lovers and mates, but the narrator, Sarah, neither actively loving nor mating in the novel's present, is saved from having to face sex squarely. Her fiancé is away for a year and she is writing both to pass the time and to examine female alternatives from which, presumably, she will eventually have to choose. Accordingly, we have analysis but no explicit presentation of sex. The narrator coolly observes her sister and roommate in and out of marriage, thinks closely about the caging of women in matrimony, and waits "to take up…life again" when her fiancé returns.

In *The Garrick Year* Drabble wryly deploys on the most subversive sexual myths of our time and moves closer to sex, which is, after all, even when not articulated, crucial in her novels. Somewhat surprisingly, the narrator is a twenty-eight-year-old female tease. Unlike *A Summer Bird-Cage* where other people's sexual relations are analyzed by a chaste narrator, the narrator's emotional life is here under scrutiny. Perhaps for the wrong reasons— revenge on an egotistical husband, a need to confirm her continued attractiveness, a desire to be gossiped about, and an urge to snap the dreariness of days spent with two small children and a dependent au pair—Emma Evans drifts into an affair which takes forever to be consummated and, alas, simultaneously finished. As a portrait of the frigid-seductive woman with a muddled concept of both male and female sexual rights, the novel is wise and complete. Emma's absurd relation with Wyndham Farrar, her actor-husband's director, involves covertly wheeling about the Cotswolds in a sportscar and dining in rustic inns. Her pathetic pleasures come from eating avocado pears by candlelight and from the knowledge that "people are talking." Excuses are offered to the lover (and the reader) for her withholding: she is tired from the babies, the doorbell rings. The problem is not temporal, which Emma herself senses when she admits:

> The reluctance was wholly on my side….I simply could not bring myself to do it. Kissing I did not mind: in fact I soon discovered that anything above the waist, so to speak, I did not mind, but that anything below was out of the question….It is quite clear, I suppose, to all, that this pace suited me far more than it suited Wyndham Farrar, men being what they are and women being what they are *said* to be.[3]

[3]Margaret Drabble, *The Garrick Year* (London: Weidenfeld and Nicolson, 1964), p. 128. (My [Virginia Beards'] italics).

The inclusion of "said" presents what the liberation theorists have gone to chapters and even books to express. Here is the woman who has internalized the values of her culture yet who, unfortunately, still wanly questions them. The lingering nineteenth-century myth that women do not enjoy sex is operating here, and the passage anticipates Germaine Greer's theory of the female eunuch. Somewhere under her stunning secondary sex characteristics, Emma's libido stirs feebly although it has been culturally maimed to the extent that she lacks the ability to express it with any sort of elan. She is not supposed to enjoy sex but dimly suspects she could. Kate Millett also discusses the myth that Emma questions when, with regard to the ethos of Friedrich Engels and J. J. Bachofen's theories about women, she writes:

> Asking themselves how women allowed their subjection to over-take them, they responded with a naiveté characteristic of their era, claiming women submitted willingly to the sexual and social subjection of pairing and then monogamous marriage because in fact women find sexuality burdensome....One is tempted to see an absurdity in such confident assumption that women dislike sex.... Engel's attitudes are affected by the presuppositions of his culture.[4]

Drabble moves from the sexually inhibited female to the sexual usurer in *Jerusalem the Golden,* and so covers still more liberationist territory. The social context of female sexuality and its usefulness as barter is the focus. Clara Maugham's development from a Midlands school girl into a slick dweller on the outer fringes of London artistic circles provides plot. Unlike Sarah and Emma of the earlier novels she is neither chaste nor too tired, and she effortlessly uses sex to gain deliverance from her humdrum provincial background. The lover who introduces her to what she considers the glittering terrestrial paradise of London is aptly named Gabriel. The pleasures, however, are neither sacred nor healthily profane. For Gabriel the liaison spells escape from dreary monogamy; Clara admits to her lover, "it doesn't matter where I come from, but where you come from, that matters to me....All you are to me...is a means of self advancement."[5]

---

[4]Millett, pp. 115-6.

[5]Margaret Drabble, *Jerusalem the Golden* (London: Weidenfeld and Nicolson, 1967), p. 204.

As a denizen of a male ordered society, both pressures from within and without exclude her from advancement in more respectable activities; thus she accommodates her oppressors by making the most of the stereotype they have stuck her with and, rather successfully, gets her pound of flesh. Her remarks to Gabriel are the culmination of years of regarding sex as a means of social improvement. At fifteen when a boyfriend took her to a bookshop in her town, she suddenly had a vision of a life of books and politics—an alternative to the plastic butter dish, telly watching style of her mother. Her delight was immense: she wanted to kiss the boy immediately, and "later that day she did, in fact, allow him to undo her brassiere strap without a word of protest" (55). Like Emma of *The Garrick Year* and Louise, the sister of the narrator of *A Summer Bird-Cage*, she uses men to gain a dubious sort of identity and security; none of these women are able to relate themselves significantly to any activity apart or different from that of being a woman. Drabble's awareness of this one-dimensional nature of many women is at the center of all her novels.

The Waterfall pushes aside the social aspects of sexual relations to examine female sexuality per se. Drabble writes of a female destroyed by her physiology and culture and rejects the cliché that eros is the way to happiness. As a radical *bildungsroman,* like its traditional prototypes *(Sons and Lovers, A Portrait of the Artist as a Young Man,* and *The Magic Mountain),* it concludes with the protagonist's intense sense of isolation. Atypically, its hero is female and its focus exclusively sexual. *The Waterfall* decimates the patriarchal cliche that women are content when loved fully and explores the paradoxical and simultaneous development of a capacity for heterosexual passion and a feeling of utter loneliness. Through the delicate tracing of the heroine's reactions to a failed marriage, the experience of frigidity and renewed sensuality and, finally, the onset of a sense of "sexual bondage" to the redemptive lover, Drabble presents a complete and eloquent imitation. *The Waterfall* is capable of affecting its reader in a way that one doubts treatises, political actions, and consciousness raising sessions rarely can.

Both technique and theme depend on the author's manipulation of female awareness. As the psycho-sexual vortex of the novel is fear, together with secrecy and dishonesty, Drabble uses a personal narrative in which Jane Gray, whose erotic development is the plot, nervously alternates from first to third person point of view according to her shifting sense of the personal, shameful, and private in what she relates. With the gradual lessening of frigidity, Drabble diminishes her use of a detached third person point of view and has Jane enter unflinchingly and honestly into articulation of passion and feeling in the first person. For instance, in the novel's beginning the intimacies of an inchoate love affair and of childbirth are sexually too volatile for Jane to tell directly; accordingly, she retreats behind third person pronouns. Narrative technique thus helps define heroine and conflict. Long after Jane's second child is born from her moribund marriage, she, now at ease with emotional intensity, thanks to her lover, confesses that the infant actually delighted her at the time of its birth but that she could not mention it:

> I am afraid now, looking back, that my failure to include her rested upon some profound and sinister cause that had nothing to do with artistic necessity: I did not want to include one man's child in the story of my passion for another man. I felt compromised. I felt condemned.[6]

The novel is constantly rewritten by its fidgety narrator, reworking her self-image under the accumulated pressure of events. Drabble's easing of Jane into first person point of view and allowing her occasional lapses into the third exposes the dynamics of frigidity and its exorcism while avoiding polemic overstatement and the sacrifice of character to idea.

Thematically *The Waterfall* refracts a vision of woman that is feminist as well as modernist. Jane Gray's problem is isolation in a world of her own hypersensitive perceptions. The novel gets beyond specific feminist issues even while clarifying them. Jane learns of passion but the desperation she experienced as a frigid, semi-catatonic wife is largely converted into the despair of one who is locked into the loneliness of "sexual bondage"—a condition possible for either sex. The protagonist lovers have little, if anything, in common. She is a poet—he is a garage owner and sports car buff. They either make love, think about making love, or do card tricks—their favorite being called "the waterfall" where the equally cascading cards become a metaphor for orgasm in coitus. When James proposes they go on a holiday to Norway,

[6]Margaret Drabble, *The Waterfall* (New York: Alfred A. Knopf, 1969), p. 50.

Jane's reaction underscores—in a modern and female echo of that
splendid sexual chauvinist John Donne—the idea that the bed
exclusively provides their adventures:

> She took it as a theme for fantasy: a dud project, delicately intro-
> duced by him to disguise their immobility, their lack of progress,
> the impossibility of their ever sharing a journey or a life or even
> a common interest: an extension of their wholly speculative con-
> nection. (179)

The sad corollary of loneliness and isolation during the non-
love making hours is evident. The most Jane concedes about her
experiences in the arms of James is:

> I was released from my enclosure, I was able to go out now with the
> children into the sun, because I was no longer bending upon these
> trivial fears and excursions the whole force of my ridiculously
> powerful passions: I had found, in James, reciprocation: I had
> found a fitting, unrejecting object for desire. One is not saved from
> neurosis, one is not released from the fated pattern…but…one
> may find a way of walking that predestined path more willingly.

The belief in determinism is also clear in Drabble's consistent
equation of sex and death. After knowing James, Jane feels that
she has been condemned "to an endless ritual of desire," that sex
is "dreadful, insatiable, addictive black," and that she is doomed.
In Havelock Ellis she discovers the definition of sexual bondage
and realizes it quite perfectly and "elegantly" describes her condition; she then "flips through the rest of the book, gazing in
amazement at all those curious masculine perversions wishing
I could attach myself to something more easily attainable than a
man." Like her predecessors both in and out of Drabble's novels,
she is trapped by the pressures of patriarchal society. Finally,
she contrasts herself with Maggie Tulliver who

> never slept with her man: [whereas Jane] did all there was to be
> done, to Lucy [James's wife], to herself, to the two men who loved
> her, and then, like a woman of another age, she refrained. In this
> age, what is to be done? We drown in the first chapter. I worry
> about the sexual doom of womanhood, its sad inheritance.
>
> (164)

The dilemma of the centrality yet inadequacy of heterosexual
relations for females runs through all of Drabble's novels but is

never as fully expressed until *The Waterfall*. The idea that human happiness is not allowed for in the universal program is ancient, but its clear working out in female terms with the mores of contemporary patriarchal society playing the Furies to the erotically hubris-ridden woman is Drabble's distinctive contribution. Being both a feminist and a compassionate pessimist who can relate isolation to causes deeper than the simply temporal and political, she has an interest also in man, society, and civilization. That she is currently working on a novel told from the masculine point of view comes as no surprise. Margaret Drabble will undoubtedly continue to explore questions that are finally human and impartial to sexual distinction.

Disorderly Company: From *The Golden Notebook* to *The Four-Gated City*

by Dagmar Barnouw

So it must be said that if a man starts thinking a bit he gets
into what one might call pretty disorderly company.

ROBERT MUSIL
The Man Without Qualities

The *Golden Notebook,* thought by most critics to be Doris
Lessing's best novel so far,[2] has been praised for its formal control. Lessing herself, in a 1969 interview at Stony Brook,[3] said she
was "very proud" of the novel's form, describing, in contrast, the
form of *The Four-Gated City* as "shot to hell." There is indeed
a marked change in attitude toward the organization of the narrative as well as toward the protagonist; yet, the narrative anarchy
and the insistence on the potential dimension in the development of the protagonist's consciousness, new in Lessing's work,

"Disorderly Company: From *The Golden Notebook* to *The Four-Gated City*"
by Dagmar Barnouw. From *Contemporary Literature,* 14 (Autumn, 1973), 491-
514. Reprinted by permission of the publisher.

[1]Robert Musil, *The Man without Qualities,* trans. Eithne Wilkins and Erns.
Kaiser (London: Secker & Warburg, 1960-61), 3 vols., I, 130.

[2]"Form" does not refer to careful organization of small structural units, for
instance, the sentence; many of her admirers admit Lessing's verbosity, her
tendency to overwrite. "Form" refers here to the larger structures, for instance,
the arrangement of the material by means of the four notebooks and the "frame"
"Free Women," 1-5. See Florence Howe, "Narrative, History and Prophecy,"
Nation, 209 (Aug. 11, 1969), 116; with slight reservations: Irving Howe, "Neither
Compromise nor Happiness," *The New Republic,* 148 (Dec. 15, 1962) 19; Fred
erick R. Karl, "Doris Lessing in the Sixties: The New Anatomy of melancholy,"
Contemporary Literature, 13, No. 1 (Winter 1972), 15. See further Dorothy

deserve serious consideration. The new, much more open narrative structures may be seen as thoroughly functional: "shot to hell," after all, points to the central concern of the novel, the descent into the self which is partly hell. Assuming, as a working hypothesis, that the indeed surprising differences between *The Golden Notebook* and *The Four-Gated City* are indicative of changes in Lessing's concept of the function and responsibility of the novelist, I should like to explore these differences in some detail, starting with a reexamination of the function of the organizational devices and their influence on intellectual decisions in *The Golden Notebook.*

Attempting to bridge the gap between experience and self-knowledge, but aware of the probably insurmountable difficulties, Anna acknowledges the division of the self by keeping four notebooks: "a black notebook, which is to do with Anna Wulf the writer; a red notebook, concerned with politics; a yellow notebook, in which I make stories of my experience; and a blue notebook which tries to be a diary."[4] After the publication of one successful novel, Anna is afraid of the premature, static quality of form that excludes truth; she works to develop a sufficiently flexible—as it turns out, elaborately sophisticated—system of cross-commentaries that is meant to restrain, but in fact exploits, irony and a skeptical ambiguity. Tommy, talking to Anna in her room before he attempts suicide, is derisive about the four notebooks, accuses her of avoiding truth for fear of being chaotic, of irresponsibility, even dishonesty *(GN,* p. 233). This accusation, so obviously well-founded, ought to be shattering for Anna. It is not, however, because she knows her failure. Tommy, having said the things that have to be said to Anna, goes and shoots himself blind; protected by his blindness that claims all his resources of intellect and will, he will then settle for the life of a progressive businessman, a life of ambiguities and compromises. Anna,

Brewster, *Doris Lessing* (New York: Twayne, 1965), pp. 139ff.; Selma R. Burkom, "'Only Connect': Form and Content in the Works of Doris Lessing," *Critique,* 11 (1968-69), 54ff.; Joseph E. Brewer, "The Anti-Hero in Contemporary Literature," *Iowa Eng ish Yearbook,* 12 (1967), 58.

[3]Jonan Raskin, "Doris Lessing at Stony Brook: An Interview," *New American Review,* 8 (1970), 170.

[4]Doris Lessing, *The Golden Notebook* (New York: Simon and Schuster, 1962), p. 406. Parenthetical page references in the text will be preceded by *GN.*

holding at a distance the memory of her descent into disintegration of the self after the "disastrous" affair with Saul Green,[5]
settles for social work and the established Progressive Party.
Molly marries money with the obligatory progressive businessman, adjusting to her own and her son's compromises. She is,
however, still afraid of whatever emotional and intellectual energy is left in Anna:

> Annoyed with herself, Molly's hands made an irritated gesture,
> and she grimaced and said: "You're a bad influence on me, Anna.
> I was perfectly resigned to it all until you came in. Actually I
> think we'll get on very well."
> "I don't see why not," said Anna.
> A small silence. "It's all very odd, isn't it Anna?"
> "Very."   (*GN*, p. 568)

Lessing's narrative tact does not permit these lines to be the
very last ones; yet, the novel does end on the "safe tone" (*GN*,
p. 51)[6] of that "odd, isn't it?"—the safety of exhaustion which has
just enough strength left for ironical ambivalence. It is true that
Anna is aware of using that "safe tone"; she also speaks to Molly
of "that awful moral exhaustion" (*GN*, p. 43) which she dreads
yet accepts as inevitable. In the conclusion—"The two women
kissed and separated"—Anna is as much defeated as Molly, and
her keener awareness of the defeat is only turned back on herself.[7]

A distinctly hostile irony is projected by the sentence that closes
the golden notebook, that unsuccessful attempt at recording truthfully whatever is Anna's share of chaos: "This short novel was
later published and did rather well." Of course it would, written
by Saul Green who has put "a curse" (*GN*, p. 523) on Anna's most
honest, most desperate attempt to understand the division. Anna's
gift to Saul, to whom she owes a new depth of descent she cannot
bear, much less, give form to,[8] is the first sentence of his novel;

[5] Irving Howe, p. 18. The relationship to Saul Green is generally seen as merely destructive; Anna's part in the failure is not recognized. See also Karl, p. 27;
Brewster, p. 147.

[6] See also pp. 135f.

[7] Florence Howe sees the ending of *The Golden Notebook* much too posi-
tively in terms of the intellectual's—Anna's—function as "boulder pusher, that
is, a teacher of the humane principles..." (p. 177).

[8] See pp. 523ff. for the description of the frightening "new state of being, one
foreign to me"; I cannot agree with Florence Howe's view of "ordered chaos
made possible" (p. 116) in *The Golden Notebook*.

it will exploit and be exploited by a literary market, as was Anna's *Frontiers of War*. Both this fact and the abstract of Saul's novel, available to the reader (*GN*, pp. 549f.), are a condemnation of ambivalence and a recognition of its power.

Ultimately, this recognition is what *The Golden Notebook* is all about. The novel offers a courageous, formally interesting, absorbing analysis of what it means to be an intelligent woman in our times; but it does not go beyond the first stage. As women have to define themselves against men—that implies an enormous advantage for the creators of male protagonists in the battles of consciousness—Anna projects herself and her creation Ella into one relationship after the other. The fact that almost all of those relationships are nothing but "affairs" is in itself information of analytical value; it ought not to be taken as literally, however, as it is in this novel. The only meaningful relationships Anna is permitted are with Michael, of whom we know not much more than that he is loved by Anna, and with Saul, of whose illness we get some glimpses but not enough to form a picture sufficiently clear to be of help in understanding what he needs from Anna. Saul is too much of a caricature anyway. Irving Howe rightly criticizes Lessing for writing "about Americans with the astigmatism peculiar to certain English leftists: she has no ear for American speech nor eye for American manners."[9] His diary entries, read by Anna, are comical rather than "ruthless," and it is difficult to see how Anna could be hurt by them (*GN*, pp. 488 ff.). Michael presumably leaves Anna in spite—or because—of his love for her; Anna makes Saul go when she realizes how extraordinarily she is going to suffer from that relationship. What has happened to the men, what will happen to them, we are not told. They are, by decree of their creator, in a much better position to combat despair than the women whom they unfailingly exploit; they also seem to be much more in control in situations of emotional crisis: Michael runs but remains calm and cool (*GN*, pp. 313 f.); Saul wants to stay quite desperately (*GN*, pp. 547 ff.) but leaves, ready for another try at exploitation of women, certain of survival: "I could see standing beside the small, thin, fair man, with his soft brush of blond hair, his sick yellow face, a strong sturdy brown-fleshed man, like a shadow that would absorb the body that cast it" (*GN*, p. 548).

The world contained in *The Golden Notebook* is too exclusive-

[9]Irving Howe, p. 20.

ly a woman's world. Irving Howe, in his very positive review of the novel, points out that "the feminine element in *The Golden Notebook* does not become a self-contained universe of being, as in some of Virginia Woolf's novels...."[10] I would agree with him, especially in view of Anna's experience with the Communist Party. Here her despair appears credible and legitimate to a high degree because the reader can himself supply knowledge of the cruel ironies, and because Lessing-Anna has clarified the obvious, but powerfully destructive, absurdities to the point where they can be presented fully and concisely. The nightmare about the execution squad with the interchangeable prisoner is a good case in point *(GN,* p. 295). But it is precisely this more comprehensive exact presentation of a human dilemma that draws attention to the unbalanced concept of the man-woman relationship. Howe himself admits to a researcher's eagerness in reference to the "other" on both sides—man's and woman's—which implies an extraordinary distance between them: "My own curiosity, as a masculine outsider, was enormous, for here, I felt, was the way intellectual women really talk to one another when they feel free and unobserved"; "For both women remain interested in men with a curiosity that is almost archeological: as if there were so few good ones left that it is necessary to hunt for them amid the ruins."[11] Howe seems to accept that fact quite calmly.

In this sense the novel's intimacy is confining and overprotective. Anna's white room, with its black and red surfaces a space bravely outlined against chaos,[12] has this quality as much as, for instance, her cooking for Michael, or, even more distinctly so, her taking care of her daughter Janet, a curiously conventional, bright little girl who seems to need as little protection as Matty's daughter Caroline. It is significant that Matty-turned-Martha will feel responsible for Caroline's polish of conventionality, recognizing it as the child's need to protect herself as a consequence to Matty's "mad" act of "setting her free" *(FGC,* p. 66.)

[10]*Ibid.,* p. 17.

[11]*Ibid.,* p. 18

[12]Cf. here Jack's room in *The Four-Gated City* (New York: Knopf, 1969), p. 42, and Bill's room in "Dialogue," *A Man and Two Women* (New York: Simon & Schuster, 1963), p. 237: "It was large, high, had airy white walls, a clear black carpet, the dark red settee, his machinelike chair, more books." Further parenthetical page references to *A Man and Two Women* and *The Four-Gated City* will be preceded by *MTW* and *FGC.*

Anna's fear of letting in chaos, "becoming that chaos" *(GN*, p. 313) is interrelated to her need to make fictitiously whole beings out of her child and the men she comes into contact with. These other selves can then be used by her to patch up, if only temporarily, the imperfections of her self. The central ambiguity of the novel is founded in the reader's inability to decide whether Anna is judged guilty of a fragmented vision by her author, or whether such judgment is rejected as meaningless, because fragmentation is inevitable. Significantly, the sexual basis of the woman's dilemma is dealt with in detail—realistically and very intelligently—in the most distancing form Anna is capable of: her fragmentary novel about Ella and Julia.

Ella, sharing Anna's needs and desires, also her particular vulnerability, is allowed to define her incompleteness more narrowly than Anna would permit herself to do. After Paul has left Ella, she "suffers sex desire in a vacuum. She is acutely humiliated, thinking that this means she is dependent on men for 'having sex,' for 'being serviced,' for 'being satisfied.' She uses this kind of savage phrase to humiliate herself" (*GN*, p. 390). Anna writes this into her yellow notebook, waiting, as it were, for Ella's next move. Ella, trying to counter the humiliation, concentrates on reminding herself how entirely personal sex had been with Paul, remembering their life together, how she had been stirred only by him, had been free of desire when he was absent. So she is able to explain to herself, make herself believe "that her present raging sexual hunger was not for sex, but was fed by all the emotional hungers of her life. That when she loved a man again, she would return to normal: a woman, that is, whose sexuality would ebb and flow in response to his. A woman's sexuality is, so to speak, contained by a man, if he is a real man; she is, in a sense, put to sleep by him, she does not think about sex" (*GN*, p. 390). This "knowledge," however, is immediately disclosed by herself (and her author) as "a set of words, the phrases of a kind of knowledge" (*GN*, p. 390). Yet, it is never made clear whether she realizes that she is caught in a vicious circle. She relies on this "set of words" to come to life, once life comes back to her, and, also, to sustain her hope that life will indeed come back to her. The self-critical comment she is allowed by her author is an elusive "But how strange that one should hold on to a set of sentences, and have faith in them" (*GN,* p. 390).

Anna shares this faith; mocking Ella gently, even granting her self-mockery, leaving her puzzled like this, leads straight back to the "safe tone" of "it is odd, isn't it?" to which Anna, after all is said, also retreats. The self-projection into Ella does not help to clarify the division; it muddles it. Anna herself repeatedly uses the abstraction "real man" (*GN,* pp. 414, 479) though she would not otherwise permit herself such escape from the obligation to define a problem clearly; Ella, allowed a lesser degree of rigor, turns into a liability.

Caught between her four notebooks, Anna cannot do without the protection of abstractions and generalizations about the "other." She is both waiting for the "real man" to come down like a *deus ex machina,* impossibly perfect, closing her wounds without getting himself infected by them, and ready to form such a man herself, forgetting for the time her own limitations as well as those of her materials. Irving Howe implicitly accuses Anna, though he explicitly accepts her on her own terms: "She wants in her men both intimacy and power, closeness and self-sufficiency, hereness and thereness. Modernist in sensibility, she is traditionalist in her desires."[13] With this, the central problem of the novel is summed up so neatly that it does not seem a problem anymore.

Michael—one of the very few times he is allowed to speak— says to Anna at the end of their "great love affair":

> "Ah, Anna, you make up stories about life and tell them to yourself, and you don't know what is true and what isn't." "And so we haven't had a great love affair?" This was breathless and pleading; though I had not meant it. I felt a terrible dismay and coldness at his words, as if he were denying my existence. He said, whimsically: "If you say we have, then we have. And if you say not, then not." "So what you feel doesn't count?" "Me? But Anna, why should I count?" (This was bitter, mocking, but affectionate.)   (*GN,* p. 283)

Anna is made to misunderstand Michael's words as withdrawal. Consequently, in her diary entry, attempting to write "as truthfully as I can," she again outlines a story about Michael and her relationship with him. It is very early morning; Anna watches Michael in his sleep, projecting past and future for him, but she is unable to see his present. What she says about their relationship, a temporary bulwark against death, is true and moving, but she still does not understand how his "why should I count?" interacts with her need to make stories out of her attachments to men. The scene is very subtly developed, and I may very well

---

[13]Irving Howe, p. 19.

have overinterpreted it in terms of an intended criticism of Anna by her creator; yet, the change in the relationships between men and women in *The Four-Gated City* could be discovered here in an embryonic stage.

Anna's story-making is, of course, one of the few defenses she has against the men who resent her using the relationship for her own desperate needs instead of understanding that need. Threatened in the very substance of her self by the exposure and rejection inflicted on her, she feels, by the man, she has to turn to that part of herself "which Michael dislikes most; the critical and thinking Anna" (*GN*, p. 283), trying to write the truth and unable to do so because this split of her self is too crude, a destruction from the outside.

Anna wants the impossible; she is not told so by her author with sufficient clarity. The scene I described is the only instance of a very tentative approach toward such clarity. Apart from that Anna is occasionally allowed to be aware of her potentially dangerous procrustean measuring of men (*GN*, p. 410), but she is made to refer it to a past Anna, when, in fact, her relationships continue to be informed by her exclusive self-projection. Most importantly, the narrative device of the four notebooks, accommodating the "crack up" too neatly (*GN*, p. 43), obscures the aspect of wastefulness implicit in such Utopian arrest of her search for the self. I cannot, therefore, agree with Frederick R. Karl's interpretation of the problem:

> When Mrs. Lessing foresees that her imperfect female characters will always select an inadequate man to make themselves miserable, she is insisting that hell is within—a visceral time bomb—and it will not be simply exorcised by anything the external world can offer. With this, we have placed Mrs. Lessing with the nineteenth-century novelists whose protagonists are themselves piecing together fragments of experience and attempting to derive some unity; she is not with the later novelists who have taken patterns of fragmentation for granted.[14]

The Golden Notebook neither denies nor accepts the existence of fragmentation; it halfheartedly flirts with some of its patterns. Hell is indeed within, but not limited to a "visceral time bomb." It is both a much more destructive and much more promising potential of human existence; and, in order to avoid such degree

---

[14]Karl, p. 19. Karl's study is one of the most interesting essays on Lessing; I shall therefore spell out my disagreements with him in detail.

of destruction and realize the promise, it has to be explored. Anna will have to be made to face chaos, though *The Golden Notebook* stops short of that.

The "small personal voice" which Lessing defended in her 1957 statement in *Declaration*[15]—the author's as well as the protagonist's—has contributed greatly to the success of her novels and stories. It has been a precise, nuanced, intelligent voice; but in its best performance, in *The Golden Notebook,* it disclosed most clearly its limitations. In the interview given in 1969 at Stony Brook Lessing said:

> Since writing *The Golden Notebook* I've become less personal. I've floated away from the personal. I've stopped saying, "This is *mine,* this is *my* experience."...Now, when I start writing, the first thing I ask is, "Who is thinking the same thought? Where are the other people who are like me?" I don't believe anymore that I have a thought. There is a thought around.[16]

This means, as Lessing herself points out, different narrative structures—the form of *The Four-Gated City* "shot to hell"[17]— and a different attitude to her protagonist. It also means a different concept of what ought to be important in the relationship between a man and a woman. Quoted out of context, Lessing's Stony Brook statement, "I'm impatient with people who emphasize sexual revolution. I say we should all go to bed, shut up about sexual liberation, and go on with the important matters,"[18] is indeed startling after the four volumes of the *Children of Violence* and *The Golden Notebook.* In its context, the apocalyptic threat of "the bomb," it expresses a logical development. "The bomb," obviously, is much more than the physical power to destroy—though the physical effects produced approach the metaphysical; it is the mental operations and manipulations sustaining it, a mental state of frenzied exclusion that has to be opposed by restructuring human relationships. In *The Four-Gated City* Lessing has accepted this responsibility.

Karl's misunderstanding of Lessing's development is so radical as to be helpful. He is shocked by the statement I quoted above:

[15]*Declaration,* ed. Tom Maschler (London: MacGibbon and Kee, 1959), p. 27.

[16]Raskin, p. 173.

[17]*Ibid.,* p. 170.

[18]*Ibid.,* p. 175.

Her turn upon herself is curious, for this conflict between collective politics and personal matters had been the crux of her work of the last two decades. Anna's psychiatrist, in fact, suggested that her political activity was an avoidance of personal blockage. The conflict was real. Now, the conflict has been "resolved." The incredibly difficult question of man-woman relationships becomes "going to bed," and sexual liberation seems an act of conscious choice, whereas before the very question of liberation raised all the familiar problems of identity and will.[19]

Neither Lessing's statement in the Stony Brook interview nor the development of relationships in *The Four-Gated City* suggests in any way that the conflict is considered "resolved"; on the contrary, it has become much more painful. It is only suggested that the locus of the conflict has shifted. Relationships between a man and a woman remain "incredibly difficult"; it is, however, no longer enough to state that fact, no matter how intelligently and lucidly. Variations of "It's all very odd, isn't it?" are not acceptable anymore because they place too much importance on premature safety (*GN*, pp. 51, 135f.). Sexual liberation is possible only if it includes the "other,"[20] the man who was so obviously not included in *The Golden Notebook;* it will have to begin again —from the beginning—as the process of contemplation of the "familiar problem of identity and will." Liberation as a conscious choice proved to be impossible in *The Golden Notebook* because the conflicts the women were caught in were kept too static. Now, though still only a potential, its very potentiality is recognized as an indispensable reality in the fight against a domineering destructive technology and the mental and physical acts that made this particular form of domination possible.

The Four-Gated City, as Doris Lessing points out with calm defiance, is a *Bildungsroman,* and as such its structure is informed by Utopia. All the protagonists of *Bildungsromane,* especially in the German tradition from Wolfram's quester hero Parsifal to Musil's Ulrich, the man without qualities, are moving toward the possibility of a conscious choice. In the nineteenth century the process of consciousness usually ended with

[19]Karl, p. 30.

[20]"All attachments are symbiotic," Karl points out (p. 27). This is, of course, the single most important problem *The Four-Gated City* is dealing with; yet, in the context of his reading of the novel, Karl sees it negatively.

the protagonist making a meaningful choice—though Utopia ended right there, if the choice (the author controlling it) was honest. In the twentieth century the protagonist has usually been shown unable to make any such decision. Honesty in this context meant renunciation in the nineteenth century; in the twentieth it has meant a fusion of hope and despair, accepting Utopia as a structural principle informing the barely begun process of the self rather than as a defined goal.

The first four volumes of the *Children of Violence* are not *Bildungsromane* in the strict sense of the concept.[21] Matty is neither moving toward a choice, a determining decision she will make at one time or the other, nor is the fact that she is incapable of such a choice integrated into the substance and structure of her development. The first three volumes offer an absorbing examination of the tragicomedy of socio-political manners a young, intelligent woman finds herself caught in, especially il-luminating because of the clearly outlined mechanism of the colonial setting. They are, however, already "dated" to a degree, belonging to that majority of novels that Anna describes in her black notebook as "a function of the fragmented society, the fragmented consciousness. Human beings are so divided, are be-coming more and more divided, *and more subdivided in them-selves,* reflecting the world, that they reach out desperately, not knowing that they do it, for information about other groups in-side their own country, let alone groups in other countries" (*GN,* p. 59). Such "novel-reports" are continuously superseded by new information about, for instance, the political-social con-sciousness in the colonies, the consciousness of women. Lessing-Anna realizes that very well. The sheer expanse of the *Children of Violence,* the inexorably detailed account of Martha's political education, is mainly justified as sustaining and making credible —in different ways—the concentration in *The Golden Notebook* and *The Four-Gated City.* The 1965 *Landlocked,* however, antici-pates, if only by implication, certain aspects of the new Martha who, on the whole, seems to have been born during that sea voyage, separating Africa from England, and *The Four-Gated City* from the rest of the *Children of Violence.*

[21]It follows from Karl's misunderstanding of the intentions of *The Four-Gated City* that he would see Matty as the protagonist of a *Bildungsroman* in the first four volumes of the *Children of Violence,* but not Martha in *The Four-Gated City* (pp. 31ff.).

Walking through London at night in the beginning of *The Four-Gated City,* Martha acknowledges precisely those dimensions of experience that Anna found overwhelming and turned away from. Though it did not expose Matty to a new stage of the self, *Landlocked* prepared her to an extent to become Martha. In this fourth volume, individuals and the relations between them are suddenly, if infrequently, penetrated by an understanding that has to be founded on an attitude toward psychological and narrative control different from that in the other three volumes as well as in *The Golden Notebook.* Matty-Martha's relationships with her mother and with Thomas Stern—both of great importance in her process of consciousness in *The Four-Gated City*— assume an illuminating immediacy, detached from any distinct perspective, even Matty-Martha's. In Mrs. Quest's dream about her own mother, which is interwoven in her daydreaming and preparations connected with the Victory Parade,[22] her relationship to Martha can suddenly be understood. This dream also provides insight into Martha's need to explore the passionate pity and fear tying her to her mother, leading her toward madness in *The Four-Gated City.*

Matty-Martha's relationship with Thomas, "sucking her into an intensity of feeling" unknown to her before (*L,* p. 81), would have been unimaginable for Anna and Michael: they never achieve such degree of mutuality. If it is almost too much for Martha to bear this intensity of openness to the "other," it is explicitly so for Thomas. He is as vulnerable as she is, and as he tries to understand her needs, she tries to understand his. Thomas' peculiar desire for women can then be accepted by Martha as arising out of his individual need; it is not "the man" who inflicts pain on the woman merely by virtue of being a man. Neither can Thomas fail her in the role of the "real man," because Martha understands the unreality of such roles. If one chooses to speak of failure at all in this context, one would have to say that they both fail their own potentiality.

Martha may be stronger and more intelligent than Thomas— Lessing's women usually are, being part of their creator[23]—but he is ahead of her on the way toward the self, having admitted

[22]Doris Lessing, *Landlocked* (New York: New American Library, 1970), pp. 60ff. Parenthetical page references in the text will be preceded by *L.*

[23]See the strangely abstracted, very much oversimplified man-woman model in "Dialogue": Bill, meant to present an extreme, yet admirable position, ap-

chaos. Sensing this dimly from the documents of madness he leaves behind, she alone understands them as "messages" (*L*, p. 272), copying them, trying to make "sense" the way she will much later try to keep some control over her own descents into the self,[24] mapping the route of his search. She takes Thomas' crumbling papers with her into her new life. Only much later will she come to understand the full meaning of his search outlined in one of the "stories" Thomas made up for himself: "'Once there was a man who travelled to a distant country. When he got there, the enemy he had fled from was waiting for him. Although he had proved the usefulness of travelling, he went to yet another country. No, his enemy was *not* there.' (Surprised, are you! said the red pencil.) 'So he killed himself'" (*L*, p. 270). She will have to recover her past.[25]

Martha, setting out on the search herself, having cast off Matty entirely for that purpose, is a strikingly different person, certain preparatory similarities in *Landlocked* notwithstanding. The change is clearly indicated by the author-narrator's attitude toward her. As narrator Lessing withdraws from the tone of omniscience, from explanations, comparisons, encouragements, and patient irony that had pervaded the first three volumes of the *Children of Violence,* the author-narrator now tries to preserve a high degree of immediacy, which is extended also to the relationships that Martha forms. Martha is given time and space for confusion, eventually even chaos. Lessing is much less protective of her than she is of any other female protagonist. Anna and the Matty of the *Children of Violence* are eminently more vulnerable, judging from their author's possessive attitude toward them alone. The degree of vulnerability seems to be connected with the insistence on "*my* experience" Lessing referred to in her Stony Brook interview. This very personal relationship between the author and the protagonist before *The Four-Gated City* is clearly reflected in Anna's creation of Ella for her yellow notebook, resembling her in mental and physical make-up, fascinat-

---

pears almost a caricature; so does Saul; middle-aged Mark, generous, understanding, still loves his wife Lynda in a way which is destructive for her and judged almost grotesquely immature by Martha (*FGC*, pp. 351ff.).

[24]See, for instance, *The Four-Gated City*, pp. 507ff., 522ff.

[25]See *The Four-Gated City*, pp. 206ff., in which Martha prepares herself for her mother's visit.

ing her by her state of being besieged: "She wore her hair tied back with a black bow. I was struck by her eyes, extraordinarily watchful and defensive. They were windows in a fortress" (*GN*, p. 393). Ella is a metaphor for Anna, including even Anna's absorbed interest in exact chemical measurements (*GN*, pp. 393 ff.), the elements in the experiment being members of a social group. Parts of the metaphor are then used independently, for instance Ella in the act of tying back her hair, fighting back chaos (*GN*, p. 394). In its mimetic simplicity this personal intimate gesture seems to defy abstraction; and the success of *The Golden Notebook* is partly based on this illusion. In reality, the abstraction and oversimplification inherent in the structural use of such metaphors—the four notebooks, the Anna-Ella projection as a whole and in details—have not been avoided. Attempting "to create order, to create a new way of looking at life" (*GN*, p. 59), Doris Lessing-Anna superimposes structures of order on chaos in a way that precludes mediation.

The structure of *The Golden Notebook*, then, hinders the process of self-knowledge. Neither the four notebooks, meant to guarantee flexibility, nor the stories, meant to guarantee multi-perspectivity (*GN*, pp. 455 ff.), fulfill their purpose; they yield only prematurely arrested analyses of relationships, closing off precariously for a time what will destroy them anyway in the end. The enemy is intensely feared but not known. In this the novel's ambivalence, really a structural problem, is essentially different from the ambivalent endings of *The Four-Gated City* or *Briefing for a Descent into Hell*, where the concept of knowledge of the self as process is consistently supported by narrative means.

Walking toward Jack's house by night, Martha is suspended between two protective enclosures that she does not want or need: Baxter's cozily shabby self-evident upper-middle-class security and Jack's starkly outlined, threatened "pure" space, determined to shut out a chaotic outside. Martha already has a very different relationship to rooms, enclosures, than Matty or Anna. Anna's room (*GN*, p. 52) resembles Jack's (*GN*, p. 43) and Bill's in colors and the feeling of lines creating space; these are all rooms of defiance, in the center of which is a desperate need for protection from unexplored chaos and unexplored fear of chaos. Martha is ready for the room in Mark's house, which is open, unthreatened, admitting the presence of thoughts distilled from past inhabitants; the sycamore tree defines the room from the outside, suggesting shifts of space in the temporal flux rather than protective static space against time (*FGC*, pp. 100 ff.).

Walking, Martha is "nothing but a soft dark receptive intelligence," open to the "invasions" of people and places she has experienced (*GN*, p. 36). She is given by her creator the freedom of "narrated monologue"[26] to a degree which has no precedent in the *Children of Violence* or *The Golden Notebook*. Seeing Jack and calling Phoebe on the telephone are like two blocks in the swiftly moving sequence of pictures and sounds. The recognizable elements of her experience seem to be changing their meaning, oscillating between fear and "a state of quiet" which, however, she is losing fast. At the telephone box where she will arrange for an appointment that will end her "aimless" open wandering through London, she feels she has lost already what she had just found: "Yes, but remember the space you discovered today. It was gone, gone quite, not even a memory, and she sunk down out of reach of the place where words, bits of music, juggled and jangled and informed. And even the calm place below (beside?) was going, it was a memory, a memory that was going" (*FGC*, p. 39). Martha's "education" in *The Four-Gated City* is toward the conscious recovery of that space with its pictures and voices that she received here by chance, made sensitive, receptive by her "aimless" walking, talking, listening. Much later, when Martha is on her first willed, and now controlled, reconnaissance descent into the self, she will remember, when she reaches that space, that she had been there and forgotten:

> If she sat quite still, or walked steadily up and down, the space in her head remained steady, or lightening and darkening in a pulse, like the irregular pulse of the sea. She had known this lightness and clarity before—yes, walking through London, long ago. And then too, it had been the reward of not-eating, not-sleeping, using her body as an engine to get her out of the small dim prison of every day.   (*FGC*, p. 472)

It takes Martha almost fifteen years and 450 pages closely packed with people, acts, and ideas to get back to where she had once been, prepared now to chart this landscape of the self in order to

---

[26]I borrow this translation from the German expression "erlebte Rede," that is, "the rendering of a character's thoughts in his own idiom, while maintaining the third-person form of narration," from Dorrit Cohn's essay, "Narrated Monologue: Definition of a Fictional Style," *Comparative Literature*, 18 (1966), 98.

be able to use it. Repeatedly pointing out the extraordinary power of conformity to certain dimensions of experience,. reinforced through centuries of standard education, to the explosive impulse contained in social ridicule,[27] Lessing moves Martha very slowly and cautiously to the point where she thinks it possible to claim credibility for the "disorderly company" she will have to ask the reader to join.[28] Martha has proved herself a very shrewd, capable, skeptical woman, living in Mark's house, coping with very different but always difficult human situations, showing a great deal of common sense. Yet, social developments, on a personal and general level, make it imperative for her to pursue her search for identity through a descent into the unexplored self.

The richly detailed story of a group of men and women living through the fifties and sixties, participating, resisting, changing, and watching themselves change, discourages the reader from more than occasional identification with the protagonist. Martha does not emerge clearly enough from the symbiotic relationships she is drawn into, formed by and forming herself during those fifteen years in Mark's house. Shedding Matty, she has overcome the need to define herself against the "other," man: now she traces the process of self-definition within the group Martha-Mark-Lynda, the permanent center around which changing constellations of young and old people, lovers, friends, and enemies revolve. This center group, however, is itself constantly changing — an important element in Martha's preparation for the descent. Martha fully understands the meaning of this fluidity in their relationship during one of the peace marches where she sees variations of Lynda-Mark-Martha, Mark-Martha-Lynda pass by in the long line of the marchers: she realizes that the only promise of permanence is in change (*FGC*, pp. 397, 518).

[27]After her first descent, Martha starts gathering information on the greatest possible variety of aspects of the occult. She begins with Jimmy Wood's "potted library representing everything rejected by official culture and scholarship" (*FGC*, p. 486)—these books, of course, feed Jimmy's mind, triggering ideas for his machines which are perfectly acceptable to and exploitable by "official culture." Martha asserts her distaste for the "dottiness," "eccentricity," "shadiness" of most of the occult, but she is also aware of her conditioned response (*FGC*, pp. 488f.); see also Francis writing to Amanda about the powerful concept "superstition" (*FGC*, p. 584).

[28]Some reviewers have not responded very generously to that invitation: see D. J. Enright in *The New York Review of Books,* July 31, 1969, pp. 22-24, and Mary Ellmann in the *New York Times Book Review,* May 18, 1969, pp. 4-5.

In this context Martha's position as secretary to Mark is of significance. She is not an independent intellectual like the writer Anna whose independence is, very importantly, extended to the economic aspect of her existence. She "serves" Mark in the archetypical role of the exploited female, the secretary. Yet, because of the individual situation in Mark's house and because of her essential participation in his work, the conception, birth, and precarious development of the four-gated city in the desert,[29] she gains moments of true independence which were inaccessible to Anna because they are essentially informed by mutuality.

The plea for mutuality, potentially dangerous because it can be perverted so easily into liberal rhetoric, gains strength and substance from the detailed accounts in *The Four-Gated City* of men and women trying to achieve it through politics, through personal relationships, failing mostly, achieving it in rare vulnerable moments. In spite of its sprawling character, the novel moves fairly fast through those fifteen years of political change and changing attitudes toward politics. Martha, having gone through her communist phase when she meets Mark, seemingly has an advantage over him, as she knows what is going to come next from remembering herself moving through the different stages of passionate involvement and disillusion. And Mark does indeed follow those stages, but he is also granted his own rhythm of change. Lynda, beyond politics from the very beginning (*FGC*, p. 165), is not judged right or wrong. Lessing refrains from making her even sympathetic; the victim is by no means idealized. Lynda may know more than Martha, who has lived through all those stages as a healthy intelligent young woman; she also may not. For all of them, knowledge is a process they are engaged in; the movement of the process differs from person to person; it is open-ended for all of them.

The greatest strength of Lessing's argument for the possibility of truly mutual relationships lies in the manner in which these three people, Martha, Lynda, and Mark, are shown to move along together for some time so that they can part without bitterness. There is none of the brilliant bitterness of *The Golden Notebook* in *The Four-Gated City:* Mark, emotionally more immature than

[29]Especially important is the part she plays in drawing Mark into the social dimension of experience: she anticipates much more realistic threats of destruction for the archetypical city; informed by her experience of the past she can insist on responsibility to the reality of the future (*FGC*, p. 134).

the two women, is a very cautious intellectual whose main virtue is to resist prematurely brilliant sentences on life; Martha is above all shrewd and common-sensical, patiently intelligent about herself and other people; Lynda, badly hurt and repressed in her specific talents, is largely inarticulate. The only certainty they have reached in middle age is their trust in the help they can give each other by understanding more and more clearly their own unresolved problems. Martha, for instance, fighting furiously with the various shapes of the self-hater (*FGC*, pp. 507 ff.) imposed on her by insufficient recovery of her past, understands now the particular form of defeat in Lynda; she also understands why Mark, too possessively "in love" with Lynda, is still unable to explore her defeat and needs to close himself off to that particular part of the search, though he accepts the responsibility for the partial results of Lynda's search and Martha's: tracing, charting on the "outside," on the walls of his study (*FGC*, pp. 282, 414) what their "working" (*FGC*, pp. 354 ff.) their way down into the self will make them see.

One could say, then, that it is not Martha who is the protagonist of the *Bildungsroman, The Four-Gated City,* but Martha, Mark, and Lynda together. This is underscored by the failure of Martha's relationship with Jack. Walking toward his house in the beginning of the novel, she knows that Jack is the only one in London who would allow her "to go on living as she was now, rootless, untied, free," which is, as far as she knows, the condition of reaching the inner space with pictures and voices:

> And she understood just why he lived as he did. She had "understood" it before; but she understood it differently now that she was in that area of the human mind that Jack also inhabited. Yes. But in that case, why did she shy so strongly away from Jack, from what he stood for—or at least, she did with a good part of herself. That part whose name was Self-preservation. She knew that. *He was paying too high a price* for what he got.   (*FGC*, p. 38)

Jack at this point knows more than Martha; making love, he has discovered that "hatred is a sort of wavelength you can tune into. After all, it's always there, hatred is simply part of the world, like one of the colours of the rainbow. You can go into it, as if it were a *place*" (*FGC*, p. 57). But Jack cannot sustain that knowledge; when Martha sees him again years later, he has "become stupid"; once "all a subtle physical intelligence," his body has been taken

over by hatred, by a degraded mind that needs to possess the
other completely by degrading her morally (*FGC*, p. 386). This
development is implicit in his relationship with women when
Martha first makes love to him: his end is the body; the silences
between her and him are not filled, contented (*FGC*, p. 62). The
comfort he offers her (the acceptance, in her body, of the passing
of time and death) isolates her further, as he makes even that acceptance part of his taking possession of her and, at the same time,
frees himself from the changes that time works on his own body
(*FGC*, pp. 54, 63, 381). The relationship with Jack is a step between Anna's love that did not reach such depth of intimacy
through the body and Martha's attachment to Mark which goes
beyond it (*FGC*, pp. 227 ff.).

The second part of *The Four-Gated City*, in which Martha
really begins her life with Mark and Lynda, is introduced by a
long quote from Robert Musil's *Man without Qualities*. It is taken
from a chapter entitled "A chapter that can be skipped by anyone who has no very high opinion of thinking as an occupation"[30]
in which Ulrich, the man without qualities, Musil's mathematician-
protagonist, is straying in his thoughts from the research paper
he is working on. He has just written down an equation of the
state of water, and so he starts thinking about water. Musil, like
any writer working with the *Bildungsroman*, concentrates on the
development of his protagonist's consciousness. Ulrich, his creation and his friend, is speculative by temperament and shares
with his author a discipline of mind and imagination that makes
it difficult for him to accept the solid established reality of daili-
ness as real. His many abilities and qualities, highly favored by
the twentieth century, have only been used to a very small degree
in his scientific work that rewarded him with a promising academ-

[30]Chapter 28: "Ein Kapitel, das jeder überschlagen kann, der von der Bes-
chäftigung mit Gedanken keine besondere Meinung hat." Robert Musil, *Der
Mann ohne Eigenschaften*, ed. Adolf Frisé (Hamburg: Rowohlt, 1970). Wilkins/
Kaiser's translation is not very accurate and misses the irony; a more accurate
reading is as follows: "A chapter that can be skipped by anyone who does not
think very highly of getting involved with thoughts." A large posthumously
published part of *The Man without Qualities* is still not available in English,
nor are Musil's socio-philosophical essays and his extensive diary commen-
taries; the translations used here are mine.

ic career. When he realizes this, he breaks off his career, taking "a year's leave from his life"[31] to test his abilities by applying them to the (assumed) reality of his time. He understands immediately that this reality is at least one hundred years behind what is being thought, behind its potential, in other words,[32] and that anyone who consistently confronts reality with modern thought processes will get involved in recreating reality, that is, will have to admit chaos. Musil developed specific verbal forms to present these thought processes; he uses the term "essayistic" to define them, and this definition has been used by critics to praise or blame the novel. But "essayistic" means much more for Musil than the assumption that the novelist is entitled to ask the reader to put up with occasional reflective passages—as the one Lessing quoted from, for instance. It means for Musil: to integrate the adventure of reason into the novel, to accept the responsibility for a verbal precision that is usually limited—to mention only examples from the German language—to philosophers of language like Ludwig Wittgenstein, Karl Kraus, or the eighteenth-century mathematician Georg Christoph Lichtenberg. Essayistic is synonymous with Utopian for Musil; that is, Utopian understood as a structural principle, informing the direction of the process of consciousness, but refraining from the imposition of a goal, which would, by definition, negate the single most important element in man's understanding and projecting reality, potentiality. The basis of Ulrich's intellectual (verbal) discipline is his "sense of possibility," his *Möglichkeitssinn*.

To return to the passage that evidently interested Lessing: Ulrich, thinking about water, follows religious, scientific, and just daily, "normal" associations connected with that concept and, as usual, is stopped by the problem of communication:

> Ultimately the whole thing dissolved into systems of formulae that were all somehow connected with each other, and in the whole wide world there were only a few dozen people who thought alike about even as simple a thing as water; all the rest talked about it in languages that were at home somewhere between today and several

[31] *Man without Qualities,* I, 49; *Mann ohne Eigenschaften,* p. 47.

[32] "dass die Wirklichkeit um mindestens 100 Jahre zurück ist hinter dem, was gedacht wird." Robert Musil, *Tagebücher, Aphorismen, Essays und Reden,* ed. Adolf Frisé (Hamburg: Rowohlt, 1955), p. 786.

thousands of years ago. So it must be said that if a man just starts thinking a bit he gets into what one might call pretty disorderly company.[33]

Admitting this "disorderly company" into the decisions defining the main structures of the novel, Musil and Lessing share essential assumptions about the novelist's function and responsibility. They are both basically unconcerned about the fate of the novel as form, declaring their quite extraordinary confidence that the novelist is indeed responsible for the whole potential stratum of an aware intelligent person's experience. It is true that Ulrich's is an exceptional mind; Mark and Martha have neither the trained mental discipline nor the dedication to epistemological problems that Ulrich has. His thought processes, immersing and dissolving the mimetic surfaces of the story he is part of, his need to shape and reshape each sentence until it is a sentence on reality, a judgment of the split between knowledge and experience, put the novel on an intellectual level which is very different from that of *The Four-Gated City*. Musil, a mathematician and behavioral psychologist—he wrote his dissertation on Ernst Mach and did considerable research in the field—deeply influenced by the Viennese School, spent three decades writing and rewriting the huge torso of his *Man without Qualities;* his idea of verbal precision and verbal discipline is, obviously, quite different from Lessing's. Yet, his primary concern as a novelist, to pursue the interrelationships between the potential and the real, is also Lessing's in her last two novels.

Musil sets the (intellectual) action of the novel in the years immediately before the First World War, 1912 to 1914; the novel, never "completed," was meant to end with Ulrich's mobilization, the apocalyptic disaster of the Great War. The First World War, as the first total war, had an effect on the imagination probably stronger than the explosion of "the bomb"; at least, the effect was intellectually more confusing and destructive. Musil always

[33]*Man without Qualities*, I, 130. "Schließlich löst sich das Ganze in Systeme von Formeln auf, die untereinander irgendwie zusammenhangen, und es gibt in der weiten Welt nur einige Dutzend Menschen, die selbst von einem so einfachen Ding, wie es Wasser ist, das gleiche denken; alle anderen reden davon in Sprachen, die zwischen heute und einigen tausend Jahren früher irgendwo zu Hause sind. Man muß also sagen, daß ein Mensch, wenn er nur ein bißchen nachdenkt, gewissermaßen in recht unordentliche Gesellschaft gerät!" (*Mann ohne Eigenschaften*, p. 113)

claimed that he was not writing a historical novel at all, as he was interested in the typical. The intellectual confusion he describes so brilliantly in his novel and in many socio-philosophical essays[34] is indeed rather postwar; his analysis is meant to show that the intellectual problems that led to the disaster of the First World War could not be resolved by it, but were intensified, and led straight into the Second World War and—had he lived to know of "the bomb"—into the Third (Atomic) World War. The split between experience and knowledge has become too wide; the caricature of knowledge, scientific technological specialization, carries a great potential of destruction. The evil is by no means science *per se* for Musil—on the contrary, it has contributed greatly to the adventure of reason—but its openness to exploitation by the stupidity of power which is made possible by extreme unmediated specialization.

Whole areas of the human mind, continents of human potential, have not been explored, and their existence is denied precisely by those who, by virtue of their intellectual training and discipline, ought to be most interested in them, but who see their intellect too much as a highly sophisticated machine, defining problems in terms of instrumental rationality. Scientific decisions are determined by the question of means rather than of ends; they are "value-free." What to do with the moon after we landed on it is a layman's question, as well as what to do with "the bomb" after it has been developed. Most of these questions will be answered by the Department of Defense, another specialist. Science, dependent on a more and more complicated technology, has changed from being man's adventure of coping with nature into an instrument of domination that constantly defeats its own purpose, as it neglects the open rational structure of coping. The concept of coping is a concept of mediation, dependent on feedback from many sources; modern science has limited the number of those sources to one, the specialist. The seemingly extreme case of the inventor Jimmy Wood, writer of science fiction and

[34]See, for instance, the essays "Mathematical Man" (1913)—"Der mathematische Mensch"; the Rathenau review, "Notes on a Metaphysics" (1914)—"Anmerkung zu einer Metaphysik"; "Helpless Europe" (1922)—"Das hilflose Europa"; the Spengler review, "Mind and Experience. Notes for Readers Who Have Come Through the Decline of the West" (1921)— "Geist und Erfahrung. Anmerkungen für Leser, welche dem Untergang des Abendlandes entronnen sind"; "On Stupidity" (1937)—"Über die Dummheit." All these essays are collected in *Tagebücher*.

consumer of old occult documents, is really a good case in point —
though Musil would probably have found him too much of a
caricature. But then, technology itself has become much more
of a caricature since the Second World War. Not only is Jimmy
completely oblivious to human values, but his real genius consists in extending instrumental reason a step into the barely
charted areas and destroying them before they can be charted
properly (*FGC*, pp. 504 ff.).

In his 1921 essay, "Helpless Europe," Musil formulated the
problem: "It is not that we have too much reason and too little
soul, rather, we don't apply enough reason in problems concerning the soul."[35] Ulrich moves in a direction informed by this
mediation. After a great deal of brilliantly detailed socio-psy-
chological satire which has some parallels in the shrewd observations on the intellectual-political life in the fifties and sixties
Lessing offers in *The Four-Gated City*, Ulrich decides that he
has to go further. So far he has been quite invulnerable, being so
irresistibly right in his sentences on a society that is constantly
one step behind some phantom "Zeitgeist," instead of controlling
it intelligently. He is watching, observing, commenting — somewhat like Martha and Mark. When he begins the next stage of
his experiment of "exact living," that is, of attempting to mediate
between reason and feeling, which will take him toward the inner
space Martha and Lynda are experimenting with — Musil calls
the exploration of that space "der andere Zustand" ["the other
state"] — he will be much more vulnerable. Taking the responsibility of this mediation so very seriously, Musil-Ulrich never
found his way out of this particular stage of the experiment. He
had intended to lead the protagonist back to a more obviously
social involvement; but the further he advanced on his exploration, the more difficult the problems became, the smaller the steps
he was able to define. As he understood psychological problems
above all as epistemological questions, he could not abandon himself or Ulrich to the descent into the self the way Lessing can make
Martha or Charles Watkins abandon themselves. Martha, it is
true, retains control, even a degree of common sense on her
descent (*FGC*, pp. 507 ff.; 522 ff.), but by no means the precisely
articulated control Ulrich cannot do without: rejecting what he

---

[35]"Wir haben nicht zuviel Verstand und zuwenig Seele, sondern wir haben
zuwenig Verstand in den Fragen der Seele." (*Tagebücher*, p. 638).

calls "pedantic precision," he searches for a "fantastic precision."[36]

Ulrich is always afraid of drowning in the wrong kind of mysticism;[37] he abhors intellectual sloppiness, which Martha will accept if she thinks it necessary; he, however, cannot, in this way, project the end separated, if only temporarily so, from the means. Attempting to mediate between mathematics and mysticism, pursuing a "taghelle Mystik," a mysticism as clear as plain daylight,[38] Ulrich will never stop doubting what he experiences in his love for his sister Agathe, his "self-love,"[39] completing him to the perfection of "the other state," the Millennium[40] of that unexplored space within. Ulrich will always maintain the distance of irony while courting most seriously the "disorderly company" he meets on his exploration of the self. It is, however, a specific kind of irony:

> This is irony: to present a clergyman in such a way that a Bolshevik is hit too. To present an oaf such that the author suddenly feels: that's what I am too in part. This sort of irony—constructive irony—is more or less unknown in Germany today. It must emerge naked from the total connection of things.[41]

This "constructive irony," as Musil further points out, has nothing to do with ridicule or condescension; it is rather a structural principle to include the reader into the protagonist's process of consciousness. It is easier to follow Ulrich than to follow Martha or Watkins because we will always be given the means to question, to doubt and to reject the "disorderly company" we have been invited to join. This, however, ought not to be misunderstood as a negative judgment of Lessing's attempts to push further into the

[36]See *Man without Qualities*, I, 294; *Mann ohne Eigenschaften*, p. 247.

[37]Musil's expression "Schleudermystik" *(Mann ohne Eigenschaften*, p. 1088) is untranslatable, combining the associations "centrifugal," "hurling," "selling out below cost-price."

[38]*Mann ohne Eigenschaften*, p. 1088.

[39]Ulrich says to his sister: "Du bist meine Eigenliebe!" *Mann ohne Eigenschaften*, p. 899; *Man without Qualities*, III, 274.

[40]*Man without Qualities*, III, 431; *Mann ohne Eigenschaften*, p. 1029.

[41]"Ironie ist: einen Klerikalen so darstellen, daß neben ihm auch ein Bolschewik getroffen ist. Einen Trottel so darstellen, daß der Autor plötzlich fühlt: das bin ich ja zum Teil selbst. Diese Art von Ironie—die konstruktive Ironie—ist im heutigen Deutschland ziemlich unbekannt. Es ist der Zusammenhang der Dinge, aus dem sie nackt hervorgeht." (*Mann ohne Eigenschaften*, p. 1603).

inner space: as her fear is more urgent, more immediate than Musil's was, her means to document it have to be more drastic, and her prescriptions for hope both more striking and more vulnerable.[42] *The Four-Gated City* is a courageous and a necessary piece of work; Enright's negative review of it in *The New York Review of Books* in fact illuminates the justification of Lessing's development from *The Golden Notebook* to *The Four-Gated City:* "That Mrs. Lessing is so shrewd about things as they are makes me resent the more sharply her uneasy excursions into things to come."[43] Uneasy these excursions may be; they are now the indispensable basis for her precise observation of things as they are.

[42]See Martha's letter to Francis (*The Four-Gated City*, pp. 596ff.). Her description of "the new children" (p. 608), tentative as it is, is still too much of a good thing.

[3]Enright, p. 23. See, however, Roger Sale in his review of *Briefing for a Descent into Hell, The New York Review of Books*, May 6, 1971, p. 15.

Doris Lessing in the Sixties: The New Anatomy of Melancholy

by Frederick R. Karl

The most considerable single work by an English author in the 1960s has been done by Doris Lessing, in *The Golden Notebook* (1962). It is a carefully organized but verbose, almost clumsily-written novel, and if we were to view it solely as an aesthetic experience, we might lose most of its force. The book's strength lies not in its arrangement of the several notebooks which make up its narrative and certainly not in the purely literary quality of the writing, but in the wide range of Mrs. Lessing's interests, and, more specifically, in her attempt to write honestly about women. To be honest about women in the sixties is, for Mrs. Lessing, tantamount to a severe moral commitment, indeed almost a religious function, in some ways a corollary of her political fervor in the fifties.

While the English novel has not lacked female novelists, few indeed — including Virginia Woolf — have tried to indicate what it is like to be a woman: that is, the sense of being an object or thing even in societies whose values are relatively gentle. For her portraits, Mrs. Lessing has adopted, indirectly, the rather unlikely form of the descent into hell, a mythical pattern characterized by her female protagonists in their relationships with men, an excellent metaphor for dislocation and fragmentation in the sixties. Like Persephone, her women emerge periodically from the underworld to tell us what went awry — and it is usually sex. Within each woman who tries to survive beyond the traditional protection of housewife and mother, there exists a bomb which explodes whenever she tries to live without men, as well as when

"Doris Lessing in the Sixties: The New Anatomy of Melancholy" by Frederick R. Karl. From *Contemporary Literature*, 13 (Winter, 1972), 15-33. Reprinted by permission of the publisher.

she attempts to live with them. Her dilemma is her personal
bomb.

In a May, 1969, interview at Stony Brook, New York,[1] Mrs.
Lessing spoke of the period in which *The Golden Notebook* takes
place as a time when "everything is cracking up....It had been
falling apart since the bomb was dropped on Hiroshima." Then,
in a statement which carries the full force of the self-hatred and
driven quality we sense in Anna and Ella, two of her narrators,
she says: "Throughout my life I've had to support parties, causes,
nations, and movements which stink." She states further: "I feel
as if the Bomb has gone off inside myself, and in people around
me. That's what I mean by the cracking up. It's as if the structure
of the mind is being battered from inside. Some terrible thing is
happening." The Bomb metaphor recalls Donne's "Batter my
heart, three person'd God; for you/ As yet but knocke, breathe,
shine, and seeke to mend,/ That I may rise...." The paradox is
similar: one may be either destroyed or resurrected by the same
experience. The difference is that Donne felt rape was another
form of chastity, and Mrs. Lessing is afraid that rape is the final
step. All her women, in one way or another, are raped. As if to
confirm the paradox in her desire for experience, she says later
in the interview· "Today it's hard to distinguish between the
marvellous and the terrible." After *The Golden Notebook,* Mrs.
Lessing tried to plumb the terrible, for her next novel, *The Four-
Gated City* (1969) is nothing but nightmare, the portrait of a city,
London, in which all four gates are guarded by Cerberus.

To continue temporarily this metaphor, the four gates in that
later novel all lead to houses of constriction, nightmare, impotence, not dissimilar to the four notebooks of the earlier novel.
At each gate, Mrs. Lessing's Martha is seeking a path, similar to
the faltering figure of Dante at the beginning of the *Inferno.* We
remember that the protagonist undertaking the Perilous Journey
in her five-novel series, *Children of Violence,* is named Martha
Quest, whose last name suggests the motif. Accordingly, if we are
to discuss Mrs. Lessing's work in the sixties—the period when
her earlier ideas found suitable techniques—we must play off
two books which converge and move away from each other, the
experimental *Golden Notebook* and the even more tentative

[1]Reported in *New American Review,* 8 (Jan. 1970), 166-179.

Four-Gated City, which crowns the *Children of Violence* series.[2] Like asymptotes, the two books approach each other without touching, all the while utilizing common images and symbols: the gate, the door, the house or room, the descent into hell, the quest. To gain a sense of the underworld, where all quests lead to further frustration, we should begin with *The Golden Notebook.*

At first, it would seem that Mrs. Lessing has picked up where Joyce has ended, with Molly Bloom's somewhat ambiguous "yes I said yes I will Yes." After all, her women, Anna Wulf and Molly Jacobs, appear to be saying "yes" to themselves and thumbing their noses at convention. But this is only an initial impression. Actually, their uncertain state of survival fits well into the ironies, paradoxes, conspiracies, lies, and deceptions that attend the world around them. About midway through the book, in the "Red Notebook 2," Comrade Ted tells of his idyllic meeting with the father-figure Stalin, whose wise presence appears to see and know all. When Anna has read this tale of Ted's meeting with Stalin, she comments: "But what seemed to me important was that it could be read as parody, irony or seriously. It seems to me this fact is another expression of the fragmentation of everything, the painful disintegration of something that is linked with what I feel to be true about language, the thinning of language against the density of our experience."[3]

In one sense, this tale, which can be read as either parody or as slavering devotion to an ideal, is the way we can read most human experience since the end of the Second World War. Mrs. Lessing tells us something about human experience in those years. She tells us, among other things that experience is infinite, variable, and messy (neither Sartre's contingency nor Marx's necessity), that all is seeming, that we cannot measure life according to pre-conceptions, that indeed we cannot distinguish between subject

---

[2]*Martha Quest* (1952), *A Proper Marriage* (1954), *The Ripple from the Storm* (1958), *Landlocked* (1965), *The Four-Gated City* (1969). Her other fiction includes: *The Grass Is Singing* (1950), *Five* (1953, short novels), *Retreat to Innocence* (1956). *The Habit of Loving* (1957), short stories), *A Man and Two Women* (1963, short stories), *African Stories* (1964).

[3]*The Golden Notebook* (New York: McGraw, 1963), p. 259. Further references to this edition will be cited in the text.

and object, that, in many ways, we are our own self-made fools. To say this is not to wallow in endless guilt about our deficiencies, but to suggest that she gives us a way of seeing the familiar and the expected. Like Anthony Powell, who views his characters mythically against endless sweeps of time, even as emerging like saurians from primeval swamps, Mrs. Lessing presents her women as Protean, as endlessly trying to recreate themselves, only to see them fall back befuddled by men like Paul-Michael or Saul Green, who need women as mothers and/ or scapegoats for their own weaknesses. The individual is always on the threshold of drowning in the collective consciousness, a political as well as a psychological point for Mrs. Lessing.

Again like Powell, with his insistent mythical-temporal references, Mrs. Lessing has mighty metaphors. The notebooks, four in number, are obviously facets of Anna's life, as clearly affirmations of her attempt to find unity as evidence of her fragmentation. "I keep four notebooks, a black notebook, which is to do with Anna Wulf, the writer; a red notebook, concerned with politics; a yellow notebook, in which I make stories out of my experience; and a blue notebook which tries to be a diary" (p. 406). In one way, these notebooks fulfill what the interior monologue does for Joyce: the derivations of this novel may be female novelists, George Meredith's feminist tracts, and Simone de Beauvoir's *The Second Sex,* but the structural conception is neo-Joycean, much as Powell's *Music of Time* is neo-Proustian despite its patina of Waugh and early Huxley.

Yet, despite those notebooks as outposts of achievement or sanity, as a means of holding on when everything else is blocked, Anna does not triumph through them. Rather, she must always return to her room—like Gregor Samsa's, her room is a fierce refuge against harsh men and events—and in her room she dreams endlessly. They are terrible things, her nightmares, which are almost comparable to Gregor's metamorphosis into a bug. One particular and recurring dream is of going under water, drowning in the very element she is trying to breast. Yet such dreams of anxiety mock Anna's conscious belief that, although ordinary, she is capable through personal exertion of moving society just a fraction. She refers herself to Sisyphus, another "boulder-pusher" who puts his shoulder hopefully to the stone even while suspecting it will roll back. One time it may not.

Her dreams and her will are always in conflict. In the "Blue

Notebook 1," Anna tells her psychiatrist, Mrs. Marks ("Mother Sugar"), of her dream of the casket. Instead of the casket holding beautiful things, it is more like Pandora's box, letting out odiferous waves of war, blood, bits of flesh, illness. Then, suddenly transformed, the contents become a small, green, smirking crocodile, whose large frozen tears turn into diamonds. The precise image is unclear, but the sardonic crocodile mocks all of Anna's dreams, hopes, and illusions. One may assume that the casket and the malicious crocodile are Anna's burdens or obstacles, always there when she seeks good faith or release.

This dream is linked to several others involving a smirking dwarflike old man, sometimes deformed, sometimes with a "great protruding penis," whose form originally took shape from a vase, like the crocodile in the casket. These interior, hollowed-out shapes, whether casket or vase, are surely vaginal, and therefore the misshapen, malicious figures who fill them are symbolic of the men intruding in Anna's life. These men are necessary for her at the same time they are inadequate, and the dreams are examples of anxiety. Late in the book, in a part that prefigures the section called "The Golden Notebook," Anna sees herself as the dwarf figure, as, what she calls, the "principle of joy-in-destruction." Perhaps she is right. What she means is that the anxiety regarding men is built into her own needs, that in some self-destructive way she is bound to seek out men who will remind her of the crocodile and the deformed dwarf with the protruding penis. All this would be consistent with her desire to live existentially, beyond the pale of normal supports.

In her Stony Brook interview, Mrs. Lessing spoke of how she uses dreams whenever she is stuck in a book. "I fill my brain with the material for a new book, go to sleep, and I usually come up with a dream which resolves the dilemma." Then she says, "The unconscious artist who resides in our depths is a very economical individual. With a few symbols a dream can define the whole of one's life, and warn us of the future, too. Anna's dreams contain the essence of her experience in Africa, her fears of war, her relationship to communism, her dilemma as a writer."[4] While simplified, this is an honest attempt to create literary material out of Freudian analysis, although elsewhere Mrs. Lessing rejects the Freudian unconscious as too dark and fearful a place.

[4]*New American Review*, p. 172.

But the dream is a warning, whether it is sugar-coated by Mrs. Marks (a female "Marx") or whether Anna wishes to see it through. The dream always brings her back to the closeness of her room, just as Martha Quest in *The Four-Gated City* is nearly always enclosed in houses and interiors. Anna writes in the "Golden Notebook" section that: "My big room, like the kitchen, had become, not the comfortable shell which held me, but an insistent attack on my attention from a hundred different points, as if a hundred enemies were waiting for my attention to be deflected so that they might creep up behind me and attack me" (p. 541). This fear of attack or rape; the use of the room as refuge—as in the later book, the houses as lairs; the insistent need to withdraw into nightmares—all these are part of the descent into hell, that mythical and yet personal seeking after self. When Mrs. Lessing foresees that her imperfect female characters will always select an inadequate man to make themselves miserable, she is insisting that hell is within—a visceral time bomb—and it will not be simply exorcised by anything the external world can offer. With this, we have placed Mrs. Lessing with the nineteenth-century novelists whose protagonists are themselves piecing together fragments of experience and attempting to derive some unity; she is not with the later novelists who have taken patterns of fragmentation for granted.

Perhaps the closest we come to Mrs. Lessing's sense of the sixties is in Harold Pinter. At first, the two seem dissimilar, and the coupling of their names may appear bizarre. But both the playwright and the novelist are heir to a development in literature that has become insistent in the last fifty to sixty years. Since Kafka and Proust, there has developed what we may call a literature of enclosure. It is a type of fiction in which breadth of space is of relatively little importance. Space exists not as extension but only as a volume to be enclosed in a room, or a house, or even in a city. Joyce's Dublin has this quality—as though the city were not open to the sky but were a series of enclosures of houses and bars and meeting places. Such a city conveys not the sense of something unfolding, but of something accruing, like an internal growth which invisibly expands to tremendous size under cover of the flesh.

Kafka's use of rooms and houses is, of course, one of the prototypes of this kind of fiction. Another is, obviously, the room of Proust's Marcel, where he stifles in heat and frustration and self-hatred. A third is the cluttered rooms of Beckett's Murphy or Watt, who bitterly malign their fate and remain immobile. Such a development in literature may, at first, appear to be a direct response to the Freudian reliance on the regressive tendencies of the adult to return to the womb, that quasi-sacred place where needs are met without effort and without external threat. Such a response is certainly there, and it is questionable if such a literature would have developed, at least in this manner, without the influence of psychoanalytic thought. To follow this argument — which ultimately is not the major one — is to see that the room is the place in which one can dream, in which one can isolate himself as a consequence of neurosis or withdrawal symptoms, all as part of that desire to seek refuge from external onslaughts which are too much for the individual to withstand. All this is certain.

But there is a further argument for the preponderance of rooms and rooming houses in Pinter and Mrs. Lessing.[5] I think we can say that the room or house signifies for them an entire culture, in particular England's shrinkage in the sixties from its postwar eminence to a minor "enclosed power." In *The Four-Gated City,* for example, Martha Quest uses Mark Coldridge's house as a way of settling her life and at the same time as an escape from a social and political world she cannot control. As a medieval family once hid behind drawbridge and moat, she hides behind the door, and thus self-concealment is both a physical and psychological fact.

Since enclosure is so significant in Mrs. Lessing's work, its features need detailed description: even though the room is a place of refuge, it is also the locale of one's descent into hell. Its physical desolation is indeed a counterpart of the character's psychological state. Further, the room serves as a tiny stage for those on a string in a puppet show. The enclosure fixes the limits of sexuality, threatens and reassures within bounds, freeing as it limits. As a consequence, the novel becomes personal, subjective, solipsistic, even when externals like political events are of significance.

The room bottles up rage, leaves no escape for anger except when it is directed back into the self. The lair is itself a physical symbol of impotence — lack of choice, will, determination; identity

[5]Besides *The Golden Notebook* and *The Four-Gated City,* cf. the rooming house milieu of *In Pursuit of the English* (1960) with similar places in Pinter's *The Birthday Party, The Room, The Dumb Waiter, The Caretaker,* and *The Homecoming.*

is indistinguishable from one's furnishings. (See Anthony Powell for this point also—most of his action takes place in living rooms and at parties; only Widmerpool has will—the rest are virtually impotent.) Clearly, the panoramic novel is snuffed out, for adventure is lost; there is no struggle. The room or house is a battleground. The family relationship is symbiotic. In such a room, eros becomes sex, spirit becomes physical, idea or theory becomes fact. Whereas space was once used for repetition of a holy act, the act of creation itself, now its repetition is one of staleness, of folding anxiety into neurosis. In the room a dumb waiter serves as a feedline, or people themselves are "dumb waiters."

Finally, in the novel of enclosure, the room is the ultimate of the profane world, negating Mircea Eliade's idea of space as being sacred. The room is geometric space, not the infinite space that Eliade sees as central to a reliving of the cosmogony: "It follows that every construction or fabrication has the cosmogony as paradigmatic model. The creation of the world becomes the archetype of every human gesture, whatever its plan of reference may be. We have already seen that settling in a territory reiterates the cosmogony. Now that the cosmogonic value of the Center has become clear, we can still better understand why every human establishment repeats the creation of the world from a central point (the navel)."[6] Keep in mind Mrs. Lessing's "four-gated city" when Eliade writes: "On the most archaic levels of culture this possibility of transcendence is expressed by various images of an opening; here, in the sacred enclosure, communication with the gods is made possible; hence there must be a door to the world above by which the gods can descend to earth and man can symbolically ascend to heaven."[7] When the room or house was sacred, one's conception of space was infinite, extending to the infinite space of the universe. Breathing in the air of this room, one could as it were breathe in something coexistent with the cosmos. Lessing and Pinter, like Beckett, provide rooms whose air is foul; space is not infinite, but geometric, and it signifies the final vestiges of the profane city.

All literature has had its enclosures, but never before has the interior been so intensely the depository of "normal" illness and anxiety. There is virtually no nature in Pinter or in the Lessing of

[6]*The Sacred and the Profane* (New York: Harper Torchbook, 1961), p. 45.

[7]*Ibid.*, p. 26.

these novels, and certainly not nature as relaxation or renewal. When Pinter wishes to speak of nature, he puts its joys, ironically, into the mouth of a killer like Goldberg, in *The Birthday Party:* "Because I know what it is to wake up with the sun shining, to the sound of the lawnmower, all the little birds, the smell of the grass, church bells, tomato juice—."[8] Here we have the typical Pinter metaphysic: the juxtaposition of dissimilars as the image or symbol of dislocation. So, too, Doris Lessing. Scribbling away in her notebooks, Anna-Ella tries to deny the outside, to negate possible renewal through alignment with external forces. Just as all anxiety comes from within—after all, nothing very dreadful really happens to her—so, also, all surcease must come from within. Thus, the modern predicament: caught in our own existential stoicism, we cling to our miseries as the sole form of our salvation.

So much is clear. What is curious is that Mrs. Lessing has picked up many of D. H. Lawrence's injunctions about mechanical sex, about enervating marriages, about the boredom of non-vital relationships, and yet she has broken with his romanticism, in which human failings, or successes, are worked out in a natural climate. To illustrate how she accepts Lawrence's indictment of mechanical sex while still accepting the machine: at one point in *The Golden Notebook*, Mrs. Lessing speaks of the vaginal orgasm, as opposed to the superficial clitoral orgasm, as something "that is created by the man's need for a woman, and his confidence in that need." She says she can always sense when a relationship is dying, for the man begins to insist on giving her clitoral orgasms, and that is a substitute and a fake. The only female sensations occur "when a man, from the whole of his need and desire takes a woman and wants all her response" (p. 186).

Through some existential process of choice or search, Anna wants to deny the historical role of women; but in her rightful desire to destroy female bondage, she does not see that the world has itself entered a new phase. And the very qualities of tenderness and satisfaction equally given and equally accepted are no longer possible for men who have sublimated their human qualities for the practical advantages of civilization. Lawrence spoke of such enervation, and he felt it had arrived. Why should we doubt that it has? In fact, by 1969, with *The Four-Gated City*, Mrs. Lessing appears willing to admit that the question has

[8]*The Birthday Party* (New York: Grove, 1968), p. 45.

answered itself. But, earlier, in *The Golden Notebook,* she has
only drawn up to the edge. Probably, her commitment to the
social possibilities of technology had blinded her to the steady
erosion of individual consciousness.

Nevertheless, *The Golden Notebook* is one of the few English
novels of the last decades to project outward rather than seek
forms of settlement. Anna's quest, already doomed to futility and
failure, must continue: as an emancipated woman, as an outsider, she must complete or doom herself with a male. She cannot
be complaisant. Even as she may suspect that the male is becoming dehumanized—she is familiar with Freud—and is capable
of relating only to profession, career, or materiality, she still
asserts choice. To justify her existence, she must deny her historical and biological role. To justify her existence, she must start
the descent that most women attempt to avoid or mitigate through
conventional marriage.

While *The Golden Notebook* stops short of the apocalypse, *The
Four-Gated City* embraces the beast. If the former limns a kind of
limbo, then the latter is indeed hell. Yet Mrs. Lessing's statements in *Declaration* do not prepare us for the sense of doom in
The Four-Gated City. In *Declaration,* she asserted her preference
for the nineteenth-century realists—Stendhal, Balzac, Tolstoy,
Dostoevsky—who despite their differences, stated their "faith in
man himself." She said, further, that the writer must not plunge
into despair, as Genet, Sartre, Camus, and Beckett have done, nor
into the collective conscience, as the socialist country writers have
done. "The point of rest [for the writer] should be the writer's
recognition of man, the responsible individual, voluntarily sub-
mitting his will to the collective, but never finally; and insisting
on making his own personal and private judgements before every
act of submission." Particularly ironic is her statement that "there
is a new man about to be born...a man whose strength will not be
gauged by the values of the mystique of suffering."[9]

By the time of *The Four-Gated City,* twelve years after *Declaration,* Mrs. Lessing has descended into despair. The four gates are
four houses, and the four houses are all various circles of Dante's
Inferno. The vision here is especially compelling because it appears to contradict the drift of her earlier work beginning with

[9]*Declaration,* ed. Tom Maschler (London: MacGibbon, 1957), pp. 194, 191.

The Grass Is Singing[10] and including even *The Golden Notebook*. In that first novel, concerned with the struggle between white interests and black survival, she demonstrated she could write a personal story against the background of complex social and political relationships. In fact, many of the attitudes and situations of that protagonist, Mary Turner, were later grafted on to Martha Quest of the *Children of Violence* series, chiefly the survival, or disintegration, of the individual amidst collective pressures. Mrs. Lessing catches superbly the degeneration of those whose relationships are based on subterfuge. Ostensibly about Mary Turner, the novel is prophetic: while trying to maintain his supremacy, the white declines, eventually fragments.

When Mary Turner "becomes" Martha Quest, tensions intensify between individual need and social rejection, between individual flexibility and social rigidity so that the first four volumes of the series, before *The Four-Gated City*, maintain an uneasy balance between stability and threat, order and potential violence. Martha herself grows up amidst the distrust between English and Africans and their mutual hatred of blacks, Jews, and change. These emotions, which she is aware of from childhood, become the major conflicts she confronts in the larger world. Already refusing the constricted role her mother forced herself to play, Martha drifts toward socialism and atheism, becomes pro-black, and attempts anything that will lead to substantial personal values. She is, of course, seeking her identity as a woman and as a person.

The first four volumes unfortunately often become trivial, especially when the main line of the narrative becomes lost in political details or in inconsequential personal acts. Mrs. Lessing knows certain things very well—the land, family relationships which have soured, the frustration of meaningless affections, the way parents hang on to their children when neither can really bear the other—but when she details the dogma of the Marxist-Trotsky-Stalin axis, the reader has no place to go. There is, nevertheless, in those early novels a curious psychological play, for those blacks hovering as dark presences in the background of white settlements are curious embodiments of Martha's slowly

[10]The title comes from *The Waste Land*, V: "In this decayed hole among the mountains/ In the faint moonlight, the grass is singing/ Over the tumbled graves, about the chapel...." The quotation is a metaphor for the Turner household and beyond that for the entire white African society.

emerging other self. Like the black natives, waiting to break out to claim consciousness, she, too, is twisting and turning in her appointed, non-conscious roles as daughter and then wife. As "Mattie," she is a girl who will fit into the colonial pattern; as Martha, she is her own woman seeking consciousness.

Closely related to the dialectic of her roles is the recurring image of the black women who refuse to be fragmented by vague choices and who breed contentedly; they are essential women, avatars of Martha's own potential future. But Martha knows that these women do not live in a blissful, untroubled paradise, that they are diseased, that they die young, that they have given themselves over completely to a natural process without sufficient individual will. And yet she envies their instinctual mode of survival, their indifference to consciousness. The temptation is to be Mattie. And yet she also knows how impossible it would be for her to try to emulate the black women. She must become Sisyphus.

These first volumes in the series, very much a product of the 1950s in their linear political and social aspirations, were evidently part of Mrs. Lessing's own experience in Southern Rhodesia and parallel in many ways arguments and attitudes put forth by Simone de Beauvoir in *The Second Sex* (1949). One might go further and say that *Children of Violence,* except for its ideology, is a working out of entire chapters in the de Beauvoir book: Childhood, The Young Girl, Sexual Initiation, Lesbianism, The Married Woman, The Mother, Social Life, The Narcissist, The Woman in Love, The Independent Woman, et al. In the latter chapter, in fact, Simone de Beauvoir writes a propos of Martha: "When she [woman] is productive, active, she regains her transcendence; in her projects she concretely affirms her status as subject; in connection with the aims she pursues, with the money and the rights she takes possession of, she makes trial of and senses her responsibility."[11]

Yet as the series continues, Doris Lessing clearly refuses for her characters the role of existential female, as later she rejected the polemics of women's liberation for a larger, more political view of life. Mrs. Lessing's Martha fears recurring history, knowing that she "could take no step, perform no action, no matter how apparently new and unforeseen, without the secret fear that in fact

[11]*The Second Sex* (New York: Bantam, 1961), p. 639.

this new and arbitrary thing would turn out to be part of the inevitable process she was doomed to."[12] This sense of nightmarish repetition, of destiny repeating itself inexorably, is of course very much part of the literature of enclosure. With spatiality, one can avoid repetition through novelty of choice or act, but enclosure negates personal expansion.

The Four-Gated City begins with suffocation and strangulation. The key images in the first pages are of grime, globules of wet, browny-grey textures, oilcloth with spilled sugar, gritty smears, grease, thumb marks. All these are "inside" images and forerun the theme of enclosure. Possibly the chief scenic effect of the book, as befitting Mrs. Lessing's continued descent into a fiercely populated hell, is either Bosch's "Garden of Earthly Delights" or his "Last Judgment." In both paintings, as in Mrs. Lessing's novel, there is the mixture of sacred and profane, of realism and fantasy, of the loving and the obscene, of large vision and carping detail, of panorama and locale. There is no single style, but a comprehensive, somewhat mannered tone. There is, also, as a sexual byproduct, the desire to wound and be wounded—both to gain delight from watching others roast over a slow fire and to be roasted oneself over the same fire. The theme of torture is never far from either Bosch or Mrs. Lessing. Both put a roof over hell. Durrell's Alexandria was also hell, but frantic sensuality was at least a temporary escape. And while Anthony Powell's seriatim novels are filled with mythical hells, whether from Homer or from Wagner, his central character, Nicholas Jenkins, remains relatively isolated from the deterioration around him. His descents are pratfalls, while others have indeed fallen. In Mrs. Lessing's novel, Martha succumbs. The theme is not so clearly decline and disintegration—as in Camus' *The Fall*—as it is the effort of sensitive human beings to survive schizophrenia.

Amidst the various denizens of Mrs. Lessing's hell, the key one is possibly Lynda Coldridge, the wife of Mark; it is to Mark's house that Martha goes seeking a refuge from external events which are themselves mad. Lynda has proven too sensitive for normal contacts—among other things, sexual relations—and her waking hours are spent in trying to hold on. At first, she survives by eating pills, but periodically she gives up these props in order to seek inner support. Yet in some curious way—and she is not

---

[12]*A Proper Marriage* (New York: Simon, 1954), p. 337.

particularly sympathetic—she is a seer, one who has a sense of impending disasters, and Martha evidently cannot forgo her presence. In fact, Lynda's very ability to "hear voices" and to experience visions is, in her society, a sign of her sickness. In other societies where such talents were indicative of the majority, she would not be sick or else her extravagances would serve a social function. One is reminded of R. D. Laing's injunction to those who would work with psychotics: "One has to be able to orientate oneself as a person in the other's scheme of things rather than only to see the other as an object in one's own world...."[13] A man who suddenly kneels down amidst a crowd to pray fervently is insane; in church, he is considered devout.

What is of interest here, however, is not simply Lynda. By herself, she is not a compelling person. Mrs. Lessing has moved beyond trying to create attractive characters whose point of view creates empathy. What is compelling is the fact that Martha Quest has given up the quest. She will never reach the Holy Grail, nor even continue the perilous journey, for she is seeking security at any level, and finds that it is easier to remain in the Coldridge house—behind that locked gate—and relate herself to Lynda's mad state. As long as Lynda is mad, Martha has Mark, while Lynda herself needs Martha's sense of order. All attachments are symbiotic. Again Laing proves instructive: "Generally speaking, the schizoid individual is not erecting defences against the loss of a part of his body. His whole effort is rather to preserve his *self*."[14] This is, by now, Martha's effort: to preserve a person who is herself "precariously structured," the overall symbol of which is Lynda's tenacious attempt to hold on without returning to the hospital.

There is some warning of this deteriorative process in *The Golden Notebook*, during Anna's affair with Saul Green and shortly after with her dream of the dwarfed man with the protruding penis: "Sitting there I had a vision of the world with nations, systems, economic blocks, hardening and consolidating; a world where it would become increasingly ludicrous even to talk about freedom, or the individual conscience. I know that this sort of vision has been written about, it's something one has read, but for a moment it wasn't words, ideas, but something

[13]*The Divided Self* (Gretna: Pelican, 1965), p. 26.

[14]*Ibid.*, p. 76.

I felt, in the substance of my flesh and nerves, as true" (p. 485). Her affair with Saul Green, destructive in virtually every way, is a forerunner of nearly all relationships Martha has in *The Four-Gated City.*

More specifically, those four gates to the four houses where Martha stays are themselves microcosms of English society, and, ultimately, of the world as Mrs. Lessing envisages it. It is a society that follows the holocaust of the Second World War and which immediately precedes the apocalyptic vision that ends our present notion of the world and the book. Yeats's rough beast has arrived. Whereas once gates were entrances that one opened while seeking something or someone, they are now barriers which close off exits or prevent egress. The four bleak houses of England are the restaurant at the beginning, where Martha would be "Mattie" (a "good fellow") and would be expected to lose herself in a dull marriage; second, the house of Mark Coldridge, a writer somewhat close to the center of power, but besieged by predatory journalists and a center of madness, inactivity, frustration, as well as some kindness; third, Jack's house—literally, that Jack built—where girls go to be broken in for their future as prostitutes, where Jack sits like a spider catching them on the fly; and, finally, Paul's house—Paul is Mark's nephew—where derelicts and misfits, sexual cripples and the maimed, as in some James Purdy story, congregate under Paul's protective wing.

The connecting link to all the houses, to all the gates, is Martha herself. At the opening of the novel, she arrives at the restaurant when she comes to post-war London, a continuation of the earlier *Landlocked.* She then seeks a job as a secretary, but accepts temporarily a post as Mark Coldridge's housekeeper. As the house becomes a walled-in medieval fortress which protects her against further action, even further thought, the job turns into a way of life. The house is Bosch's hell, Gregor Samsa's room, the Invisible Man's basement cell, but it is also a refuge. Perhaps a modern view of hell is no more than this, Sartre's *No Exit,* a place in which one loses himself, his will, his determination, and exchanges choice for a lair. Dostoevsky pressed this option in the Grand Inquisitor scene, and the contemporary response is clear. Freedom, as Martha once quested after it in the stifling atmosphere of the white man's Africa, is not worth the struggle; we are, she appears to accept, all caught in a larger scheme anyway, and it is better to be besieged than to besiege. Using Mark's house as a base of operations—settling in for the rest of her useful years—Martha occasionally ventures out, to have casual sex with Jack and to continue the debasement of her former intentions. Or else she gravitates to Paul's house, a kind of live-in encounter group, in which the maimed attempt to support each other; all experience there is "tripping," hallucinatory.

Shut in, besieged, surrounded by madness, frustration, sickness, inadequate, furtive sex, gated, with hyena-like journalists howling outside, with nuclear bombs in production, with marches and counter-marches, with threats always looming—whether Russia, fission, or personal schizophrenia—Martha has to put herself together in some fashion. If she is enclosed in four houses, she is also Janus-faced: the softness of Mattie is the reverse of the questing Martha. The houses are both integrative and disintegrative, much as the notebooks in *The Golden Notebook* represented two opposing strains: those parts of Anna-Ella which could be consolidated and those pieces which defied stabilization. The apocalyptic epilogue of *The Four-Gated City* represents, in some ways, the "golden notebook" section in that book. The content of both is seeking form. In geometry, the circle indicates perfection, completion. But Mrs. Lessing utilizes not circles, but "fours": four notebooks, four gates or houses, and epilogues or "golden" episodes. The "fours" indicate all directions, negate completion, baffle expansion, intensify the enclosed quest. There is no magic in four. And the content finally achieves a form that allows no exit, except through the apocalyptic vision of a new, technological world which ends the novel.

The hopeful, striving Martha of the earlier books in the series is clearly very different from the Martha of this novel and also different from the Anna-Ella of *The Golden Notebook*. Like the rest of us, Mrs. Lessing has changed her former vision, in which political and social action—the image of Sisyphus pushing that boulder—was possible, even though results were miniscule and possibly not even visible in one's own lifetime. Now the world has turned upon itself, in a repetitive cycle of violence: *Children of Violence* ends in a final disaster in which radioactivity, lethal gas, nerve gas, and the other by-products of a run-away society have ended life as we know it. Like Antony Powell, as his series darkens, Mrs. Lessing gets gloomier and murkier, heading toward that vision which has rarely been sympathetic to the English temperament. It is chiefly a continental design, the sense of final things in Mann, Kafka, Conrad. Deeply humanistic, Mrs. Lessing takes up the familiar question of technology in conflict with the rest of life and foresees, in striking images of disintegration, science as inexorable, while human values, never more than tenuous, are trapped in Atreus-like houses in which people devour each other.

The symbol of breakdown in morality and in humanity is Jimmy Wood, a mild-mannered scientist and writer of space fiction who is a human computer. Jimmy represents the bland forces of military, science, and government which, with velvet glove, offer salvation while they are missing a human dimension: "It was as if Jimmy had been born with one of the compartments of the human mind developed to its furthest possibility, but this was at the cost to everything else." Jimmy specifically has been designing machines which can tamper with the human mind, making improvements on existing machines which destroy part of the human brain by electric charges. In addition, he has developed on government request machines to destroy the brains of dangerous persons, who would then vanish without protest. Further, Jimmy has worked on and perfected a machine for "stimulating, artificially, the capacities of telepathy, 'second sight,' etc." So that the machine would always have fuel, it is necessary for governments or the military to have on hand a "human bank" which the machine could utilize. Such a human radio or telephone, or whatever, would provide an extension to the machine and prove more flexible; after that, it is up to the military to find a specific use.

In a way, Jimmy Wood's invention works, for certain people do have psychological reactions as telepaths. The drift is toward the interchangeability of people and machines, until life itself is indistinguishable. The final sections of the novel concern a letter from Martha, now old and worn-out, addressed to Francis Coldridge, Mark's son. At the time Martha is barely surviving in Robinson Crusoe style on a "contaminated island" off the coast of Scotland. Britain has been poisoned; the political center has shifted to Africa and to the Chinese. The time is less than thirty years from now. In her *New American Review* interview, Mrs. Lessing spoke of *The Four-Gated City* as a prophetic novel. "I think that the 'iron heel' is going to come down. I believe the future is going to be cataclysmic."[15]

[15]*New American Review,* p. 175.

In *The Golden Notebook,* the key issue was human relationships, especially the relationships between men and women as a
key image of modern humanity or inhumanity. Sexual liberation,
from the female side, and sexual restructuring, from the male,
were necessary. But in 1969, Mrs. Lessing said: "I'm impatient
with people who emphasize sexual revolution. I say we should all
go to bed, shut up about sexual liberation, and go on with the
important matters."[16] Her turn upon herself is curious, for this
conflict between collective politics and personal matters had
been the crux of her work of the last two decades. Anna's psychiatrist, in fact, suggested that her political activity was an
avoidance of personal blockage. The conflict was real. Now, the
conflict has been "resolved." The incredibly difficult question of
man-woman relationships becomes "going to bed," and sexual
liberation seems an art of conscious choice, whereas before the
very question of liberation raised all the familiar problems of
identity and will.

The Four-Gated City is, in several ways, a curious finale to the
Children of Violence series. It appears to cap the "enclosure"
theme, so that Martha ends up, in Mark's house, as exhausted
and otiose as the narrator in Proust or one of Beckett's dying
gladiators. Up to this point, Martha, like Powell's Nicholas
Jenkins, had been involved in a *Bildungsroman.* Far more than
Jenkins, however, Martha has rubbed her nose into the filth of
events. Observer more than participant, Jenkins moves easily in
his own version of the dance of time. But while he waltzes or re-
laxes into old familiar motions, as appropriate to someone who
glides through an established society, Martha contorts her body
into the brittle shapes of modern dance, as befitting someone who
must always create the society in which she is to move.

Self-evidently, she is involved in constant assertions of her
mind and body, while Powell's protagonist has a ready-made
group into which he always fits. And although he acts as a voice
of decency and constraint among those who indulge in desperate
ventures, he is too reserved to take any chances for himself. (We
remember he is Sloth in the tableau of the Seven Deadly Sins.)
Mrs. Lessing, born in Persia of British parents, then coming to
England as an alien from Rhodesia, where she had lived from
her fifth through her thirtieth year, is herself the prototype of
the unsettled artist. Not unusually, her Martha must go through

[16]*Ibid.*

all the awkward, anxiety-producing movements of the dance of time. There is no point at which she can stop to say: "I have arrived, I can see all around me." For her, all experience is a series of new starts. Powell's Jenkins need never start anew, for all the flotsam and jetsam from the past are at hand to create continuity in one fluid, dance-like step. Only events interfere.

In addition to these twists and turns, Martha must struggle through male-female relationships which could stifle her at any given point. In *Martha Quest,* she must deal with a series of narcissistic young men whose need is not for her, but to assure some nagging fear in themselves—whose own hesitancy about their manhood shades every aspect of their relationships and turns most sexual episodes into mother-child encounters. With herself unfulfilled as a woman, Martha must avoid her "biological destiny," which would mean the end of all; at the same time, she finds such lack of will attractive as an alternative to setting herself constantly against her destiny. This feeling is particularly acute, as we mentioned before, when Martha views the easy compromise of the black women, who give in early to their destiny and live without seething.

Yet Martha fights off the situation in which "men seemed to press a button, as it were, and one was expected to turn into something else for their amusement"; that is, "married, signed and sealed away."[17] In her relationship with her mother, in particular, one sees what Martha has to fight through even before she comes up against the young men. She detests her mother as only those can who have translated their hatred into pity. That is to say, she must fight against her mother in herself; she must be aware of sliding back. For Mrs. Quest is a mother, not a human being or person, and Martha must resist the same role for herself. Not only has Mrs. Quest been destroyed by racism—like most of the other settlers, she accepts a schizoid, paranoiac routine in which blacks both serve and persecute her—but she has been destroyed by her sexual, emotional, psychological repression. Having been miserable, she rejoices in her philosophy of misery; and needing to justify her own choice, she must destroy her daughter's alternatives.

Therefore Martha's rebellious assertions of will are the substance of the first four volumes of *Children of Violence.* To understand this fact is to see how contrary *The Four-Gated City*

[17]*Martha Quest* (New York: Simon, 1952), p. 268.

really is, for there all relationships are symbiotic. No one stands without using another as crutch; no one is sick or well without influencing the sickness or well-being of another. And these relationships are not of the sort that build a whole or unify a group which can stand together; they are an infection, a slow stain throughout the society. A good image of such suppurating love and affection comes when Mark Coldridge approaches his symbiotic other half, the mad Lynda:

> He kissed her. Lips, a slit, in the flesh of a face, were pressed against a thin tissue of flesh that saved them from pressing a double row of teeth which had lumps of metal in them. Then these lips moved to touch her own slit through which she was equipped to insert food or liquid, or make sounds. A kiss. That part of Martha which observed this remarkable ritual was filled with a protective compassion for these two ridiculous little creatures—as if invisible arms, vast, peaceful, maternal, were stretched around them both, and rocked them like water.[18]

The imagery is remarkable for its quality of lost identity, of submergence in another, of rejection of self. From here, the novel ends with the apocalypse; the ultimate bomb goes off, and a profane society has embraced its doom.

None of this is witty, or even ironic. Perhaps because she was an outsider, Mrs. Lessing has always been earnest and has never traded on the English tradition of social comedy, or muddling through. Both Anthony Powell and C. P. Snow, in their vastly different ways, belong to that mode, as do most of the 1950s "Angries" writers. In her rather grim, relentless manner, Mrs. Lessing has tried to be both panoramic (about racism, communism, bombism, all the "ologies" and "isms") and subjective. Her length indicates as much: *The Four-Gated City* runs one quarter of a million words, and *The Golden Notebook* is about as long. And yet with all her prolixity, she has almost nowhere to go. She is getting less personal, as she suggests in her *New American Review* interview, and she has destroyed the objective world. There is always science fiction, but in that mode those intense human relationships which are the strength of her earlier work can have no outlet. One wonders as he holds these two considerable achievements in hand if still another novelist is succumbing to apocalyptic visions as a way of settling personal problems.

[18]*The Four-Gated City* (New York: Knopf, 1969), p. 468.

The Case Against McCarthy:
A Review of *The Group*

by Norman Mailer

It had to happen. It was in the command of all the ironies that there would come a day when our First Lady of Letters would write a book and lo! the lovers would stand. Arthur Mizener would stand to be counted, and Granville Hicks, Clifton Fadiman, W. G. Rogers, and Gilbert Highet, Edmund Fuller, all those Virgilia Petersons, Dennis Powers's and Glendy Culligans. The reviews came in on wings of gold, "Brilliant" "Sheer" "Superlative" "Highly" "Generous" "Wonderfully Worth" "Great Joy To." Not since Elizabeth Janeway wrote *The Walsh Girls* has any lady-book been given such praise by people such as these. Yet it has happened to Mary, our saint, our umpire, our lit arbiter, our broadsword, our Barrymore (Ethel), our Dame (dowager), our mistress (Head), our Joan of Arc, the only Joan of Arc to travel up and down our raddled literary world, our poor damp kingdom, her sword breathing fire while she looked for a Dauphin to save us, looked these twenty years, and brought back nought. Even the patience of Joan cannot endure. She found a Dauphin at last in the collective masculinity which is to be scraped together out of eight Vassar girls, class of '33. "Miss McCarthy has come through brilliantly," writes David Boroff. "It is sheer exhilaration to watch her nimble intelligence at work, great joy to read her rich and supple prose. *The Group* clearly is one of the best novels of the decade." What has Mary done that now she is guilty by association with the Boroffs and the Fullers and the

"The Case Against McCarthy: A Review of *The Group*," From Norman Mailer, *Cannibals and Christians* (New York: The Dial Press, 1966), pp. 133-40. Reprinted by permission of the author and the author's agents, Scott Meredith Literary Agency, Inc., 845 Third Avenue, New York, New York 10022.

Hicks? Is this true guilt or innocence in disarray? Can she be conspiring with the epigones? Is the witch plotting how *not* to give the goose away? What a case!

Barrister William Barrett, late of Heidegger Row, finds for the defendant:

> The novel opens with a wedding and closes with a funeral. The two scenes, particularly the first, are beautifully composed tableaux, magnificent photographs of an occasion with all the details meticulously assembled, including those that give the picture its haunting period quality. Between these two scenes, in which all of the group are assembled, the tangled skeins of eight different lives unwind, and interweave. Yet the eight different stories have the unity of a novel, for they turn around the pivotal figure of the group, Kay Strong....Kay is the bellwether of the group in their struggle for emancipation. Though the girls are all solidly middle-class, and six of them from the Social Register, they insist on meeting life free from parental protection or guidance. Kay's death at the end—whether by accident or suicide—is a symbol of a kind. It is now 1940, the time of the Battle of Britain, and she falls from the window of her room in the Vassar Club while doing some volunteer airplane spotting. "In a sense," somebody remarks at her funeral, "Kay is the first war casualty." This is Miss McCarthy's neat way of ringing out the old years of the New Deal and ushering in the new period of the war.

Mr. Norman Podhoretz is a villainous, impressive, and magnetically disdainful prosecutor. What demolishment in his summation!

> Any Vassar girl of the Class of '33 who could so violate her true nature as to have a wedding like that was bound to jump out of a window sooner or later. The leopard ought to know better than to think he can change his spots.
>
> It is this aspect of the Thirties that Miss McCarthy finally hates the most: the atmosphere of the period demanded of all the leopards that they work as hard as they could at doing something about their spots. Wilfully blind to the spirit of moral ambition and the dream of self-transcendence that animated this demand, she can see nothing in it but foolishness and insincerity—despite the fact that she herself was produced by that spirit and was beautified once by the dream. The Muses have rewarded her for the *trahison* she is now committing by presenting her with a flatly written and incoherently structured book, a trivial lady writer's novel that bears scarcely a trace of the wit, the sharpness and the

vivacity which glowed so often in her earlier work. A well-deserved fiasco, if you ask me.

Well, what is one to do? It is a busy season and the aspect most annoying of this trial is the time it will take to render a fair verdict for the defendant. The case begs for a brief of ten or fifteen thousand words. Yet it is a matter of dispute whether it is worth anything like this at all. Still, it is annoying to pass judgment lightly, for the defendant has curious merits and odd charms, little glints of gold in a ton of clay.

It is as if one were panning a sample. The nuggets are few, but the ore washes oddly. Only a step away, a shovelful deeper, perhaps there is high rich count. *The Group* is thus a book which could be said to squat on the Grand Avenue of the Novel like a shabby little boutique, a place which offers treasure in the trash. One has even had to ignore rumors that the nice shabby saleslady—alias Joan of Arc—is a princess whose family lost its fortune in the revolution; one hears other reports that she is also a miser and the swag is buried in the cellar.

That is why a concentrated act of detection is necessary. For this little shop don't belong on the Avenue, and it's got to be improved or else ripped down. Yet the saleslady is a good worker considering she's a princess; even a literary commissar might regret an act of *inégalité* here.

Which last remark must of course reveal the bias of the judge and the true nature of this court. Miss McCarthy has been summoned to a Tribunal, and will be offered revolutionary justice. All stand. The defendant's Fellow-Worker's Court will now find:

Ergo: *The Group,* as all good literary workers keeping up the work must know by now, is a collective novel about a near (or let us say quasi-) revolutionary period in American life, the nineteen-thirties; its heroines are eight nice girls, all or conceivably all of them Episcopalian at some time or another (one needs a revolutionary statistician to set these matters straight), all of them Upper-Middle Class and all of them civilized to that point of Christless High Church rectitude whose communal odor is a cross between *Ma Griffe* and contraceptive jelly. So it is no easy task Miss McCarthy has set herself. She has eight well-to-do young ladies moving through the thirties on the very outer fringe of events, and none of them has an inner passion large enough to take over the book and make it run away. Indeed the only character one would not likely flee at a cocktail party, a rich arrogant green-eyed beauty named Eastlake, decides to separate from the book herself. She takes off for Europe after the first few chapters and does not get around to coming back until the book is almost done. She has in the interim become an open lesbian as opposed to—would it be a Closet King? Which encourages the single medical prescription one can elucidate from the book: It tacitly states a mixture of passionless goodness and squashed mendacity, precisely the lot of average nice rich bright young Protestant girls, is so regurgitative a violation of their nature that cancer or psychosis are now house percentage against any decent woman. No wonder Miss Eastlake left—she would have been unconvincing if she had remained. Still, Lady McCarthy is an unhappy hostess. What if you were to give a party for Christine Keeler and invited all your friends. Then Christine didn't show. What a party!

So, here, let's refine Comrade Mary's problem a little further. A collective novel in which the most interesting character is missing, a collective novel in which none of the characters have sufficient passion to be interesting in themselves, yet none have the power or dedication to wish to force events. Nor does any one of the characters move critically out of her class by marrying drastically up, or savagely down. Not one of the girls even exhibits an engaging bitchery. (The nearest to this existential condition, Norine Schmittlapp, is more pig than tootsie.) Correlatively, no one of the girls falls deeply and tragically in love. The formal heroine, Kay Strong Petersen, entered as evidence previously by Barrister Barrett, does indeed fall literally out of a twenty-story window in the Vassar Club; clearly, she is a suicide-by-accident before the failure of her love, but she is somehow too horsey, and all-but-dyke, to buy a single revolutionary tear—one receives instead the impression that she might smell like a locker room of dedicated handball players—gloom, determination, and the void ooze from her persona. The nicest of the heroines by sentimental measure is Polly, but she and her husband are too nice; one cannot even cash an allusion to the *Ladies' Home Journal*—some checks should not be spent. There is of course a second nice heroine named Dottie. She is clean, Boston clean; her conscience moves with the drilled but never unimpressive grace of a fine ballerina. Indeed she has the grace to come to orgasm on the night she gives her first flower to still another in the endless gallery of Mary McCarthy's feverish, loud-talking, drunken, neurotic, crippled, and jargon-compensated louts. Did our First Lady of Letters never meet a gentleman on the flying trapeze? No, McCarthy's lout smells like fertilizer and he ploughs Dottie under—there is a good novelistic harvest for the next twenty pages. We are given Dottie's purchase of a diaphragm at her lover's demand; her subsequent repudiation—he is not at home when she calls; her act of renunciation—she quits her purchase beneath a bench in Washington Square Park; and her moment of final suspense when chapters later she confesses to her mother (who has a first-rate sense of modest conscience) that she is still in love with the lout. Her mother's conscience takes the inner journey from Boston to a village garret and she begs her daughter not to marry the new man she has taken in compensation (a nice rancher who is never to appear in evidence), but instead advises Dottie to go back to her lover of one night and find out what is finally in her love. It is the voice of a most refined moral instinct, and Dottie says no. Dottie ducks. She is our second-best nice heroine, but one crack on the mouth and she's out.

Thus it goes. There's Helena with the finest mind in the book, a quiet girl who rides her considerable culture like a consummate horseman. But she is a eunuch for others, void of relation. There's Pokey Prothero, rich, society, dumb, sexy, potentially interesting, but never given attention; there's Priss, a young New Dealer who has no breasts but breastfeeds her baby—one can hardly remember more about her. Finally there's a real duncey broad who becomes a literary agent. One can't even recall her name.

Now, this sparse gallery offers a flaccid springboard from which to jump into a major novel of the thirties. But Mary McCarthy is too much of an old pro not to see the odds. Her characters will come from one class and make no heroic journeys to other classes, they will not look to participate in the center of the history which is being made, and they will be the victim of no outsize passion. Nor will they be made sufficiently eccentric to separate clearly from one another. They will be called Lakey and Kay, Pokey and Polly, Dottie, Helena, Norine, and Priss. (And Duncey.) Nor will there be an attempt to avoid the proportions which are consequent. She will take these women, nearly all finally dull, because they have neither the interest to break out of the cage of their character, nor even the necessity—the cage is not that cruel, the girls are merely premature suburbanites—and she will obey the logic of the intricately educated and dull, she will follow them through their furniture and their recipes, she will give us lists of categories that no sociologist would ever dare. This is the most dangerous hurdle of them all, this is the one any professional knows to avoid unless he is willing to dare a real fall. Because lists and categories in novels must be consummately perfect, each detail quivering with the illumination of a touch of true love, or a hint of the deep, or indeed you are dead. Lists and categories are always the predictable refuge of the passionless, the mediocre, the timid, and the bowel-bound who will not make another move until they have exhausted the last.

These are real odds, what! These piss-out characters with their cultivated banalities, their lack of variety or ambition, perversion, simple greed, or depth of feeling, their indifference to the bedrock of a collective novel—the large social events of the season or decade which gave impetus to conceiving the book in such a way. Yes, our Mary's a sneak. Like any First Lady she disapproves of unseemly ambition, and yet she is trying a novel which is all but impossible to bring off in a big way. No ordinary ambition here. Megalomania indeed. Her little boutique on the Avenue is going to open in competition to Proust's Tiffany.

Well the Court would not certify her as mad. The odds are a hundred to one or a thousand to one against bringing off the book, but it is possible. At least it is existentially possible. For until some great new realist arises, some modern Zola, we will not know. The work of realism was done for the nineteenth century, but whether it can be done for the middle of the twentieth century we shall indeed not know unless the attempt is made. So may have reasoned McCarthy. If one takes a little stillwater of society and captures it in its proportions, its style, its affairs, its moods, *its very relation to reality* (which is to say the mode by which it attempts to perceive reality), if one brings it to life in such a way as to transcend the journeyman novelist's little spill of life (his verisimilitude and occasional good moments) and instead creates a work which is true in its very relation to the perception of reality (one repeats the notion) then a magic is worked. The little book of realistic details has of a sudden its resonance, it has come to life, it is a Being, a psychological reality which lives afterward in our brain, touches our motives, affects the history we in turn will make. Any book can do this if it is pure enough and true enough to create a turn of being in the mind of the reader. So goes the existential premise.

Say, then, did Lady M. bring it off? And the answer is that she came just far enough to irritate the life out of us, because it was just far enough to reinvigorate the premise—it is the grand premise of the novel—but she did not climb high enough nor cleanly enough in the deep councils of her sleep to get up over the first ridge and start a base camp from which one could decide if the mountain is to be negotiated from this direction. She got just so far symbolically as the episode in one of her scenes where the butler comes in to whisper to his mistress that the child of the visiting lady has had an unfortunate accident in his pants. Yes, Mary deposited a load on the premise, and it has to be washed all over again, this little long-lived existential premise.

All right, but why did she fail? Where did she fink the job? And this is how ten thousand more words are demanded and one thousand must suffice. But first let credit be given to her formal virtues. Because her sense of detail, while suffering from a fatal if tiny taint of the monotonous and overindulgent, is still her single most impressive achievement. Her book fails as a novel by being good but not nearly good enough, it fails for a variety of temperamental and characterological reasons soon to be listed, but it is enormously successful as sociology. It will continue to exist as a classic in sociology long after it is dim and dull as a novel, it will survive in Soc Sci I at every university and junior college: the specific details are to be mined by the next twenty-five classes of PhD's.

And at its best, *The Group* is far better than that. It is skillful, intricately knitted as a novel, its characters while not always distinguishable from one another are true in their reactions, or at least are true in the severe field of limitation she puts on their comings and goings, their paltry passions, their lack of grasp, their lack of a desire to grasp. It is all true what she does, it is just not true enough. Her eye sees with a knife's edge, but her hand, overwary of drama and surprise, blunts the stroke. The book like a person in depression is dull in its basic condition—it comes to life only by a stirring, a moment of inspiration, then it lapses into dullness again. And details sweep in and sweep away the possibilities for each little scene to become sufficiently alive to wake up the others. She is to be given respect for conceiving a novel such as this and laying out the ground plan, she is an engineer *manque* in literature, but her failure diverts judgment away from her technique and over to her character. She is simply

not a good enough woman to write a major novel; not yet; she
has failed, she has failed from the center out, she failed out of
vanity, the accumulated vanity of being overpraised through the
years for too little and so being pleased with herself for too little;
she failed out of profound timidity—like any good Catholic-born
she is afraid to unloose the demons; she failed out of snobbery—
if compassion for her characters is beginning to stir at last in this
book, she can still not approve of anyone who is incapable of performing the small act exquisitely well; she failed by an act of the
imagination; she is, when all is said, a bit of a duncey broad herself, there is something cockeyed in her vision and self-satisfied
in her demands and this contributes to the failure of her style.
The long unbroken paragraphs settle in like bricks. They are all
too equal to one another—it is the wrong book in which to lose
one's place; there is even mild physical boredom in the act of
reading as if one were watching a wall being stacked up rather
than seeing the metamorphosis of a creature.

Finally she suffers from a lack of reach. She chooses to be not
close enough to the horror in the closet. Her nice girls are ref-
ugees from the schisms, the wrinklings, and the crater mold of
the Upper Middle Class, that radiation belt of well-to-do Protestants full of Church, rectitude, exclusion, guilt, and insanity.
Is there a nice rich Episcopalian family or fine Presbyterian clan
in our American world which does not have its important secret
member raving mad? Nice girls live on the thin juiceless crust of
the horror beneath, the screaming incest, the buried diabolisms
of the grand and the would-be grand. One does not have to have
that in one's novel, but one has to have a sense of that madness if
the book is to be resonant. Yet Mary is too weak to push through
the crust and so cannot achieve a view of the world which has
root.

Ultimately, novelists must believe that the people who run the
world are essentially good, are an expression of God's work (a
conservative view), or in antithesis must decide that the Devil is
at the shoulder of every ruler (which is where the Bolsheviks and
the Black Muslims come together). One can presumably write a
great novel from either point of view or some conciliation of the
two (Proust, Henry James, James Joyce, Andre Malraux come to
mind) but one cannot make a Being of a realistic novel if it has no
root. Then there are merely sniffings, snippings and clippings,
codicils of taste, and quick exits for bad taste. Mary's vice is her

terror of being ridiculous, and so she is in danger of ending up absurd, an old-maid collector of Manx cats, no tails and six toes, an anomaly of God. It even invades her vision. One called her cockeyed for a cause. There is an atrocious anachronism in the book. Her characters while engaged in the activities of the thirties have a consciousness whose style derives directly from the fifties. One has to keep reminding oneself that these events did not take place ten years ago, but thirty years ago, and this is unforgivable. It is like wrapping a tuning fork in velvet. Her little book so full of promise and quiver ends up soggy and damp. What rings true does not please the ear, what pleases is not quite true. So the book seems stuffed with cotton and catalogues as Podhoretz was quick to accuse.

Yet when all is said, *The Group* has one fresh virtue. It has something new in it; it has a conception of the novel which is Mary's own, a tool by which to cut an ascent into some of the sheer ice faces of the social world. And that is her method. Her Method. For she has divined the first law of our social world, which is that we learn by what we can glean from a hundred alienations of context, from a thousand suffocations of our emotions. So we are deep in an affair, close to growing nearer or being spoiled for love another year, and then our context is ripped. A commercial is on the air. A recipe is to be discussed at dinner. Ten years later we hear of the beloved at a cocktail party. Was it this girl or that? The names have slid around into one another or have divided. Memory is in mitosis. Mary may be the first American to try this in a thoroughgoing way. Everything in the profound materiality of women is given its full stop until the Eggs Benedict and the dress with the white fichu, the pessary and the whatnot, sit on the line of the narrative like commas and periods, semicolons, italics, and accents. The real interplay of the novel exists between the characters and the objects which surround them until the faces are swimming in a cold lava of anality, which becomes the truest part of her group, her glop, her impacted mass.

If, at the highest level, she has failed and even failed miserably to do more than write the best novel the editors of the women's magazines ever conceived in *their* secret ambitions, it is nonetheless possible now to conceive that McCarthy may finally get tough enough to go with the boys. She has been a very bad girl these years, mean and silly, postured and overpetted, petty in the extreme, but now there's a hint she may be capable some day of taking a real step, a suggestion that the Saints will preserve our Mary-Joan and bless her with a book which can comprehend a man. Does anyone know where society will end if the heroine of *The Company She Keeps* should encounter Julien Sorel?

But that drama of conjecture is moot. For the present, a decision: Mary McCarthy is judged Guilty of Meretriciousness and equally: Guilty of conspiring not to give the goose away, which means thus, Guilty of refusing to reveal that the genteel lords and ladies who manage America are the psychic descendants of Conrad's Kurtz. "Ah, the horror, the horror," and she will not take a burning look.

Mary McCarthy: Society's Demands

by Patricia Meyer Spacks

Trying to circumvent society, women always fail. They also fail, some novelists suggest, if they attempt to embody society's values. Mary McCarthy's fiction belongs to an era in which, one might think, the problem of vocation has been solved. Her heroines hold jobs, can even have careers. Yet, with infinite possibilities of doing and being, they perceive vividly how rigid laws control them within every possibility. In *The Company She Keeps,* the heroine wishes to conform—although what she wants to conform to is never precisely clear; or, rather, it keeps changing, thus blurring. She also wishes the imaginative vision characteristic of Edith Wharton's heroines; but the focus and meaning of that vision aren't clear either.

Society in a Wharton novel is "the best people." Mary McCarthy considers the ambiguity of *best.* In her superficially unrestricted world a woman can lead a "free" life without penalty, but her heroines too need the approval of "the best people"—lacking any assurance of who exactly they are. New alignments take place; men and women define themselves in relation to changing standards, shifting assumptions. One may know them by the company they keep; but *The Company She Keeps* reveals the full ambiguity of *that* idea. Political allegiances now become part of social status, the choice of a psychoanalyst creates a label as precise as that determined earlier by receiving or failing to receive an invitation to a ball. Edith Wharton notes a mother's alertness to what name (first or last) a hairdresser uses in referring to the customer's daughter; Mary McCarthy shows a woman worrying over the impression she will make on her fellow pas-

"Mary McCarthy: Society's Demands." From Patricia Meyer Spacks, *The Female Imagination* (New York: Alfred A. Knopf, Inc., 1975), pp. 254-60. Reprinted by permission of Alfred A. Knopf, Inc. and George Allen & Unwin Ltd.

sengers in a club car. Attitudes toward international affairs, personal philosophies, jobs, clothes: all function as social counters. Some ideal of social conformity rules as definitively as in Edith Wharton, although reality, utterly different, utterly unpredictable, comprising a moral chaos, shapes individuals in more various ways. Rules are no longer clearly defined: a shabby coat may confer more status than a lavish one. Great tension therefore prevails, rewards and punishments remain obscure. Mary McCarthy examines meticulously the painful ambiguities of personal experience in a setting that implies rigid demands without ever clarifying the nature of those demands.

Margaret Sargent, the central character of the six loosely related episodes of *The Company She Keeps,* young, intellectual, attractive, presents a life history in some respects resembling Mary McCarthy's own. Three episodes concentrate directly on her experience, telling of her first divorce, her seduction by an unattractive man on a train, and her psychoanalysis; the other three centrally concern her male companions: a crooked art dealer for whom she works, a professional host who wishes to help her, a Yale man, temporarily Margaret's colleague, whose political opinions become his means to success. The young woman leads a varied life, surrounded by and interested in diverse people, engaging in various occupations and roles.

Especially roles: far more definitive than occupations. The novel studies woman-as-actress and how society conditions her to this position. Not that society conditions only women—the three sketches focused on men emphasize that men, with similar problems, show similar effects. Margaret, an actress, lives among actors. Mr. Sheer, the crook seems bizarrely different from others but bizarrely resembles everyone else. "Masquerade was life to Mr. Sheer. He could not bear to succeed in his own personality, any more than an unattractive woman can bear to be loved for herself." To risk the self for judgment would be dangerous; to discover the self, impossible. As Mr. Sheer becomes more successful in legitimate business, he begins to despair. His associates protect him from the consequences of his trickery; his efforts at risk taking (playing the stock market, seducing a client's wife) backfire—the client has been yearning to ditch his wife, the gallery Sheer works for covers his losses. Unable to tolerate the pain of being a commonplace self, Mr. Sheer begins to risk his body. Acting the invalid if he can't act the confidence man, arranging to have portions of his anatomy (appendix, gall bladder, teeth) removed, he dramatizes the self-destructiveness implicit in the steady presentation of false faces to the world.

All the stories, like parables, implicitly claim universal relevance despite their reliance on specific social detail. Pflaumen, the perfect host, inhabits a narrative in the second person singular. The "you" designates Margaret Sargent, but the strained technique justifies itself by suggesting that the reader too struggles in the same social structure and dilemmas. Pflaumen's genius derives from his capacity to create "the illusion of a microcosm,... the sense of a little world that was exactly the same as the big world, though it had none of the pain and care. Each of Pflaumen's guests had been selected, as it were, for his allegorical possibilities." The allegories played out around Pflaumen's table involve clashes of value (or displays of clashing values: a rather different thing), the inception of love affairs, rivalries, enmities, the assigning and acceptance of work to be done; and a steady drama of social emotion—appreciation (of food, wine, wit, beauty), political passion, literary, musical, and dramatic interest. All feeling is merely part of the show—a fact accounting for the manifest uneasiness of participants in the display.

"Portrait of the Intellectual as a Yale Man" enlarges the arena and shifts the terms, but not the point. Pflaumen generates suspicion; Jim Barnett, the Yale man, dispels uneasiness by his very existence. The apparent type of healthy American conformity, his vigorous wholesomeness, the earnestness of his conviction, validate his radical opinions. "He made you think of Boy Scouts and starting a fire without matches...and the Our Gang comedies and Huckleberry Finn....He might have done very well as the young man who is worried about his life insurance, the young man who is worried about dandruff, the young man whose shirts won't fit him, the young man who looks up happily from his plate of Crunchies..." However imaginable in all the stereotypical roles of American folklore and advertising, Jim in fact plays another part: "he was worried about Foster and Ford and the Bonus Marchers and the Scottsboro Boys." He acts a charade of radicalism, making the parade of commitment into another stereotype; working for *Destiny* (a thinly disguised version of *Fortune*), he achieves all he wants: money, freedom, the chance to dramatize himself as a divided man. Seeing his wife as "the Average Intelligent Woman, the Mate," he feels gratified that "his domestic life was wholesome and characterless, like a child's junket....He had a profound conviction that this was the way things ought to be, that this was life." His insistence on finding reassurance everywhere makes him reassuring to others; in all his shifts of opinion, the world remains to his perception profoundly logical: endangering no one, he moves to inevitable success.

In the course of his rise Jim goes to bed once with Margaret Sargent, whom he judges, with considerable condescension, as foolhardy, rash, extreme. She defends unfashionable opinions though obviously scared, gets herself fired from a job she needs, lacks the worldly wisdom which comes naturally to him. But his brief liaison with her assumes for him "an allegorical significance" as a turning point in his career. He conducts endless imaginary dialogues with Margaret; sleeping with his wife, he pretends she's Margaret: the thrill of adultery without penalty. Gradually he realizes how much he resents her, because her existence comments on his: she has the power to make his life seem "a failure, not a tragedy exactly, but a comedy with pathos." Despite the persistent unreality of her own experience, she represents for him, ironically, the reality principle. Her presence makes him dimly realize that he only plays roles, limits his psychic expenditure, relies on pretend money while convincing himself that it is real.

As in *Middlemarch*, the novelist suggests that men and women endure similar social pressures, suffer similar problems. Men here seem no more reprehensible than women in the solutions they discover—identical solutions: acting parts in self-created dramas that society applauds or, unhappily, fails to applaud. Margaret's apparent moral superiority to Jim Barnett, in her superior faithfulness to a political position, wins her no applause. Although it makes Jim uneasy, it seems a trifle foolish: no testimony to the virtue of women, evidence rather of one woman's lack of practicality, eventually meaningless even to herself. Jim Barnett, however morally inadequate, achieves "success." Margaret Sargent feels more and more utterly a failure.

Why does Margaret go to bed with Jim Barnett? We never know. In another part of the narrative, though, we learn how she finds herself in bed with an even more unlikely companion, a "porcine" businessman in a Brooks Brothers suit whom she meets on a train. Her sexual career proceeds from one arbitrary event to another. She divorces her husband because she feels compelled to enact the drama of divorce; by the time she leaves for Reno, she realizes that she'll never marry her lover, and she already enjoys and fears her fantasized role as Young Divorcée. Her involvement with the businessman occurs on a trip west to tell her aunt of her approaching second marriage, which never takes place either. In her psychoanalysis she recalls a long sequence of meaningless love affairs, and finally a severely limiting, childless marriage to an architect who tyrannizes over her. Through sexuality she tries to resolve her uncertainty about her femininity: "what she was really asking all along was not that the male should assault her, but that he should believe her a woman." Men "could only respond by leaping at her—which, after all, she supposed, was their readiest method of showing her that her impersonation had been convincing." But the response remains unsatisfactory: conscious of herself as actress (by acting a role too well she ends up with the improbable Mr. Breen), she wants an audience—not fellow performers on the same stage.

The nature of the response to dramatic performance in society comprises the most complicated and compelling issue in *The Company She Keeps,* Men and women, equally driven to "perform" in the social world here depicted—stage metaphors dominate every section of the novel—are alike obsessed with audience response. Yet Margaret, the only woman with more than a walk-on part, suffers more sharply than her male counterparts: not because of her superior sensitivity (though that is a hinted possibility) but because of the social significance of her sex.

Mr. Sheer, Pflaumen, Jim Barnett want, and to varying degrees get, applause. The tragic side of Mr. Sheer's comedy emerges when he's reduced to applauding himself, giggling at the dangers of his surgical operations, because no one else will provide the kind of admiration he craves. Pflaumen offers the artifacts of his apartment, his wines, his menus, his maid, as objects of praise; all represent himself. He gets what he wants, grudgingly given because of his glaring need. Jim Barnett cannot achieve the success of creativity—his great book remains unwritten—but he wins the success of the world: universal admiration and sympathy. Men, in other words, applauded by self or others, achieve, if not happiness, at least a measure of satisfaction specifically from their self-presentation to the world at large.

The comparable satisfactions of women, if Margaret is representative, never compensate at all for their private miseries· Society, in encouraging a sense of infinite possibility for women

(Margaret's available roles seem more abundant than Jim's), only intensifies the individual's awareness of inadequacy. Jim Barnett and Pflaumen may wish to do and be more than they can do and be, but their community asks of them no more than they offer. Margaret, on the other hand, can never escape the feeling that something more is wanted: her audience's reaction never satisfies her. If they seem thrilled by the high drama of her divorce, they probably won't be thrilled tomorrow. If someone takes her to bed in a Pullman berth, he vulgarizes her; if he admires her high style he makes her feel ridiculous; if he sends her a telegram of sympathy, she throws it out—standing in, as it were, for her audience, of which she remains always vividly conscious. Her social milieu, intricate and ill-defined, but very precise in her imagination, both creates and reflects her. She may appear to move outside it, as in the brief encounter with Mr. Breen, but she soon manages to incorporate such happenings within her understanding of her social definition. Driven by the obligation to be "interesting"—to herself first of all, that self epitomizing her society—she finds the possibilities always diminishing. Never can she predict fully the consequences of an act: this she discovers with her divorce. A psychoanalytic hour miniaturizes her total experience, as she says what seems interesting, what seems to insist on her "specialness," only to discover unforeseen uncertainties as the result of such self-assertion.

The Company She Keeps studies female *hubris*—not the arrogance of overweening self-assertion beyond the laws of God and man, but the apparently more modest assertion of insistent self-display as the perfect representative of society. *What* Margaret is seems fully defined by *where* she is, in time and space: this fact generates her pain. She articulates the complicated and often contradictory values of her world, demands of herself that she articulate them flawlessly. If these values have little solidity, she too will be utterly fluid. Her highest achievement is insight, for which she prays: "If the flesh must be blind, let the spirit see. Preserve me in disunity." But what she can see remains severely limited. Like her creator, she has an acute eye for social detail: her malicious portrait of her analyst and her self-castigating description of her own middle-class life display the same sharp perception of the relation between minutiae and meaning. She sees her own posing and the poses of others, but no possibility for authenticity; she feels doomed to be "the equivocal personality who was not truly protean but only appeared so," taking pride only in the fact that "she could still detect her own frauds."

What Margaret can perceive is limited, as she and her world are also limited. Her irony belongs to the society described: smart, witty, self-deprecating, destructive. Yet clear seeing represents a genuine value. McCarthy as author demonstrates how imaginative vision, even operating in a context of severe moral disorder, can assert at least limited meaning. The multiple points of view, the varied fictional techniques of the novel provide stylistic equivalents for the multiple roles available to the heroine. Her inability to make any final commitment reflects her society's lack of clarity and testifies her willingness and capacity to survive, to endure the suffering of her many selves despite her open-eyed perception that her environment provides only temporary illusions of meaning. Interior insight confirms exterior disunity, the imagination promises nothing: except the heroine's faith, her only available faith, in her perceiving self.

Iris Murdoch: The Novelist as Magician/
The Magician as Artist

by Linda Kuehl

Form, Iris Murdoch warns, is the artist's consolation and his temptation: he is tempted to sacrifice the eccentric, contingent individual while he consoles himself with the secure boundaries of structure. As she sees it, this constitutes a crisis since the contemporary novelist tends to produce fiction in the shape of tiny, self-contained, crystal-like objects. Diagnosing the tyranny of form as an ill that must be cured, she postulates a return to the novel of character as it is manifested in the works of Scott, Jane Austen, George Eliot and Tolstoy, for these nineteenth-century writers were so capable of charity that they gave their people an independent existence in an external world.

Because Miss Murdoch clings to the faith that people are unique and precious, and persists in our inhuman age to advocate the creation of such characters, it should be illuminating to examine her own fiction accordingly. Surely few modern writers are as concerned as she is with the plight of the novel. Few have contributed so many dazzling, not to say intelligent, essays on the subject. And few have worked within forms as inventive as her own original metaphysical fantasy.

This genre is stamped by a combination of pyrotechnics and philosophy, a design of bizarre effects intended to convey reality as contingent and eccentric. It employs stock fairy tale, mythic and Gothic devices and transforms them into literary correlatives of the author's philosophical vision.

These elements are most skillfully worked out in her second, fifth and seventh works, respectively, *The Flight from the Enchanter, A Severed Head,* and *The Unicorn.* The question is whether they evidence a talent for serious fiction or merely for sensational effects. Even more important, does Miss Murdoch's nostalgia for nineteenth-century characterization satisfy the twentieth-century dilemma between fictive form and the human person?

The Novelist as Magician

The Flight from the Enchanter, A Severed Head and *The Unicorn,* all invoke eerie, twilight regions, netherlands where characters act out their fantasies remote from the daylight world of everyday human affairs. To heighten the nightmare, the author relies upon haunting settings and emotionally charged atmospheres, such as Victorian mansions, Gothic castles, weird landscapes and interiors.

The castle or mansion, a stock convention of the Murdochian fantasy, isolates the characters from the outside and intensifies the sense of foreboding which is a leitmotif to the action. There is the exotic palazzo in *Flight* that ensconses Mischa Fox; Rembers, in *Severed Head,* the Victorian retreat for sinful collusions; and Gaze Castle, in *The Unicorn,* where shadows and gloom hover with foreboding, where comings and goings remain clandestine, and muffled voices and suppressed emotions threaten to erupt with sudden violence.

Miss Murdoch's fondness for such backgrounds extends beyond the cliché manor, since its paraphernalia reappears wherever she depicts human transgressions. The coastland in *The Unicorn* is her most extraordinary landscape. Marked by megaliths, dolmen, carnivorous flora and cliffs of black sandstone, the terrain is appalling. Yet, even ordinary sites like a London flat, Liverpool Street Station or an elegant mews undergo unearthly transformation. Here the trappings remain fairly constant: the prevalence of candlelight, fog, sulphurous odors, incense fumes; the general impression of exotic disarray; the womb-tomb feeling emphasized by recurring words like cavern, cave, dim, opaque and remote.

These settings provide environments for tales of enchantment which involve two groups of characters, those who enchant and

those who are enchanted, in an intricate network of flight and
pursuit. The enchanters are mysterious, magical figures who
represent the forces at work in an ambiguous universe, while
the enchanted suffer from ignorance and impotence and so regard these powerful beings with fascination and loathing. The
mansion or castle in which much of the action transpires is a
metaphor for the universe and its atmosphere an emblem of a
limbo closer to hell than heaven. The enchanters and their subjects are engaged in a futile symbolic struggle between knowledge
and illusion.

Miss Murdoch projects her fantasies through the psyches of
her enchanted characters: Annette Cockeyne, Nina, Rosa and
Hunter Keepe, and John Rainboro in *Flight,* Martin Lynch-
Gibbon of *Severed Head,* Marian Taylor and Effingham Cooper
of *The Unicorn.* These are impressionable observers, in fact
voyeurs. They convert the unknown into vague concepts of
destiny, demons and portents, perceiving themselves as spellbound victims of arbitrary powers. In order to preserve their
own romantic dreams, they collaborate in each other's illusion.
To endure their own drab routines, they anticipate, often plunge
into liberating adventures.

The observer's obscure internal terror is indicated by a prevailing notion of being spellbound. Futile attempts are made to
break the spell that would enable one to awaken from the numb-
ing paralysis and cross into one's own verifiable world. But
lethargy is inescapable, an automatic response to higher powers,
and the enchanted feel trapped into enacting dramas which they
neither understand nor control. Like sleepwalkers, they move
along predestined paths, bewildered by the arbitrary and incom-
prehensible game, with the self-righteous irresponsibility of a
victim. Martin Lynch-Gibbon, middle-aged wine merchant of
Severed Head, epitomizes the good-natured acceptance of this
condition by following assigned tasks according to the concep-
tions others have of him and by acting out fated roles heedless of
commitment.

Martin, who persistently seeks a masterful mistress, is just one
of Miss Murdoch's posturing Courtly Lovers. Effingham Cooper
of *The Unicorn* pursues the sequestered beauty of Gaze Castle.
John Rainboro of *Flight* muses about being an abject suitor com-
miserated with by the world as well as by his lady. Complementing
this prostrate admirer, the female plays the reverse role by toying

with her Courtly Lover. There are two examples of the woman as aggressor in *Flight:* Annette Cockeyne, a "perpetual virgin," dreams of heroically conquering the evil that enslaves men's souls, thereby setting them free; and Rosa Keepe, a "perpetual siren," suffers the conflict between saving her lovers and destroying them. Both the self-asserting female and the self-deprecating male collaborate in one another's illusion and so maintain their respective poses.

Another mode of preserving illusions is the romantic escape from drab routine into some vague but promising excitement. This impulse is exhibited by Marian Taylor in *The Unicorn* when she arrives at Gaze Castle after fleeing from an unrequited love affair and the post of school-mistress. In the author's words, "she had wanted always, as she obscurely knew, some kind of colourful, uplifting, steadying ceremony, some kind of distinction of life which had so far eluded her." But Marian's hopes are not fulfilled even when she finds herself in a fascinating milieu. Like all the enchanted characters, she is an initiate which means that she can never penetrate the enchanter's sphere.

By focusing upon the voyeurs' zest for intrigue through their imaginings about the enchanters, Miss Murdoch stimulates the reader's curiosity. The enchanters—Mischa Fox of *Flight,* Honor Klein of *Severed Head,* and Hannah Crean-Smith of *The Unicorn*—are bizarre extensions of their subjects' most profound wishes. Their own disguises vary with the erratic impressions of the enchanted who enfold them in mystery through allusions to their suspect reputations and legendary pasts, exotic and menacing comportments, mythic dimensions and curious accomplices.

The public reputation of Mischa Fox, the first of the enchanters, is that of international press lord and rogue. He is threatening because his methods are so devious, his connections and achievements, dubious. Mischa's more primitive though equally awesome counterpart in *Severed Head* is Honor Klein, a don of anthropology, who frequently leaves Cambridge to visit her barbarous tribes. Inspiring more romantic love is Hannah Crean-Smith, the sleeping beauty enchantress in *The Unicorn.* Local legend has it that she is imprisoned in Gaze Castle for the duration of a seven year curse that will end in disaster. Like Mischa and Honor, Hannah's fame is self-proliferating. She possesses such magnetism that others automatically cluster around her.

In *Flight* and *Severed Head*, the enchanters appear ominously exotic. One manifestation is a visible foreignness, as, for example, Mischa's Oriental magic and Honor's mid-European brusqueness. Another is an elusive holiness: Mischa is likened to a sage and priest, Honor to a goddess and "Hebrew Angel." Both she and Mischa, who are frequently referred to as demons and ghosts, take on the power of merciless deities.

The enchanter's most enigmatic and compelling aspect is a mythic dimension symbolically conveyed through his gaze. Mischa's power is insured by the shocking effect of one brown and one blue eye whose unflecked shades give "the impression of two faces super-imposed." This double profile signifies omnipotence and omniscience, both of which are further accentuated by his habit of withdrawing into shadows whenever the enchanted attempt to fathom his look.

Mischa is a precursor of Honor Klein, particularly with regard to his unnerving countenance, the harbinger of her Medusa stare. She is a quadruple version of the Gorgon monster, a synthesis of Greek, Freudian, Sartrean and Murdochian views. The Greek myth, first of all, serves as the source for both Honor's hideous demeanor and her supernatural prowess. Freud's influence is in the direction of sexual imagery: his link between the castration fear and the sight of the female genitals is rendered graphically, especially in the scene where Honor severs a napkin with a Samurai sword as Martin looks on terrified. Honor also embodies the Sartrean individual — sovereign, self-realized, inviolable — one who has achieved, in Sartre's term, "self-coincidence"; hence, Medusa-Honor surpasses Freud's sexually stimulating creature to become the uncompromising antagonist of falsehood and deceit. Finally, with self-coincidence as a stepping-stone, Honor transcends Sartre's isolated though realized being to attain "co-existence," a word Miss Murdoch introduces in her first novel, *Under the Net*, to denote love, or the unselfish apprehension of another person's reality. Thus, *Severed Head* ends with the promising co-existence between two separate individuals, Honor and Martin.[1]

The petrifying Medusa stare is rendered more indirectly in *The Unicorn* where it is abstractly signified by the forbidding Gaze Castle which cloisters Hannah Crean-Smith. This enchant-

---

[1]A. S. Byatt, *Degrees of Freedom* (London, 1965). In Chapter VI, Miss Byatt presents an excellent discussion of the Martin-Honor relationship.

ress has some of the hypnotic qualities of her predecessors, as, for instance, Mischa's mystical grace and Honor's commanding hauteur. Essentially, however, she is a spiritualized Medusa, a strange golden-eyed patrician whose vaguely feudal air kindles romantic dreams in the impressionable observers. Conjectures about Hannah range from a Platonic vision of Ideal Beauty to a Christian symbol of saintliness to a psychological representation of the dissociated neurotic to a sentimental version of the supernatural princess.

This kind of conundrum is kept alive by curious accomplices, the final dimension of Iris Murdoch's enchanters, who have special though equivocal access to their masters. Peculiar in their own right, they transmit their conjectures to outside observers, thereby contributing further complications about the enchanter's identity. Hannah's intimates include Violet and Jamesie Evercreech, Denis Nolan and Gerald Scottow, parasites whom Marian Taylor holds accountable for her mistress's ambiguous imprisonment.

In *Severed Head* and *Flight,* Palmer Anderson and Calvin Blick are the respective accomplices who contrast with the enchanter's basic nature, thereby serving as reverse sides of the same coin. Palmer, the beautiful, gentle psychiatrist, is the opposite of his half-sister Honor, the ugly, caustic anthropologist. Significantly, it would seem, his modern wizardry fails where her uncivilized methods succeed. The contrast also operates by way of Calvin, "the dark side of Mischa Fox's mind." As Mephistophelian minister, he clandestinely launches the action in *Flight* by providing others with "grotesque pretexts for doing what [they] really want to do." Whether or not Mischa actually issues directives, Calvin is responsible for doling out and nurturing illusions and consequently keeping the enchanted characters whirling in perpetual frenzy.

Calvin Blick's diabolical schemes lead to a final element of Miss Murdoch's fantasies, for her own plots do, in fact, evolve from grotesque pretexts. Each is an intricate pattern of bizarre details uniquely and painstakingly arranged to establish a chaotic veneer. The primary ingredient is a repertoire of melodramatic effects presented through essentially two techniques: a direct assault upon the reader's nerves and a strategy of insinuation. The first uses cloak and dagger violence and shock: sensational events that one does not expect or that one nervously hopes will not occur. The second technique relies upon coincidence, riddles, ironic reversal and sexual perversion, all suggested through obscure hints and traces.

Her direct assault upon the reader's nerves is obvious in *Flight, Severed Head* and *The Unicorn* which together contain six attempted and actual suicides, three murders, numerous physical attacks, imprisonments, banishments, desertions, abductions, rescues and escapes. Of course, the treatment varies in each book. *Flight's* psychological orientation compels the enchanted characters to enact their neurotic impulses as their counterparts in *Severed Head* also do but with one important difference. Whereas in *Flight* violence functions as a natural extension of the characters' unconscious feelings, in *Severed Head* it is the primitive intrusion upon a civilized drawing room milieu. Therefore, Rosa's jealous lunge at Annette and the catastrophe she instigates at Mischa's party are shocking but not extraordinary events, while Martin's attack upon Honor in the cellar and their ensuing struggle is preposterous because such behavior is astonishing from a wine merchant and a professor of anthropology. In *The Unicorn,* violence is even more routine though less explicable than in *Flight,* Gaze Castle being the kind of milieu where anything other than the "Gothic and grotesque" appears unreal. Here we find a society based upon unintelligible rules, so that numerous melodramatic acts occur with no discernible reason. In fact, violence is never motivated. For example, why does Hannah attempt and finally commit suicide, or why does she try to murder her husband and succeed in killing Gerald? Why does Denis kill Peter, or why does Pip kill himself? These and other deeds happen as a matter of course and go unpunished.

Miss Murdoch is probably infamous for her strategy of insinuation, which is the reverse of the direct assault and which may be roughly defined as a technique whereby she creates an atmosphere of the uncanny. The first three conveyors of this method, namely coincidence, riddles, and ironic reversals, are intended to produce the sense of entrapment. Coincidence generates what Freud calls the "factor of involuntary repetition." Translated into literary terms this means that the author repeatedly entangles her enchanted characters in unwieldly and inescapable situations, in recurrent interruptions, discoveries, pursuits and predestinations. To intensify the oppression of fate, she also scatters riddles without explanation. Moreover, she weaves her novels around central riddles which she never solves yet continually entices the reader into solving. Thus, *Flight* hinges upon whether Mischa Fox is actually the enchanter; *Severed Head* upon Honor Klein's demonic intentions; and *The Unicorn* upon Hannah Crean-Smith's choice between internment and freedom. As for ironic reversals, these can be light, as the discovery that Annette has inadvertently taken milk of magnesia tablets instead of sleeping pills in an attempted suicide; or grave, as the realization that Rosa, who fancies herself "half lady of the manor and half social worker" is enslaved by the Polish brothers.

Miss Murdoch's fourth strategy of insinuation pertains to sexual perversions. She exploits these through cryptic but pointed remarks, intimate and knowing glances, and hesitating yet lingering caresses, all tokens of suppressed appetites and passions that consume enchanters and enchanted alike. Of these perversions, homosexuality and lesbianism are the most insidiously pervasive. Assuming various guises, specifically surrogate father-son and substitute mother-daughter, older-younger woman and master-servant alliances, they render every character and relationship suspect. Reinforcing the Gothic decadence are the implicit *ménage à trois* and incestuous liaison. Spouses consort with mutual lovers and siblings experience intense sexual attachments. This erotica rarely becomes overt but rather signals psychological torment. That such hints remain covert is typical of Gothic fiction where implication is more dynamic than fact.

In summary, then, Iris Murdoch transforms the clichés of the novelist's trade into her own unique genre, the metaphysical fantasy. We have seen how Gothic setting, flamboyant characterization and melodramatic plots give rise to ornate networks of intrigue. What we have yet to see is whether hers is a talent for serious fiction or merely for sensational effects. That is, are *The Flight from the Enchanter, A Severed Head* and *The Unicorn* legitimately contingent and eccentric or are they random and anomalous?

The Magician as Artist

Miss Murdoch's enthusiasm for nineteenth-century characters prompts her desire to give "a lot of people" an existence separate from herself and to permit them to roam freely and cheerfully through her pages. Unfortunately, she seems unable to do this,

for in each successive novel there emerges a pattern of predictable and predetermined types. These include the enchanter or
enchantress—occult, godly, foreign, ancient—who is torn between exhibitionism and introspection, egotism and generosity,
cruelty and pity; the observer, trapped between love and fear of
the enchanter, who thinks in terms of ghosts, spells, demons and
destiny, and imparts an obfuscated view of life; and the accom-
plice, a peculiar mixture of diabolical intention and bemused
charm, who has dealings with the enchanters and power over the
observers. Therefore, while characters may possess a unique
manner or bearing, each belongs essentially to one of the three
aforementioned sets. Mischa Fox, Honor Klein and Hannah
Crean-Smith comprise the first; Rosa and Hunter Keepe, Annette Cockeyne, John Rainboro, Martin Lynch-Gibbon, Marian
Taylor and Effingham Cooper the second; and Calvin Blick,
Palmer Anderson and Gerald Scottow the third. All three groups
— enchanters, observers and accomplices—make up a scheme
symptomatic of the author's failure to break away from the tyranny of form. Though she produces many people, each is tightly
controlled in a superimposed design, each rigidly cast in a classical Murdochian role.

Related to her inability to portray free and independent persons is her technique of molding characters into legendary figures. In *Flight,* for example, she starts out to employ the myth of
Mischa Fox in order to expose mythology but actually expends
more energy in making him mysterious than in using him to unravel the phenomenon of enchantment. By teasing the reader
with riddles and allegories—Is Mischa a press lord with far-
reaching influence in Establishment circles? Is he a dictator or
perhaps a personification of the Welfare State? Is he an Existential God ruling haphazardly in a hypothetical universe?—she
ends up corroborating the myth. The reinterpreted Medusa myth
incarnated by Honor Klein in *Severed Head* raises further problems. As a composite of Greek references, the Freudian castration
complex and incest taboo, and a Sartrean Godhead, she becomes
weighted with too much "significance." Consequently, the human
figure—the ugly spinster with a passion for Samurai swords,
savage tribes and trenchant relationships—is over shadowed.
And the reader therefore wonders how a masculine female don
embodying a Gorgon monster who represents genitalia can
arouse real passion in Martin Lynch-Gibbon. Here again Miss

Murdoch has given into form by playing with clever allusions and images, even going to the extreme of naming Honor as "altogether a Medusa."

She also invests her characters with excessive philosophical connotations. For instance, Hannah Crean-Smith is a cipher for the following: Is she a Circe, a Christian martyr, an incarnation of the Greek concept of Até? Is the remedy for her condition freedom, humility, patience or contrition? Yet these riddles are irrelevant since Hannah is too obscure, unemotional and over-intellectualized to invest them with real meaning. Though striking as the image of ravaged beauty, she never comes alive as an actual person, so her own actions and the response she elicits from her parasitic admirers amount to fanfare. Moreover, since a cipher can tell us nothing about sin and suffering or innocence and wickedness, the reader feels cheated as he was in *Flight* and *Severed Head*. Insofar as he has been lured to expect some unifying meaning, but disappointed by discovering that there is no such meaning, he comes to realize that Miss Murdoch has been trifling with her audience as well as her people.

She also builds character through literary allusions. I have touched upon this technique with regard to Honor Klein, yet it is even more apparent in her treatment of Hannah whom she unwisely associates with *"la princesse de Clèves,"* unwisely because the heroine of Madame de Lafayette's novel is a truly tormented figure struggling between duty and conscience, who finally chooses austere, religious seclusion in order to become a paragon of virtue. Whereas in the seventeenth-century novel the ultimate question as to whether or not she made a "good" choice stems from an essentially human drama, in *The Unicorn* the previously mentioned questions about Hannah evolve from metaphysical ideas and literary associations. To borrow Calvin Blick's phrase, she is a "mechanical device" for the presentation of undeveloped ideas which do not quite assume the proportions of serious allegory since their existence is never justified.[2]

If Iris Murdoch is unable to give her characters a free and independent existence because they are cast in predetermined roles and are invested with intellectual concepts and associations, she also limits them through her ambivalent detachment. Ideally,

[2]Robert Scholes, *The Fabulators* (New York, 1967). Scholes' contrary opinion is interestingly stated in his fifth chapter, "Fabulation and Allegory."

this moral neutrality[3] is calculated to create a distance between the author and her characters and, in so doing, establish an impartiality towards the ideas they embody. Implicit here is the author's nostalgia for old-fashioned characterization, that "Godlike capacity" which she attributes to George Eliot who so respected her characters as to make them separate from her own conflicts and prejudices. Moral neutrality is, therefore, Miss Murdoch's means to resist using art as mere expression of self and her effort to become, like Shakespeare, invisible.

Her neutrality, however, does not empower her to bring Eliotesque people into being. Rather, her characters become tokens of an anti-rational argument about character itself, embodiments of the "messy, boundless...infinitely particular, and endlessly to be explained." As personifications of a theory, specifically accumulations of exotic detail, inexplicable motives, and weird fantasies, they are reduced to arbitrary and anomalous caricatures. Because the detached author permits them the freedom of thinking, doing and saying anything, they fly apart, or, to use George Eliot's own words, they have no "equivalent centre of self from which the shadows fall with a difference." Miss Murdoch's characters suffer from too much potential, too much contingency, too much eccentricity. And, so, while she seeks that "enticing mystery of the unknown" that is found in a writer like Alain-Fournier, she fails to approximate his mysterious depths. Instead, we must settle for a surface of sensational and immediate effects, inventive to be sure, which provokes playful suspense.

Neither does her neutrality eventuate in charity and tolerance. On the contrary, it results in moral confusion. To begin with, she takes an almost voyeuristic delight in her Mephistophelian characters and their wicked impulses, in satanic Calvin Blick, impish Jamesie Evercreech, and sinister Gerald Scottow, not to mention those three disreputable enchanters. These people are equipped with superior intellect, wile and charm which qualifies them to manipulate the observers whom she deflates by jesting at their protests of innocence, premature boasting, flagrant illogic and incurable pedestrianism. Paradoxically, Miss Murdoch's surreptitious bias is balanced by a converse prejudice on behalf

[3]Olga Meidner, "The Progress of Iris Murdoch," *English Studies in Africa* (March, 1961), p. 31. Miss Meidner terms this "moral indecisiveness—a kind of moral 'neutralism'."

of her observers. "An odd sort of Anglo-Irish snobbery" emerges, as the critic, Gabriel Pearson, puts it,[4] from her equation of the foreigner and supernaturalism on the one hand and the English-man and pragmatism on the other. Because the first group, the inaccessible enchanters, usually possess Oriental, Jewish and Slavic features, they divulge the author's surprisingly shallow conception of the non-Anglo-Saxon as symbolic of dark and evil universal forces. And, while the victimized Anglo-Saxons falter and fail, they nevertheless benefit from a timely rescue by their protective, maybe chauvinistic, author. Of course, this conflict between the two sets represents a grave contradiction to Miss Murdoch's notion of the unclassifiable individual. Still another violation of complex individuality is her almost categorical por-trayal of women as aggressors and men as Courtly Lovers. In her scheme of things, the female dominates, destroys and rescues, while the supplicating male serves and endures. In this way, she violates her own dictum of moral neutrality by being neither moral nor neutral and, in turn, undermines the human aspect of her fiction.

Besides being damaged by predetermined roles and ambiva-lent detachment, her characters are additionally dehumanized by the mechanical parts they are forced to play in the labyrinths of intrigue. Here again the private personality is sacrificed to the overall pattern. Miss Murdoch's Gothic and fairy tale people are designed not to break out of the fantastic into the concrete world beyond but are ordained to remain within her dream-prisons. Were she really interested in dramatizing the flight from enchantment, she would have focused upon the struggle against illusion. Instead, however, it is enchantment itself that fascinates her, and consequently she prefers to entangle rather than to dis-entangle her characters.

The tyranny of intrigue over characterization is obvious in the purely arbitrary pretexts of the novels. Situations evolve from mechanical maneuvering. For instance, the events in *The Uni-corn* occur because of the deterministic principle that the her-oine's fate will be disclosed at the end of seven years, and they terminate because that is the traditional time span in fairy tales. This capricious notion, like Mischa's offer in *Flight* to purchase

[4]Gabriel Pearson, "Iris Murdoch and the Romantic Novel," *New Left Review,* XIII-XIV (January-April, 1962), p. 143.

the defunct journal, *Artemis,* from Rosa and Hunter Keepe and Antonia's request in *Severed Head* for a divorce from Martin, trigger equally prearranged episodes.

Miss Murdoch's excessive intrigue necessitates inflexible super-structures, and these superstructures are another token of the dominance of form. *Flight's* structure is circular. At the end of the novel, Rosa Keepe's panic is assuaged when Peter Saward shows her a picture of Mischa's birthplace: "Here is the old market square and here is the famous bronze fountain, and here is the mediaeval bridge across the river...." By pacifying Rosa with a romantic escape from reality, the novel ends nearly where it began, with another exploitation of Mischa as a mythic or story-book character. Although *The Unicorn* concludes with various melodramatic events, its structure is also circular in the sense that the characters have not progressed beyond their initial be-nighted outlooks. When Marian Taylor and Effingham Cooper arrive at Gaze Castle, they are filled with sentimental expecta-tions concerning Hannah; when they depart, they hold propor-tionately apocryphal views. Marian still misunderstands the heroine's suffering and Effingham now distorts her "as a doomed figure, a Lilith, a pale death-dealing enchantress: anything but a human being."

Unfortunately, this kind of structure falsifies both novels. *Flight* becomes a grotesque joke contrived by an author with a flare for sensationalism. So does *The Unicorn,* though the joke is even more outrageous because the later book promises so much more at its inception: an eerie castle, a tormented beauty, a be-witching cast of eccentrics. Yet, after titillating the reader with horror and black magic, Miss Murdoch disappoints by supplying no better resolution to the implications of the story than a *deus ex machina.* This takes the form of murder and suicide, though neither has any meaning in and of itself and neither sheds any light upon the main issues of sin and suffering. Moreover, in both *Flight* and *The Unicorn,* the observers' final ignorance furnishes no insight in reverse into the enchanters' true identities even though such information is warranted in view of all the hints and traces which have been previously planted.

While Miss Murdoch employs a circular structure when she wants a grim ending, she uses a vertical one for optimistic finales. Both are equally random since they are not outgrowths of char-acter but superimpositions. The promising confrontation between Honor Klein and Martin Lynch-Gibbon, which serves as the climax to the vertical plot of *Severed Head,* is ludicrous. However self-consciously ironic the author tries to make them sound, their sentiments are absurd as these statements testify: "We have lived together in a dream up to now. When we awake will we find each other still?" and "Well, we must hold hands tightly and hope that we can keep hold of each other through the dream and out into the waking world." Of course, a romantic relationship between Martin and Honor is unfeasible. As a lovable buffoon, he has not been prepared for such a drastic change, and, as a hideous Medusa, she is too freakish to excite any man. That the author was aware of this disparity is apparent, for she had to force her resolution by gratuitously introducing the myth about Gyges and Candaules. Had Martin been impaled upon Honor's Samurai sword, *Severed Head's* conclusion would have been more consistent with the tone of the rest of the novel.

Whether Miss Murdoch uses the circular or the vertical design, her provocative method of alternating between violence and shock on the one hand and of insinuating supernaturalism and eroticism on the other rasies expectations which she does not fulfill. Therefore, the reader feels cheated as if by one of Honor's dark gods. It has all been a sham: the coincidences do not add up to Gerald Scottow's inflated concept of "great patterns in which we are all involved," but to painstakingly plotted events intended to tantalize the reader; the riddles do not amount to the crucial questions about metaphysical ambiguity but to teasers planted at regular intervals to seduce the reader further; the ironic reversals do not signify twists of fate that render people absurdly impotent but clever tricks that build up tension and suspense for their own sake; and, the sexual perversions do not expose sinister ambivalences in human relationships but erotic dabbling.

Finally, Miss Murdoch's Gothic settings complete the tyranny of form over character. In representing the receding background of an impenetrable reality, the scenery is merely decorative and, in making pretexts for intrigue, hints of future violence and traces of past horrors, it supplies merely facile excuses for sensationalized behavior. Most important, though, in symbolically exteriorizing states of mind, it dwarfs the characters by stressing their stock Gothic and fairy tale characteristics. Though these isolated effects are skillful, often the evocative vocabulary—i.e.,

dim, haze, cavern, cave—becomes monotonous and the sym-
bolism—e.g., Liverpool Street Station standing for Hell—too
obvious. Were Miss Murdoch intentionally imitating Anne
Radcliffe's extravagant manner of steeping the reader in beauty
and terror, her settings might be considered successful. Her aims
being far more serious, however, her results fall short of the mark.

Measured by her own standards, *The Flight from the Enchanter,*
A Severed Head and *The Unicorn* fail because each sacrifices free
and independent characters in carefully contrived forms. As we
have seen, she reduces her people to predetermined and predictable roles and submerges them in weighty and unrealized philosophical concepts and mythic-literary allusions. Also, she
mistranslates moral neutrality into cold, ambivalent and sometimes immoral detachment. And even her designs suffer because
she indulges in playful excursions, sensational effects and fanci-
ful settings for their own sake.

Iris Murdoch is a paradox indeed: typically modern insofar
as she arranges her characters contrapuntally to illuminate the
universal predicament and curiously old-fashioned to the extent
that she employs traditional Gothic and narrative devices. Consequently, she appears to be irreconcilably divided between a
contemporary proclivity towards novels of ideas and a nostalgic
commitment to novels of character. As a philosopher, she naturally inclines towards the first, causing her to create people who
either have ideas to articulate or who are idiosyncratic enough to
voice her own ideas. However, as Philip Quarles notes in Huxley's *Point Counter Point,* this comprises only "about .01 per cent
of the human race" which is why "the real, the congenital novelists
don't write such books." But whereas Huxley admits through
Quarles that he never claimed to be a congenital novelist, Miss
Murdoch states in her literary essays that she wishes to write
fiction entirely free from rationalism. In attempting to do so, she
deliberately sabotages any ideas that might bear the imprint of
"insight," by embracing ideas not her own, and, especially, by ap-
propriating literary devices from conventional fiction. Seen in
this light, the melodramatic and frivolous elements in her fiction
camouflage her bent to write like Aldous Huxley by using devices
borrowed from Anne Radcliffe. Ironically, though, her works
come through neither as novels of ideas, for they are too obscure,
nor as novels of character, for they are just too playful.

Of course, being a perceptive critic, she is profoundly conscious that she has not succeeded in conveying the unique and precious qualities of the human person. Yet, however brilliantly she articulates the dilemma in her essays, it is doubtful that her thinking about fictive form has been at all radical. Her nostalgia for traditional but outmoded techniques makes her position obsolete. Like Sir Walter Scott who lived in Old Abbey because he fancied a bygone era, Miss Murdoch's great betrayal of character is partially the onus of an anachronistic literary theory. By opting for nineteenth-century characterization, she avoids radical solutions to issues that cannot be satisfied through orthodox means since modern novelists no longer create people like Anna and Vronsky, Dorothea and Causaubon. Her own Mischa, Honor and Hannah could possibly exist in Huxley's books, but hardly in Tolstoy's or George Eliot's.

The disappointing thing about Iris Murdoch is that she continues at the rate of almost one per year to write novels according to the dictates of an obsolete standard and within the context of tired patterns. Indeed, *The Italian Girl* and *The Time of the Angels* are tarnished replicas that lack the spontaneous, entertaining and often ingenious qualities of their predecessors. And her latest book, *Bruno's Dream,* though an attempt to scale universal ambiguity down to human proportions, has the characters talking too much about things like "the metaphysics of a kiss" and doing too little actual kissing. Which makes one wonder: why does so astute and reputable a moral philosopher dedicated to art continue to produce the kind of novels that make some critics suggest that her real province is either detective or science fiction? One may only hope that she will reassess her faith in traditional forms. At the very least, one looks forward to a more serious consummation of this talented philosopher-novelist's wit, intelligence and inventiveness.

Women in the Novels
of Ann Petry

by Thelma J. Shinn

Ann Petry is black; she is also a woman. Yet her novels are
not limited ethnically nor sexually. Her first novel, *The Street*
(1946), tells the story of a young black woman in Harlem; her
second, *Country Place* (1947), tells of two white families in a small
Connecticut community; her third, *The Narrows* (1953), tells of
a black man and a white woman in Massachusetts. Petry has penetrated the bias of black and white, even of male and female, to
reveal a world in which the individual with the most integrity is
not only destroyed but is often forced to become an expression
of the very society against which he is rebelling. She shows that
the weak, regardless of race, are misled by illusions and stifled
by poverty.

Particularly for Lutie Johnson in *The Street,* the struggle for
survival alone is so demanding that even her *attempt* to struggle
also for some status as a human being—despite poverty, racial
and sexual stereotypes, and loneliness—gives her more stature in
her failure than most people earn in victory.

Lutie can scarcely be said to be attracted to the stereotypes
which would define her as a black woman. Her tension grows out
of the seeming inevitability of her conforming to the stereotypes
despite all efforts she may make to break free, because she is born
into a life that gives her new goals but fails to give her any way to
achieve them. She has been born and raised in Harlem; her
mother is dead, and her father is a drunken bootlegger who is
more a burden than a protector. What family values she has are
inherited from her wise and understanding grandmother. She is
separated from her husband and trying to support herself and

"Women in the Novels of Ann Petry" by Thelma J. Shinn. From *Critique,*
16, no. 1 (1974), p. 110-20. Reprinted by permission of *Critique.*

her son, Bub. Loneliness, poverty, the apathy and violence of ghetto life, and prejudice oppose every step she tries to take to improve herself.

Lutie faces a very different set of problems than do most American heroines. She never has the alternative of remaining dependent; even the desirable dependency of marriage is closed to her: "The only way of getting out was to find a man who had a good job and who wanted to marry her. The chances of that were pretty slim, for once they found out she didn't have a divorce they lost interest in marriage and offered to share their apartments with her."[1] She must make her way in the world on her own. Since survival—preferably at a human level—is her foremost problem, her "values" seem mainly materialistic; she dreams of a better job, a cleaner apartment, a more decent neighborhood.

However, Lutie is "handicapped" by a sense of moral integrity which reveals much of what a woman could be if social pressures did not destroy her first. Lutie will not live with a man, for instance, without the sanction of marriage, even though most of the women around her do so freely and thus escape the necessity of supporting themselves. She maintains her moral stand—and it is moral because she believes it to be—even in the face of New York divorce laws which at that time made re-marriage nearly impossible.

She is also held back because she refuses to prostitute herself. Every route off "the street," which symbolizes the poverty and its concomitant evils which she is trying to escape, seems to be through offering herself to some man for the alternative he can offer her. Again, such behavior is expected of her: "Sure, Lutie thought as she walked on, if you live on this damn street you're supposed to want to earn a little extra money sleeping around nights. With nice white gentlemen" (57). But she refuses to conform.

Nor are Lutie's strengths all negative. She is attractive and hard-working, has struggled through high school and business school to be eligible for a better-paying job—although the next civil service rating that she is currently struggling to earn will still not pay her enough to enable her to move. That she is warmly loving and sensitive to the feelings of children can be seen when

---

[1]Ann Petry, *The Street* (New York: Pyramid Books, 1961), p. 55. Subsequent references are to this edition.

she is working as a maid for the rich white Chandler family. When Mrs. Chandler's brother commits suicide on Christmas morning, the parents forget about Little Henry, and Lutie turns to him:

> She picked him up and held him close to her, letting him get the feel of her arms around him; telling him through her arms that his world had not suddenly collapsed about him, that the strong arms holding him so close were a solid, safe place where he belonged, where he was safe. She made small, comforting noises under her breath until some of the whiteness left his face. Then she carried him into the kitchen and held him on her lap and rocked him back and forth in her arms until the fright went out of his eyes.   (35)

She not only loves her own son but also tries to treat him with the respect due another human being:

> She wanted to put her arm around him and hug him, for he still had tears in his eyes, but he had obviously been screwing up his courage to the point where he could tell her whatever he had on his mind, even though he wasn't certain what her reaction would be. So she turned toward him and instead of hugging him listened to him gravely, trying to tell him by her manner that whatever he had to say was important and she would give it all her attention.
> (48)

Her compassion and understanding extend not only to those she loves but even to those she hates or those who have hurt her. A critic has admired Petry's own "genuine and generous and un-discriminating...creative sympathy" by which she "*becomes* each character she mentions,"[2] and Lutie shares with her creator this empathic insight: "As she changed her clothes, she thought, this is the same thing that happened to Jim. He couldn't stand being shut up in the little house in Jamaica just like I can't stand being shut up in the apartment" (56). Thus, she understands the tensions that drove her strong, unemployed husband to another woman while she worked at the only job she could get—as a maid in Connecticut—and came home once a month.

Yet this strong, moral young woman—attractive and willing to work—finally conforms to the worst stereotypes of the black woman. She lives in a dark, garishly-painted apartment (she had

---

[2]David Littlejohn, *Black on White* (New York: Viking Press, 1966), p. 155.

asked for white walls) and, leaving her son alone, goes to a bar:

> No matter what it cost them, people had to come to places like Junto, she thought. They had to replace the haunting silences of rented rooms and little apartments with the murmur of voices, the sound of laughter; they had to stay and empty two or three small glasses of liquid gold so they could believe in themselves again.   (95)

As much as she tries to be a good mother, she strikes her son twice, once when she sees him lighting a cigarette for her father's blowzy mistress, Lil: "And what was far more terrifying giving Bub a drink on the sly; getting Bub to light her cigarettes for her. Bub at eight with smoke curling out of his mouth" (12). The second time she strikes him publicly, when she comes home to find him shining shoes with a box he made himself: "It's also that you're afraid that if he's shining shoes at eight, he will be washing windows at sixteen and running an elevator at twenty-one, and go on doing that for the rest of his life" (47). Finally, she even commits murder, when the man she has hoped to borrow money from locks her in his apartment and intends to sleep with her and then to pass her on to his white boss, Junto. Ironically, she is borrowing to pay a lawyer to save her son from reform school, but even the lawyer knows that Bub would be freed without his assistance. Lutie does not know, but she still refuses to prostitute herself. When she rejects Junto and then Boots as well, Boots tells her: "I don't take that kind of talk from dames,…not even good-looking ones like you. Maybe after I beat the hell out of you a coupla times, you'll begin to like the idea of sleeping with me and with Junto" (265). In angry defense, she grabs a heavy iron candlestick and attacks him: "A lifetime of pent-up resentment went into the blows.…First she was venting her rage against the dirty, crowded street. Finally, and the blows were heavier, faster, now, she was striking at the white world which thrust black people into a walled enclosure from which there was no escape" (266).

Lutie becomes exactly what her society has defined her to be through its stereotypes. In a similar though more gentle way. Betty Friedan has asserted that the society of the 50's created a mystique and real women filled its role: "When a mystique is strong, it makes its own fiction of fact. It feeds on the very facts which might contradict it, and seeps into every corner of the culture, bemusing even the social critics."[3] Lutie Johnson, the very woman who set out to contradict her stereotype, becomes a vehicle of her society. Would we have preferred that she slip quietly into being one of the "little lost girls" working for Mrs. Hedges and Junto as prostitutes? Or like the self-effacing Min who melts into the background because of a "shrinking withdrawal in her way of sitting as though she were trying to take up the least possible amount of space" (20) but who survives because she has learned that "a woman didn't stand much chance alone; and because it was too lonely living by herself in a rented room. With a man attached to her she could have an apartment—a real home" (86)?

Lutie Johnson, alone now in Chicago, running from the law, has abandoned her child, the person she loved most in the world. Her problem is compound: she is black and a woman. But the integrity she shows; the strength, love, compassion, and understanding she demonstrates, despite her failure, show what can come from one woman. Her destruction by a society which prefers to foster the survival of the passive Mins argues strongly for a needed change in that society. "The protest," a critic has pointed out, "is that decent human beings are ruined by social forces they cannot come to terms with."[4]

To show that her arguments do not stop with blacks or with the ghetto, Petry follows *The Street* with *Country Place* (1947), which, we are reminded, takes place in a small Connecticut town and in which "the cast...is almost entirely white."[5] Although her narrator is a male, Petry announces through him that the topic of women will be discussed:

> It is only fitting and proper that I should openly admit to having a prejudice against the female of any species, human or animal; and yet, like most of the people who admit to being prejudiced, I am not consistent, for I own a female cat, named Banana. Though I am devoted to her, I am well aware that she is much closer to the primitive than a male cat.[6]

[3]Betty Friedan, *The Feminine Mystique* (New York: Dell, 1963), p. 53.

[4]Chester E. Eisinger, *Fiction of the Forties* (Chicago: Univ. of Chicago Press, 1963), p. 70.

[5]Littlejohn, p. 154.

[6]Ann Petry, *Country Place* (Boston: Houghton Mifflin, 1947), p. 1. Subsequent references are to this edition.

His cat reveals other characteristics as well: "Like most females she makes no effort to control her emotions" (2). Of course, our narrator sees men in animal terms as well—especially when those men are involved with a woman: "Ed at that moment was like a tomcat walking stiff-legged toward a female—ready, waiting, hungry" (15).

The novel centers around a mother and a daughter, Lil and Glory, and their respective in-laws. Glory is married to Johnnie Roane, who is just coming home from the war, and she has been living with his mother while he was gone. Lil is married to Mearns Gramby, the richest man in town, who married her when he was forty-seven and took her to live with him and his mother. The story is really of the infidelities of Lil and Glory with the same man—Ed Barrell, the town rake—and of the mothers of their respective husbands. In *Barbary Shore,* Mailer did not write of the effects of the war on the women back home as he had planned; in *Country Place* Petry completes the task for him. She not only demonstrates the collapse of tradition but also shows what society has become; Lil and Glory are vehicles of their society as Lutie is of hers, without, however, her underlying integrity.

Johnnie Roane comes home from the war eager to see his young wife, Glory, and through her to forget what he had been through: "this gives you back some of what you lost—this makes you forget wars and rumors of wars" (30). Glory is wearing a flimsy "Victory" nightgown: "designed by someone who had never been to war, but who knew that wars were won and lost in the bedrooms" (31). Glory is not ready to accept him back: "Women aren't made the same as men," she tells him; "They don't enjoy sexual intercourse" (39).

The cliché, of course, is only an excuse. Glory is a product of the collapse of traditions, and Johnnie's absence has brought out the worst in her: "Instead of a sharp line of demarcation between right and wrong, Gloria and her generation had found only the vague blur made by erasures—it was all that remained of a moral code after the impact of two world wars" (86). Glory has the additional handicap of being beautiful—a handicap also for Lutie, who was "too good-looking to be decent." Glory lacks the moral foundations Lutie gained from her grandmother. Her mother, Lil (interestingly, the name Petry gave to the mistress of Lutie's father), has quickly dismissed her as soon as she marries Johnnie, saying: "I won't have to think about you any more. I can put my mind on myself" (72). Glory is left thinking: "What was it like?

Oh, like expecting to find a strong hand which would help you
down from a high and lonely place, and then, just as you reached
for it, the hand was withdrawn—deliberately, coolly" (72).

Added to these weaknesses in her heritage is her boredom with
housewifely tasks after being so popular in high school: "sometimes she quarreled with Johnnie just to break the monotony of
their existence" (44). When Johnnie goes into the army and she
gets a job at Perkin's store, she feels "free for the first time in her
life" (44-5). She makes a decision: "But she knew what she wanted.
She did not intend to return to a life of cooking and cleaning in
that frame house of theirs...She was the prettiest girl for miles
around and all the men who came in the store paid homage to
her" (46). The contrast between her beauty and popularity and the
dowdiness of wives who shopped at the store was too much for her:

> A few more years and that's the way Johnnie will have me looking.
> I'll have four or five children and never quite enough money to go
> around. I'll be riding buses to get to the markets where the food is
> cheapest; and wearing a house dress under a winter coat; and I'll
> put on wrinkled cotton stockings in order to save my best ones for
> Sundays; and carry a cloth knitting bag instead of a pocketbook.
> I'll start for home at this hour of the day so's to have the supper
> ready for Johnnie and he'll wolf it down and grunt and reach for
> the newspaper. Then he'll take his shoes off and sit sprawled in a
> chair half-asleep until time to go to bed.   (74)

The picture she draws, pessimistic though it is, seems haunting-
ly accurate. The male druggist narrator, although he "found it
easy to think of Glory with contempt" once she starts seeing Ed
Barrell, cannot improve on the picture much:

> Yet I could not help wondering if she would have remained faith-
> ful to Johnnie if there had been no war to interrupt the normal
> course of their life together. Under other circumstances, she might
> have remained one of those pretty, more or less useless girls who
> get married and cook unappetizing meals and keep a house mid-
> dling clean, and then later on have children, not because they want
> them but by accident—born of a moment of careless, lazy passion.
>   (98-9)

When Glory is given the slightest hope of an alternative to
her all-too-normal life, she cannot see that she is choosing an
illusion. Rather, she has been brought up to believe in illusions;
as Mrs. Roane says about the "fancy ladies" at a trial in town:

> I think that's why so few girls in Lennox used to get in trouble back in those days. They could see for themselves what could and did happen. Nowadays it's not so easy for a girl to see that. I blame the movies more than anything else. They make it easy for a girl to believe that somewhere there's a beautiful carefree life if they could just find it.   (126)

Just so does Glory see the glamour of an affair, even up to the time she watches Johnnie fight with Ed after he finds them together in a cabin:

> The expression on her face held him [Johnnie] motionless. Her lips were parted, she was bending forward, her eyes fixed on him. He had seen that same expression on her face when they used to go to the movies. She would sit on the edge of the seat, not moving, lapping up the gaudiest kind of melodrama, so entranced that you knew that she had transformed herself into the glossy heroine on the screen.   (194)

So has Glory followed the dictates of her society and made herself a heroine in her own life.

Glory lives in illusions today because she cannot face the realities of tomorrow; her mother, Lil, is living the future of the illusory choice. She had supported herself and her daughter as a seamstress: "And you needed sleep so badly you could cry because you had been sewing all day long and your back ached from bending over the machine; your eyes hurt from putting some special piece of handwork...on...for some rich bitch who wouldn't want to pay but a fraction of what it was worth" (166). Knowing that the only alternative for her lies in a good marriage, Lil manipulates and plots to win the rich Mearns Gramby—only to find her life "geared to Mrs. Gramby's. 'Mother doesn't go out in the evening any more. We must stay home with her!'" (167).

Mearns has other ways to keep Lil in line: he never gives her any money unless she "humbly" requests it, and then he expects "a proper show of gratitude" (214). She has a mink coat but nowhere to wear it. She turns for comfort to Ed Barrell because "she needed the undivided attention of a lover; needed and wanted that attention to use as a bulwark against the indifference and the hostility she had found in this house" (162). Barrell, however, wants only "to get her undressed and in bed with him in the shortest possible time" (162). Lil, it seems, cannot win; but she is very good at losing. She even loses when Mrs. Gramby dies, because the will—which Mearns had a hand in as well—gives her anticipated inheritance to the servants.

The older generation of women—Mrs. Roane and Mrs. Gramby—are somewhat more favorably presented. Mainly, however, they serve to show the collapse of values. Mrs. Gramby does have the capacity to see her own mistakes—she recognizes that she has over-protected her son—and to admit that, if Lil were

> someone else's daughter-in-law, I would say that I could see how she came to intimacy with that bowlegged man. For she must have been desperately disillusioned, too, what with the bedroom door kept open at night, the cats stalking in and out, the cats sleeping on her bed, no money of her own, no place of her own in another woman's house.   (214)

Petry shows once again that the sordidness of reality, the inequities and false illusions of society, and the inadequacies of the possibilities for women rob strong and weak alike of a chance for personal development and a sense of security.

The picture does not brighten in Petry's last novel of this period, *The Narrows,* which brings together the whites and the blacks in another small New England town and shows that when individuals publicly oppose society—when a black man dates a white woman—the problems increase astronomically.

In Link Williams, the young black hero of the novel, Petry has succeeded in creating in depth a man of integrity and stature, no mean feat for a woman writer. But Link, too, is driven to violence and eventually destroyed despite—or because of—his integrity. His death seems to be the inevitable outcome of his love for Camilo, the daughter of a multimillionaire gun manufacturer and wife to the "Captain." Camilo is white, rich and bored, a beautiful blonde who is used to having her way. Perhaps she is trying to compensate for not becoming an English instructor at Barnard, a job she was tentatively offered before she married: "It was something that I did by myself with my own brain. Don't laugh at me. I would have been good at it. I would have been somebody in my own right and instead—instead."[7] Whatever the reason, she gives herself to Link with such "absolute and complete surrender, the abandonment to surrender," that he feels her very nature would have forced him to end the affair what-

---

[7]Ann Petry, *The Narrows* (Boston: Houghton Mifflin, 1953), p. 95. Subsequent references are to this edition.

ever the outside pressures might or might not be: "it would eventually have been a matter of survival, a refusal to be suffocated, owned, swallowed up" (317). When he does break with her, however, she is sure that the reason is another woman, and she forcefully fulfills the role of the woman scorned: she screams, tears her clothes, and accuses him of rape.

Camilo conforms to female stereotypes—some of the most negative, in fact—just as all of Petry's other women do eventually, whether or not they struggle against such conformity. A good example is Link's "aunt" Frances Jackson, whose first description is given by Link himself: "F. K. Jackson is right at least ninety-nine point nine times out of a hundred. It's very difficult for us average humans to love a female with a batting average like that" (14). Frances then fills in the portrait herself:

> I see my father...and he's saying, "Frank, you know you've got a man's mind," Anywhere I go here in Monmouth, I can always see myself—too tall, too thin, too bony. Even at twelve. And too bright, able, and unable and unwilling to conceal the fact that I had brains. When I finished high school I went to college, to Wellesley, where I was a kind of Eighth Wonder of the World, because I was colored. I hadn't been there very long when the dean sent for me and asked me if I was happy there. I looked straight at her and I said, "My father didn't send me here to be happy, he sent me here to learn."... A college graduate. All hung over with honors and awards and prizes. And I knew I'd never get married, never have any children. So I was going to be a doctor....My father was alone here and I couldn't bear to leave him, and there was the business he had built up so slowly and so carefully. So I became an undertaker too.
> (234-5)

She knows that her future has been determined for her; despite her intelligence and talents, Frances is doomed to live her life as circumstances have shaped it.

Ann Petry does not ignore the particular problems of blacks; her protrayals, especially of Link Williams and Lutie Johnson, in both their individual triumphs and their socially-caused failures, display potentiality enough for admiration and oppression enough for anger to satisfy any black militant. Her first concern, however, is for acceptance and realization of individual possibilities—black and white, male and female. Her novels protest against the entire society which would contrive to make any individual less than human, or even less than he can be.

Character and Themes in the
Novels of Jean Rhys

by Elgin W. Mellown

Jean Rhys, born in the West Indies in 1894, published five books between 1927 and 1939. Her first collection of stories was sponsored by Ford Madox Ford, and her four succeeding novels were praised by reviewers in England and America. But because of the outbreak of war in 1939, her books were not reprinted, and she dropped out of public attention. Then, in 1958, the BBC broadcast a dramatized version of her novel, *Good Morning, Midnight.* Its critical reception encouraged Miss Rhys to publish some short stories which she had written and to begin work on the novel which in 1966 gained the highest praise of any of her writings, *Wide Sargasso Sea.* In it she tells the story of the first Mrs. Rochester, the shadowy figure whom Charlotte Bronte only lightly sketched in *Jane Eyre.*

Wide Sargasso Sea is both an imaginative *tour de force* and a novel valuable in its own right. It places the earlier novels in a new perspective which shows that Jean Rhys is a master of her genre. In her novels she depicts the character of one particular type of woman, while exploring certain human themes and constantly attempting to develop a close relationship between style and content. Her books have now been reprinted in England and America and are being translated into both European and Oriental languages. Yet even with this ever-increasing popularity Miss Rhys has remained a very private person.

Jean Rhys was the daughter of a Welsh doctor and his English

"Character and Themes in the Novels of Jean Rhys" by Elgin W. Mellown. From *Contemporary Literature*, 13 (Autumn, 1972), p. 458-75. Reprinted (with slight changes by the author) by permission of the publisher.

Creole wife.[1] She came to England with an aunt in 1910 to attend school in Cambridge; from there she went on to the Royal Academy of Dramatic Arts. When her father died—she was then seventeen—she went to work as a chorus girl in a theatrical troupe which toured the provincial theaters, living between engagements in London. In 1918, then twenty-four years old, she "married a Dutch poet and for ten years lived a rootless, wandering life on the Continent, mainly in Paris and Vienna."[2] In these years she began to write; and in 1922 or 1923, when she and her husband were living in Paris, Mrs. George Adam, wife of the French correspondent of *The Times,* brought her stories and sketches to the attention of Ford Madox Ford. Caught up in various legal and economic problems which finally led to a divorce, Jean Rhys lived for a time with Ford and his common-law wife Stella Bowen, the Australian painter.

The complex relationships in this *ménage à trois* have been described generally by Stella Bowen in her autobiography, *Drawn from Life,* obliquely by Jean Rhys in her first two novels, and directly by her husband, Jean Marie Langlet, in his documentary novel *Sous les Verrous.*[3] Apart from the personal relationship, Ford was probably the most important literary influence upon Miss Rhys. In the last issue of the *Transatlantic Review,*[4] he published under the title "Vienne" a few sections of a novel called "Triple Sec" which she was then writing; and sometime between 1925 and 1927 he arranged for her to translate Francis Carco's novel *Perversité,* involving himself in the project to such an extent that both Carco and the American publisher, Pascal Covici, thought

[1]Biographical information is taken from Francis Wyndham, "Introduction" to Jean Rhys, *Wide Sargasso Sea* (New York: W. W. Norton and Co., 1966; New York: Popular Library, n. d.), pp. 5-13; Marcelle Bernstein, "The Inscrutable Miss Jean Rhys," *Observer* (London), 1 June 1969 [magazine section], pp. 40-42, 49-50; and John Hall, "Jean Rhys," *Guardian* (London), 10 January 1972, p. 8. There are also references to Jean Rhys in Arthur Mizener, *The Saddest Story: A Biography of Ford Madox Ford* (New York and Cleveland: World Publishing Co., 1971), pp. 344-50.

[2]Wyndham, p. 5.

[3]Édouard de Nève [pen-name of Langlet], *Sous les Verrous. Roman* (Paris: Librairie Stock, 1933).

[4](Dec. 1924), 639-45.

Ford himself was the translator.[5] He also wrote a lengthy preface
to Miss Rhys's first book, a collection of short stories entitled *The
Left Bank,* which Jonathan Cape published in 1927. In the same
year Ford broke off his relationship with Miss Rhys, and she re-
turned to England. She married again (her second husband died in
the mid-1940s, whereupon she married his cousin, who has since
died); and between 1928 and 1939 she wrote four novels: *Postures,
After Leaving Mr. Mackenzie, Voyage in the Dark, and Good
Morning, Midnight.*[6]

Although each novel centers upon one woman, the four individuals are manifestations of the same psychological type—so much
so that if we read the novels in the order of their internal chronology,
we find in them one, fairly sequential story, albeit the principal
figure suffers a change of name from novel to novel. This story
begins in *Voyage in the Dark,* in the autumn, 1912. The narrator
and central figure is Anna Morgan, a chorus girl in a touring company at Southsea. She is an orphan, having been brought from her
home in the West Indies two years earlier by her stepmother. In
Southsea she is picked up by Walter Jeffries, an older man, who
meets her later in London and seduces her. He takes care of her,

[5]During "the winter months of both 1924-25 and 1925-26, Ford and Stella" lived
in Toulon where one of their friends was Francis Carco (Frank MacShane, *The Life
and Works of Ford Madox Ford* [New York: Horizon, 1965]. p. 194). Always the
entrepreneur of literary talent, Ford evidently wanted to help bring Carco's novel
Perversité (Paris: J. Ferenczi et fils, 1925) before the English-reading public. At
any rate, on 7 January 1926 Carco wrote to Ford thanking him for his interest (David
Dow Harvey, *Ford Madox Ford, 1873-1939. A Bibliography of Works and Criticism* [Princeton: Princeton Univ. Press, 1962] , p. 97); and in 1928 Pascal Covici
published an English translation with Ford's name given as the translator. But in
letters to Edward Naumburg, Jr. (Harvey, p. 97) and Isabel Patterson (Richard M.
Ludwig, ed., *Letters of Ford Madox Ford* [Princeton Univ. Press, 1965] , pp. 176-
77), Ford declared that the translation was actually made by Jean Rhys. To Miss
Patterson he wrote, "I could not have done it myself half so well if at all because
translating is not one of my gifts and I do not know the particular Parisian *argot*
that Mr. Carco employs." In March, 1972, Miss Rhys told me that she translated both
Perversity and Édouard de Nève's *Barred* (London: Desmond Harmsworth, 1932).

[6]*Postures* (London: Chatto and Windus, 1928; American title—preferred by the
author—*Quartet* [New York: Simon and Schuster, 1929]), *After Leaving Mr.
Mackenzie* (London: Jonathan Cape; New York: Knopf, 1931), *Voyage in the Dark*
(London: Constable, 1934; New York: William Morrow, 1935), and *Good Morning, Midnight* (London: Constable, 1939; New York: Harper, [1967]). Page references with abbreviations are noted parenthetically in the text and are to the following editions: *Q—Quartet, A—After Leaving, G—Good Morning* (New York:
Vintage Books, 1974), *V—Voyage* (New York: Popular Library, n.d. [1976]).

and she falls desperately in love with him. Their liaison lasts until October, 1913, when Walter breaks it off. Anna drifts from one man to another in the demimonde of pre-war London. In March, 1914, three months pregnant by an unknown man, she begs money from Walter for an abortion. She almost dies from the bungled operation; but as the novel ends, the doctor who has been brought to her assures her friend Laurie that "She'll be all right.... Ready to start all over again in no time, I've no doubt" (*V*, p. 160).[7]

The story resumes in *Quartet*. The time is now the early nineteen-twenties, and the heroine, twenty-eight years old, is named Marya Hughes. She is married to a Pole, Stephan Zelli, and they live in Paris. Stephan, a mystery man, appears to be a fence for stolen *objets d'art*. He is arrested for larceny, and the destitute Marya is taken up by a British couple, Hugh (H. J.) Heidler and his wife Lois. She lives with the Heidlers, and soon H. J. makes love to her with the knowledge and connivance of his wife. But Lois' permissiveness is only a matter of necessity, and she becomes so unpleasant that Marya moves into a hotel where H. J. visits her. Although Marya is repulsed by the situation, she transfers her love-dependency from Stephan to H. J. and cannot break away from him. When Stephan is released from prison, he has to leave France; but before he leaves, Marya sleeps with him. Heidler, because she has "betrayed" him, breaks with her and sends her to Cannes on a pension of three hundred francs a week. The novel ends in a flurry of melodrama: Stephan and Marya return to Paris; he threatens to kill H. J.; she cries out that she will betray Stephan to the police; Stephan throws her aside and goes off with another woman of the district, thinking to himself, *"Encore une grue"* (*Q*, p. 186).

In *After Leaving Mr. Mackenzie* the central figure is named Julia Martin. The place is again Paris; the time, April, some four or

---

[7]The story, "Till September Petronella" *(London Magazine* [Jan. 1960], 19-39; rpr. *Tigers Are Better-Looking, with a selection from* The Left Bank [New York: Popular Library, 1976]), set in London, 28 July 1914, gives a less desperate picture of Anna—here named "Julia Petronella Gray"—as she encounters various men. Jean Rhys fuses several periods in this story: the description of Petronella's lover "Marston" corresponds to descriptions of Ford, while the French girl who helps Petronella choose her dresses is named Estelle. Obviously it is more than a mere coincidence that Ford's *New Poems* (New York: William Edwin Rudge, 1927) contains a poem commemorating a past love affair—"There shall no refuge be for you and me/ Who haste away....But in the deep remoteness of the heart,/ In the deep secret chambers of the mind /.../ Lo! you, enshrined."—which is entitled "To Petronella at Sea" (p. 35).

five years later. Since the previous October when her lover Mr.
Mackenzie left her, Julia has been living on the weekly three hundred francs which his lawyer sends her. (This sum for an ex-mistress
seems fixed in Miss Rhys's mind.) Now the allowance is stopped with
a final payment of fifteen hundred francs. Julia in a fit of rage returns the check to Mackenzie; on the same night she meets George
Horsfield. He gives her money and persuades her to return to London. She does so in order to meet her first lover, W. [?Walter] Neil
James—who gives her money—and to see her sister Norah and
her mother, an invalid who dies while Julia is in London. Norah
and her paternal Uncle Griffiths send Julia away after the funeral;
she takes Horsfield for her lover and then returns to Paris. The
novel ends with her begging one hundred francs from Mr.
Mackenzie.

The story reaches its conclusion in *Good Morning, Midnight.*
Sacha Jansen, living in bitter retirement in Bloomsbury on a
pension from an unidentified person (it is now two pounds ten
a week) and trying to drink herself to death, is sent to Paris for a
visit by her friend Sidonie. Sacha walks through the streets she
knew in earlier days, the familiar places and even remembered
faces bringing back events of the past. Her memories sound a
bittersweet melody above the harsh, inescapable present, for
Paris is unchanged, while she has aged and faded and become a
mere shell of hate. In a cruel, reversed mimicry of her own life,
a young gigolo attaches himself to her. She tries to persuade
him that she does not want him and that she is not wealthy. He
attempts to make love to her in her hotel room, and she wounds
him as she herself has been wounded by offering him money as
a bribe to leave her alone: "You can have the money right away,
so it would be a waste of time, wouldn't it," she says (*G*, p. 183).
But he leaves without forcing himself on Sacha and without taking her money. His not making use of her, which negative act is
a recognition of her as an individual whose wishes are to be
respected, brings her out of the isolation and hatred which have
for so long surrounded her; and out of compassion she gives herself to the man in the adjoining room whom she has previously
despised. The story in the four novels is that of the spiritual
progress of a woman from the joy of childhood into the ordeal
of adolescent love and sexual experience, through a resulting
bitterness, grief, and selfish isolation, toward a position which

will allow her to develop a compassionate understanding of the human situation.

In his *New York Times* review of *Wide Sargasso Sea* Walter Allen pointed out that Charlotte Brontë's Mrs. Rochester summed up "the nature of the heroine who appears under various names throughout Jean Rhys's fiction...[;] she is a young woman, generally Creole in origin and artistic in leanings, who is hopelessly and helplessly at sea in her relations with men, a passive victim, doomed to destruction."[8] The woman upon whom Jean Rhys centers her attention is indeed always a victim. Stella Bowen saw this quality in the novelist herself and described her as being "cast for the rôle...of the poor, brave and desperate beggar who was doomed to be let down by the bourgeoisie."[9] There is never an escape for the Rhys heroine: happiness is always followed by sadness, and her last state is always worse than her first.

Yet we must qualify these generalizations. This figure of degraded womanhood is not static, but develops from novel to novel, the development being, at least in part, the author's movement away from autobiography toward an ever more complete, imaginative rendition of the single character. Thus, in the first novel, *Quartet,* Marya Zelli, unlike the later heroines, has a strength and vivacity that are sapped but not completely perverted because she is an autobiographical projection, so much so indeed that she fails as a fictional creation: the novelist bestows qualities upon Marya that she would not actually have possessed. Miss Rhys seems only gradually to have learned which of her own experiences properly belonged to the character whom she was to sketch over and over in her novels. She also learned to conceal this recognition and, in a calculated play for verisimilitude, to give the impression of complete subjectivity. If we wish to appreciate Jean Rhys, we must sidestep our first impression that we are reading her autobiography and examine the novels as imaginative works. Only then can we see her most important literary achievement: the portrayal of a psychological type never before so accurately described. These *complete* descriptions make the character more than a psychological type: she is rather woman in one of her archetypal roles.

[8] 18 June 1967, p. 5.

[9] *Drawn from Life, Reminiscences* (London: Collins, 1940), p. 167.

The most basic experience treated by Jean Rhys concerns the
woman's childhood. Its peace and security are associated with a
warm climate, in contrast to her adult insecurity in a cold northern world. This pattern is most obvious in *Voyage in the Dark*:
Anna constantly shivers and suffers in the English climate. Her
love affair with Walter Jeffries springs from an adolescent desire
to find that warmth and security which she knew in childhood in
the game of sexual love with a partner old enough to be her
father. This theme is tentatively announced in several of *The
Left Bank* stories, while in *Wide Sargasso Sea* it becomes a poi-
gnant memory of the frustrated nymphomaniac who is brutally
restrained in the cold isolation of Thornfield Hall.

This archetypal woman never finds a man who will faithfully
continue to fulfil her needs. Marya knows such happiness longer
than any of the other women, but even Stephan, her older, lover-
husband, eventually fails her. Her need is both psychic and physical, for Miss Rhys was one of the first women novelists in England
to acknowledge a woman's desire for sexual love; and when
Stephan is imprisoned for a year she must allow herself to be
taken by another man who is, as always, older and, as always, a
brute. Instinctively knowing that her man will desert her, the
woman increasingly debases herself in a desperate attempt to
hold on to him, the inevitable result being that her abandoned
position increases his revulsion. The Rhys woman may be a mistress in name, but in fact she is always a victim of love because
she is at the mercy of her uncontrollable desires.

An adjunct theme has to do with woman as creator. These tor-
tured women cannot reach maturity by giving birth to a child
which, depending on them, will force them into adulthood; and,
having no husbands to provide for them and with no way of earn-
ing a living other than by selling their bodies (which must thus be
kept free of a dependent child), they must abort any life that
may spring in their wombs. If they do give birth, as Julia Martin
does, then they are unable to keep the child alive. Woman as
creator and sustainer of life has no part in the archetypal figure.[10]

These women are forever alone outside the realm of everyday
society and cut off from the ordinary patterns of life. In them we
see a literal meaning of the term *demimonde,* for theirs is only a

---

[10]Here is one of the clearest distinctions between the writer and her heroine:
Jean Rhys gave birth to a child (is indeed a grandmother) and also created the
fictional character who is the subject of this discussion.

partial existence. They know that they are alive because they suffer and because money passes through their hands. The respectable world views such women as commodities to be bought and as hostages who must pay their way. As Maudie says in *Voyage in the Dark*, "Have you ever thought that a girl's clothes cost more than the girl inside them?...People are much cheaper than things" (*V*, p. 39). In this understanding of life lies the origin of one of the novelist's most important themes, that personal identity is determined by economic wealth. This attitude appears to link Miss Rhys with that realistic tradition which Defoe and Richardson represent, and certainly her stress upon this theme brings her obvious romantic impressionism into line with the harsh realities of modern economic life. But she goes further than any of her predecessors. In her novels all of the prevailing moral values come solely from this single standard, with no attention given to any of the other arbiters of morality which earlier authors recognized, if only to pay lip service to them. The Rhys woman reasons that, since her physical existence depends upon money, everything else does too—character, morals, ethics, even religious values. And since she knows too that money is merely an artificial thing, that which men give to women when they make love to them, or when they send them away, she cannot respect that respectable society which values it: she describes those persons who have a devil-may-care attitude to money as *chic*. Herein lies Jean Rhys's twentieth-century development of the realistic tradition. Her women do not identify themselves as the owners of plantations in Virginia, or as the mistresses of the squire's household, positions valued by a money-minded society no matter how they may have been gained. Rather these women find their identity and a truth for themselves by flaunting their disdain for the money upon which society is based. Julia Martin throws away the check and, aware of her sister's and uncle's absolute disapproval of her, spends her last shillings on roses for her mother's cremation, while Marya and Stephan recklessly spend their last francs on an unneeded, luxurious meal. Stella Bowen wrote about this attitude in reference to Jean Rhys herself, and her comments quite accurately describe the world of these novels:

> All the virtues, in her view, were summed up in "being a sport," which meant being willing to take risks and show gallantry and share one's last crust; more attractive qualities, no doubt, than

patience or honesty or fortitude. She regarded the law as the instrument of the "haves" against the "have nots" and was well ac-
quainted with every rung of that long and dismal ladder by which
the respectable citizen descends towards degradation.

It was not her fault that she knew these things, and the cynicism
they engendered had an unanswerable logic in it. It taught me that
the only really unbridgeable gulf in human society is between the
financially solvent and the destitute. You can't have self-respect
without money. You can't even have the luxury of a personality.[11]

While these novels are thus linked one to another not only by
the central character but also by this harsh, economic view of life,
they are not merely psychological studies or economic tracts, but
carefully designed dramas of character development. In *Wide
Sargasso Sea* this growth is obvious—after all, Jean Rhys chose to
enter a progression of events with a predetermined ending (that
is, the novel *Jane Eyre*); but this novel is a special case, and the
earlier ones present more typical situations faced by the novelist.
Although character development is less accomplished in *Quartet*
and *After Leaving Mr. Mackenzie* than in the next two novels,
by the end of *Quartet* Marya has changed to the extent that she
admits her love for Heidler and reshapes her relationship with
Stephan. In the second novel there is a more significant change:
initially Julia is smartingly alive to the cruelties of life. Then,
after a not too subtle flashback to the first time she was "happy
about nothing; the first time [she was] afraid about nothing"
(*A*, p. 159), a memory which is linked to her catching butterflies
which broke themselves to pieces in trying to escape from the box
in which she imprisoned them, there follows the incident of
George Horsfield touching her arm as they sneak together up the
dark stairs of her Notting Hill boarding-house. She screams
and awakens the landlady and of course is asked to leave. She is
the butterfly broken by her own struggles against the imprison-
ing walls of her society and—no less—of her defenseless sensitivity. But at the end of the novel she is rejected by a young man
who, having followed her on a dark street, sees her revealed by a
street lamp:

> He gave her a rapid glance.
> "*Oh, la la,*" he said. "*Ah, non, alors.*"
> He turned about and walked away.
> "Well," said Julia aloud, "that's funny. The joke's on me this time."
> (*A*, p. 187)

[11]Bowen [*Drawn from Life*], pp. 166-67.

She no longer *feels* the criticism which would have destroyed her earlier, nor does she feel any pity for a starving man whom she sees; and she realizes that she is ending "where most sensible people start, indifferent and without any pity at all" (*A*, p. 188).

Perhaps it was this dead end of emotion in her second novel which caused Miss Rhys to turn away from a biographical chronology in her third, *Voyage in the Dark*. It chronicles Anna's never-ceasing descent on the scale of personal and social values, a history of degradation all the more chilling because so obliquely told. Not for this author the gloating of the pornographer over salacious incidents: such matters may be the stuff of life, but she is the artist concerned with character portrayal, her style being completely shaped by its demands. We experience only what Anna experiences; and if we want to see her in the eyes of the world, we must make our own deductions and extrapolations.

But while there is more action in *Voyage in the Dark* than in any of the other novels, *Good Morning, Midnight* is actually the most accomplished of the four novels in terms of character development. Marya and Julia both come to terms with themselves, Anna is a drifter who is shaped by the persons whom she meets, and none of the three ever truly achieves an adult relationship with another person. It remains for Sacha Jansen, the longing-for-death dipsomaniac, who has deliberately frozen over the wellsprings of love to live only through her memory of the past, to develop into an adult by going beyond her adolescent hate-fear of other human beings. Yet this change comes only on the last page of the novel and is more suggested than defined. Having wounded the Russian gigolo as deeply as she herself has ever been wounded, and having seen him turn the other cheek, Sacha leaves her door open, inviting the man next door whom she has so long avoided·into her bed. The novel ends as she looks up at him:

> He doesn't say anything. Thank God, he doesn't say anything. I look straight into his eyes and despise another poor devil of a human being for the last time. For the last time....
> Then I put my arms around him and pull him down on to the bed, saying: "Yes—yes—yes...." (*G*, p. 190; exact punctuation)

I think that these echoes of Molly Bloom's voice are deliberate and that they serve to tell us more about Sacha than Jean Rhys was willing to state directly. Sacha overcomes the drift toward death that obsessed the earlier manifestations of the Rhys woman by finding this compassion, and in some way it so alters her character that she is no longer a subject for the novelist. The four novels work as a unit which (like certain other contemporary, quasi-autobiographical novels) ends because the material has been brought to a logical conclusion. Significantly the last of the novels, *Wide Sargasso Sea,* is set in a distant land in a non-contemporary time.

Reviewers of Miss Rhys's books, even of her first, praised her technique,[12] although none realized that it is based on the consciously manipulated point of view. Like her contemporary Ernest Hemingway, Jean Rhys learned to allow her characters to create themselves through their own narration of their stories. The technique derives of course from Browning's dramatic monologues—Jake Barnes comes to life in the same way that the Duke of Ferrara does—and in the more successful stories of *The Left Bank* the young writer makes a comparably adroit use of the narrator. In "Illusion" the "exceedingly nice" Miss Bruce,[13] an English artist resident in Paris, is stricken with appendicitis and rushed to a hospital. The narrator, in searching out personal necessities for Miss Bruce in her apartment, comes upon the sensible lady's secret, an armoire of bright frocks. The story is only an amusing vignette with overtones of Krafft-Ebing—until one realizes that the author has caught one's attention because she has made the narrator so ambiguous that not even his sex can be determined. Similarly in "The Blue Bird" Carlo (*née* Margaret Tomkins) tells her story of hopeless love for a "Bad Man" to the narrator who is certainly female but whose exact relationship to Carlo is never explained.

The stories of *The Left Bank* are generally told by a sexually ambiguous persona who is alive to pathos, keenly aware of her own sensibilities, generally conscious of the emotions of others, and always completely amoral in her evaluations. They are experimental pieces, and one would like to know how much Ford worked with his young protégée on them. He commented in his

---

[12]D. B. Wyndham-Lewis, "Hinterland of Bohemia," *Saturday Review,* 23 April 1927, p. 637; "Miss Rhys's Short Stories," *New York Times Book Review,* 11 December 1927, p. 28; among others. *The Left Bank* was widely and favorably reviewed.

[13]Jean Rhys, *The Left Bank and Other Stories,* with a Preface by Ford Madox Ford (New York: Harper and Brothers, [1927]), p. 30.

"Preface" that, when he tried to get Miss Rhys to introduce topographical details into her writing, "she eliminated even such two or three words of descriptive matter as had crept in...."[14] If she refused direct suggestions, she profited however from Ford's example, particularly in that technique which he called *"progression d' effet,"* the idea "that every word set on paper—*every* word set on paper—must carry the story forward and, that as the story progressed, the story must be carried forward faster and faster and with more and more intensity."[15] In *Quartet* the forward movement is too fast and the ending degenerates into melodrama. Still, there are isolated passages in which every word contributes to the total effect—Marya's confession to Stephan of what happened while he was in jail is one of these:

> "Yes. There was a letter from him [Heidler] at the hotel to-day. But first...I must tell you...When I'd been there with them...a little time, Heidler started making love to me...And so I went to her, to Lois, and I told her what was happening and I asked her to let me have the money to go away....And she said...that what was the matter with me was that I was too virtuous and that she didn't mind....And that I was a fool not to trust Heidler....And that night she went out somewhere and left me alone with him...."
> (*Q,* p. 179; punctuation as in first edition [1928])

The passage also illustrates the distinction which Ford made between the spoken language and "English-literary jargon."[16] Marya, Julia, Anna, and the other characters speak or think in the language appropriate to their individual voices, but when Miss Rhys is outside the character, giving us, as in this passage from *After Leaving Mr. Mackenzie,* the character's inarticulated and actually unrecognized feelings, she uses a literary language which is unrelated to the character. Julia sets off for Montparnasse with high hopes, but (as we saw in the passage quoted above) a young man turns away from her in repugnance, and after this rebuff she begins to feel a total indifference to humanity:

[14]Ford, Preface to *The Left Bank,* p. 26; also in *Tigers Are Better-Looking,* pp. 161-162.

[15]Quoted from *Joseph Conrad, A Personal Reminiscence* (London: Duckworth, 1924), p. 210, by Frank MacShane, ed., *Critical Writings of Ford Madox Ford* (Lincoln: Univ. of Nebraska Press, 1964), p. 87.

[16]In his letter to Anthony Bertram, 14 Aug. 1922. *Critical Writings,* p. 100.

The Place du Chatelet was a nightmare. A pale moon, like a claw,
looked down through the claw-like branches of dead trees.
    She turned to the left and walked into a part of the city which
was unknown to her. "Somewhere near the Halles," she thought,
"Of course, at the back of the Halles."
    She saw a thin man, so thin that he was like a clothed skeleton,
drooping in a doorway. And the horses, standing like statues of
patient misery. She felt no pity at all....
    It used to be as if someone had put a hand and touched her heart
when she saw things like that, but now she felt nothing. Now she
felt indifferent and cold, like a stone.

                        (*A*, p. 188; punctuation as in first edition [1931])

    In these passages there is a device which Jean Rhys may have
picked up from Ford, although she could have found it in many
contemporary French novelists (Carco, for example): it is the use
of the ellipsis to indicate those pauses which are a part of the
spoken language, or to show a sequence of events or ideas, or
some type of change, which the novelist does not want to follow
through in detail. The technique is appropriate for the inarticulate, drifting heroine, but is much less satisfactory for such characters as Lois and Heidler, who are always self-conscious and
aware of themselves.
    But Jean Rhys only gradually learned her technique, and her
first two novels are flawed by her failure to control the point of
view. In both she is the omniscient, third person author, even
pausing—in the Ford manner—to address the reader directly,
as here, at the opening of the second chapter of *Quartet:* "Marya,
you must understand, had not been suddenly and ruthlessly
transplanted from solid comfort to the hazards of Montmartre"
(*Q*, p. 15). But this point of view is so patently that of the main
female character and so biased in her favor that the abrupt shifts
into the thoughts of another character—often the one against
whom the heroine is reacting—destroy the continuity of the narrative and weaken its psychological verisimilitude. *Quartet* is
the worst offender because Miss Rhys alternately uses the views
of Marya, H. J., Lois, and Stephan, and even enters into the consciousness of strangers passing by. The problem is less critical in
After Leaving Mr. Mackenzie since the cast of characters is smaller,
yet the movement from Julia's thoughts to those of the persons
whom she meets distracts the reader, not least because these

characters enter the narrative only because they have some relationship with Julia; they do not exist in their own right.

The solution to this narrative problem comes in *Voyage in the
Dark*. The novelist realized that her concern with one character
demanded that she write in the first person, utilizing only those
sensations, impressions, and experiences which the first person
narrator could reasonably have had. Anna Morgan and Sacha
Jansen know only that they suffer and that therefore they exist;
anything outside themselves exists only because they happen to
think about it, or because it impinges upon their consciousness.
The controlled point of view which holds to the consciousness of
the central character is not only a functional way of telling her
story, but also expresses her solipsistic philosophy. The aesthetic
value of both *Voyage in the Dark* and *Good Morning, Midnight*
is raised because the first person point of view is the technical
correlative of Jean Rhys's understanding of life.

I have delayed looking at *Wide Sargasso Sea* because it is a
masterpiece that need not be discussed except on its own terms,
as well as the logical outgrowth of the developments in the previous four novels. In it we are told the story of Rochester and his
first wife prior to (as well as during) the time period of *Jane Eyre*.
Miss Rhys accounts for their early lives, their marriage, and Bertha's subsequent madness and incarceration at Thornfield Hall,
ending this "secret history" with the death of Bertha in the fire.

Wide Sargasso Sea is composed of first person narratives by
Antoinette Cosway Mason Rochester (only her husband calls
her Bertha) and by Edward Fairfax Rochester, along with a one-
page conversation between Grace Poole and Leah, the maid. The
sections narrated by Antoinette—the first, part of the second, and
the third—are in the past tense and appear to have been written
at Thornfield Hall; or, perhaps more logically, to be Antoinette's
recollections during her moments of lucidity at Thornfield Hall.
The last section takes us through Richard Mason's visit to the attic
room to the moment before Bertha-Antoinette slips out of the
attic with the lighted candle to set fire to the Hall. The sections
narrated by Rochester are also in the past tense, but are subtly
different. The whole story is known to Antoinette as she writes,
and we, knowing its end but not its progress, must accept the
workings out of its details because we recognize the inexorable
conclusion looming before us. Rochester's narration however

takes place at the moment that events occur, and consequently
we share with him his revelations and growing horror. Thus the
two voices tell us one story, giving us not merely the contrast of
their attitudes, but more important for the effect of horror which
it produces, the contrast of the victim who knows her fate with
that of the victim who must gradually learn his. Antoinette knows
from the start that she is doomed and that any act is futile, while
Rochester imagines, even as his destiny bears down upon him,
that he is a free agent.

The biographical details which Jean Rhys provides for Charlotte Brontë's characters are as complex as any actually given by
the Victorian novelist. Annette Cosway, an English Creole in
Jamaica who is widowed about the time of the Emancipation
(1834) when her daughter Antoinette is ten years old, lives with
her daughter and imbecile son Pierre for five years on the run-
down plantation Coulibri, an object of ridicule and hate to the
free Negroes. Finally she manages to marry the wealthy Mr.
Mason; they live together in the refurbished plantation house
until they are driven out by rioting blacks. The house is burned,
Pierre is killed, Antoinette is injured and becomes seriously ill,
and Mrs. Cosway-Mason goes mad. She is kept in private confine-
ment where she is the sexual prey of her Negro attendants. She
dies while Antoinette is at convent school, as does Mr. Mason, but
not before he settles thirty thousand pounds on Antoinette.
Richard Mason, her stepfather's son, arranges for Rochester, the
impoverished younger son of Thornfield Hall, to marry Antoinette; he comes out to Jamaica and is married after only a few
weeks' acquaintance. Antoinette gives herself body and soul to
him, Richard having already given her money to him with no
settlement made in her behalf. Rochester realizes that he does
not love Antoinette, although he is sexually infatuated by her.
Her passion for him corresponds—so much so that his basically
Puritanical nature is revolted, and he is ready to turn away from
her in disgust when he is told by her colored half-brother that he
has been tricked into marrying the daughter of a mad nymphomaniac. His sudden revulsion throws Antoinette into a sexual
panic; we gather that she is indeed unfaithful to him; and to protect his "honor" as well as to "punish" Antoinette, Rochester
brings her to England and imprisons her in Thornfield Hall,
his own father and elder brother having died and the estate
having devolved upon him, ironically removing the necessity

for his marrying the heiress. During the voyage to England Antoinette actually goes mad and subsequently knows only intermittent moments of sanity in her garret prison.

Here, then, spelled out clearer than in any of the previous novels, are the details of the life of the now familiar Rhys heroine: a happy childhood in a tropical state of nature, growth into adolescence without the presence of a father, a complete submission to physical love, the inevitable loss of that love, and the consequent misery. In one sense, then, as Walter Allen noted, Antoinette Cosway *is* the embodiment of Marya, Julia, Anna, and Sacha. On the other hand, however, her character lies in a somewhat different sphere from theirs. They are shadows of an archetypal figure, and their precise outlines (because we see them always from the inside, so to speak) are often indistinct. Their indefiniteness contributes not a little to their universality. Antoinette, while a manifestation of the same archetypal figure, is however a positive character who is not to be confused with anyone else. She may be representative of nineteenth-century Creole girls at the mercy of fortune-hunting younger sons, and she may even be an example of tropical hot blood reacting to the icy restraint of the north, but she is not, like the other Rhys heroines, Woman with a capital *W*.

Interestingly enough, Rochester does not share this individuality. The novelist's men all have basically the same psychology: they are creatures with physical desires who have the power of simple, logical thinking. Rochester differs very little from Stephan Zelli (the outcome of both stories results from their notions of honor), while his ability to separate physical relationships from psychic ones parallels this trait as it appears in Heidler, Mackenzie, and even Anna's first lover, Walter Jeffries. A man's heart, according to Jean Rhys, is never much involved with his physical desires.

The technique of the novel reinforces the different approach to the male and female characters. The man considers himself to be a free agent in the present moment, not fearing the future and not completely at the mercy of the past. But the woman knows instinctively that she must act out a preordained role and that, no matter what present events may indicate, her end is inevitable. While the first four novels incorporate these psychological concepts, only in *Wide Sargasso Sea* is the technique completely appropriate to the author's basic concept of life. This harsh, realistic view is at times heavily Freudian, the spectre of Nietzsche being never far away; and it appeals only to the strong-minded reader who, like the author herself, can look directly at the human comedy. Because this attitude to life is so convincingly presented through all the means at the novelist's command, we realize that while *Wide Sargasso Sea* captures us initially because of our interest in the story—its explanation of events about which we have always wondered—and because of its ability to provide that *frisson* that readers can never resist, its ultimate aesthetic value comes from its complete unity. Technique, content, and characterization work together to delineate a mature artist's view of life.

It is perhaps too soon to assign Jean Rhys a definite place in literary history, although we can notice her relationship to her contemporaries. The story of her life inevitably makes us compare her to Katherine Mansfield. Both women were ex-colonials who never forgot the islands where they were born. Both of them— like many another colonial newly come to London or Paris— discovered a madder music in a bohemian life morally more lax than that which the natives of Swiss Cottage or the Boul' Mich ever enjoy. And although they both wrote about the helpless woman who needs the love and protection of a man, they were themselves solitary artists who knew their true life best when they were seated at the lonely writing desk. Yet the differences in their personal attitudes make their writings quite different. Katherine Mansfield, in spite of her labors to master the Continental tradition of writing *contes* and her desire to be like a Chekhov or a de Maupassant who could fleetingly turn the brilliance of his genius upon prosaic events, illuminating and fixing them forever as he saw them, never departs from the traditional moral stance of the British novelist, except, from time to time, to slip from it into sentimentality. Jean Rhys, in contrast, employed not only the *mise en scène* of the Continent, but also the European *Zeitgeist*—its new ideas in psychology, its aesthetic application of certain philosophical ideas, and, most of all, its between-the-wars appreciation of the plight of the individual, the isolation of existentialism. Caught up in such ideas, she quickly leaves behind her the traditions of realism as practiced by earlier British novelists and, neither commenting upon nor manipulating her characters according to any moral pattern, allows them (or more accurately, the single character) to express what is. Relentlessly she develops her single vision of a world in which free will is a myth and the individual has no power to control his destiny. She pays little or no heed to the reader's resulting depression or occasional mystification and never, like Mansfield, utilizes an irony to exalt the reader. Katherine Mansfield often puts him on the side of the gods where he can feel superior to the self-deluding Miss Brills who flounder before him; Jean Rhys does not salve our pride, but aims through her various technical devices to make us experience the degradation and humiliation of her characters. In the Rhys world there is no superior vantage point for anyone.

Comparisons with such female writers of the period as Virginia Woolf and those whom Lionel Stevenson has aptly named "A Group of Able Dames" in *The History of the English Novel: Yesterday and After*[17] offer little help in defining the place of Jean Rhys in literary history. There are certain similarities between the content of her novels and those by Djuna Barnes, particularly in the post-war Parisian setting and in the fascination with bizarre psychological types, and also those by Radclyffe Hall. The stress which Jean Rhys and Radclyffe Hall gave to misunderstood and socially unacceptable aspects of female psychology helped open the way for that unabashed treatment of all types of characters which we accept and even demand from novelists today. Of course Radclyffe Hall's evangelical intentions of propagandizing for oppressed women put her novels in a different class from Jean Rhys's; and certainly Radclyffe Hall, in spite of her flaunting of sexual mores and her sophistication, never departs from her traditional—even county-English—morality: she is always concerned with her characters as moral entities. Such a concern is completely missing from Jean Rhys's fiction. In it we find a portrayal of human beings, particularly of one type of woman, functioning in an economic society, who are seen from a physiological and psychological point of view. Whatever moral values are present are derived from the characters themselves.

These types and their world are now perhaps commonplaces of contemporary literature. Even in 1940 Stella Bowen could write that "this world...has...found an impressive literature in the works of writers like Céline and Henry Miller."[18] Other names

---

[17]*The History of the English Novel: Yesterday and After,* XI (New York: Barnes, 1967).

[18]Bowen, p. 167.

might now be added to this list, including that of Tennessee Williams, whose novel *The Roman Spring of Mrs. Stone* reads in some ways like a slick-magazine version of *Good Morning, Midnight.* Most of these authors would be European or American, rather than British. In spite of all the changes which have taken place in literature and in the other forms of our modern culture, the contemporary British novelist has not completely abandoned traditional moral values. Perhaps the literary heritage of the "great tradition" of morality is sufficient to outweigh the new forces in society.

Yet if Jean Rhys's philosophy has not been adopted by other British novelists, that fact says nothing about her abilities as a novelist. Her five novels are models for anyone who wants an original understanding of life and of human nature, and who desires the aesthetic pleasure one finds in a perfect correlation between technique and content.

Muriel Spark's Fingernails

by Malcolm Bradbury

"The sense of a system saves the painter from the baseness of the *arbitrary* stroke, the touch without its reason."

HENRY JAMES, PREFACE TO *The Tragic Muse*

I

Muriel Spark has always struck me as an interesting and decidedly amusing writer, but not always a particularly distinguished one; yet something has been happening in her recent work that makes her increasingly approximate to that condition. The development is hard to define, but it has to do with an increasing authority and assurance in her manner of presenting her work, an increasingly high-handed manner with her readers, and an increasing sharpness, if not cruelty, in her narratorial relationship with her characters. It also has to do with an economical paring down both of the rhetoric and the matter so that the natural form of expression becomes not the contingent novel but the tight *novella*. In some ways it represents a decided limiting of the pleasures—especially the comic pleasures—that have been present in some of her earlier novels, and there may be paradoxical grounds for hoping that in due course a certain relaxation will occur and some of the impurities—themselves, one always felt, carefully invigilated impurities—of the previous books will return. Still, we are not all that used to works of high aesthetic achievement and poise, and this, over her last three novels, from *The Public Image* (1968) on, she has offered us;

"Muriel Spark's Fingernails" by Malcolm Bradbury. From *Critical Quarterly*, no. 14 (Autumn, 1972), 241-50. Reprinted by permission of the author and the publisher.

these are books that possess a high tactical authority and a singular clarity so that every compositional decision, every rhetorical device, every perspective in every sentence has the high economy of, for example, one of Hemingway's better stories, the same air of exchanging language at the very best possible rate. Of course the ends are different, and in many respects they are, in Miss Spark's case, much more flamboyant. For Muriel Spark has not ceased, in this process of artistic self-purification, to be a comic writer. The tactics of indifference which give poise to her aesthetic manner transfer themselves through to an appalling moral manner: they become a sort of splendid impudence in which we encounter a decidedly strange view of the world and of human potential and the human condition.

Perhaps this is another way of saying that Muriel Spark's aesthetics and her religion, her Catholicism, are closely involved —a point that has been tellingly made by David Lodge in an interesting essay on her work.[1] This might serve to remind us to what an extraordinary extent it is the Catholic novelists who have contributed self-conscious aesthetics to the English literary tradition and have, in so doing, given those aesthetics a casuistical, or Jesuitical, streak. Concern with the analogue between God's making and the writer's tends wonderfully to generate a large frame of reference for art and a sense of high presumption, in more than one sense of the word, in the writer; meanwhile Protestants have realism. At one end of the debate is the Joycean extreme, the secular casuistry by which he is able to speak of the wholeness and the objective existence of a fiction, a suspended aesthetic stasis, dramatically self-validating, while the novelist, Omnipotent creator, stands outside, "indifferent, paring his fingernails." At the other is the doubt that invests much French Catholic fiction and is best embodied in Mauriac's famous statement, which is not without paradox: "the heroes of our novels must be free in the sense that the theologian says man is free. The novelist must not intervene arbitrarily in their destinies." Mauriac's view is the more humanistic, and it gives an uneasy liberalism to his work; but it is the line from Joyce that gives formal purity, the wholeness of a symbolist art. These matters

---

[1] David Lodge, "The Uses and Abuses of Omniscience: Method and Meaning in Muriel Spark's *The Prime of Miss Jean Brodie,*" in *The Novelist at the Crossroads* (London, 1971), pp. 119-44.

are very much in play with Muriel Spark, who is in no conventional sense a humanist, and whose fingernails deserve our
closest attention. In England, where closer influences on her
work seem to lie, not dissimilar issues have their place in the
writing of Graham Greene and Evelyn Waugh — Greene being
closer to Mauriac's edgy humanism, and Waugh to an art, however unlike Joyce's, of indifference or detachment. Greene is,
to humanist eyes, capable of being a quirky writer, but he is deeply rooted in the substance of a knowable world, which means that
only on occasion do these aesthetic matters protrude far enough
to win our attention. The obvious case of that is *The End of the
Affair;* there the narrator, Bendrix, a professional writer and a
secular realist, competes with an alternative plot-maker, God,
who attempts to intrude the improbable, in the form of miracles,
into an ostensibly realistic universe. This is somewhat the sort
of dilemma that Waugh hints at on one occasion in his writing —
in *Brideshead Revisited,* where the possibility of an oblique,
divine purpose in the chaos of modern history is intimated,
again through a secular hero himself trying to attach significance
to a contingent or even a downhill and saddening plot.

But what Muriel Spark is closer to is the assuredly comic Waugh,
the writer who, despairing of God's sensible presence in modern
history, feels free to represent it as chaos, as a vulgarized non-
sense, without any really significant moral substance. Faith may
enter, but the idea of it as a possession that redeems this world is
not given; it is as often as not an attribute of those who suffer or
are historically victimized, a stay or a remarkably oblique alternative. But men are in ignorance of true things, and that
aristocratic belief generates comic spectacle in the form of a
macabre dance. It is this that passes on into the famous macabre
of Muriel Spark, a *memento mori* writer if ever there was one.
Indeed her novel of that title is her most Waugh-like, and also
its own testament; a farce which uses the continuing obsession of
its senile cast with the things of time and history, it at once gives
a comic unreality to those things — for the agents, by performing
them, parody them — and invokes a cool, instructive pathos as
we contemplate the human failure to consider what really matters.
In this, the book resembles very much that kind of tragicomedy
we call black humour — a line to which Waugh has, to my eyes,
significantly contributed for the age. But one must not leave
unremarked an essential difference; Muriel Spark has become

that much more the aesthetician, and not only because she has something of the disposition of a poet and is, too, one of the more intelligent of our modern novelists. To Evelyn Waugh, it seemed, the discontinuity between what God has in mind and what man is is so remote that plots are at a discount; and he is pre-eminently a novelist of the contingent. But Muriel Spark senses a necessity, a need for wholeness and coherence. Indeed, that increasingly has become her preoccupation; and the pre-occupation not only links her fairly closely with some of the more energetic developments in contemporary fictional aesthetics (I had almost said with Professor Frank Kermode) but gives her novels a teleological or, as we are learning to say, an end-directed economy which makes them into very exact, very formal and very duplicitous objects.

To a point they always were; there are a number of themes and modes that occur throughout her work. One of these is a decided curiosity about the relation of an author to a fiction and the characters he invents; another is a comic interest in social milieu generative of extravagance of one sort or another; a third is an obsession with the breaking or collapse of innocence, and a related interest in figures of camp or high style. But in these earlier novels she is extremely interested in—and capable of being amused by and amusing about—an extended social world, and the formal concerns are, so to speak, not greatly more than the procedural speculations of a writer technically and theologically self-aware and, though in ways decidedly quirky or ambiguous, morally concerned for the persons in her charge. At times this thrust seems to take the form of a desire to free her people from their inexorable puppeteer. "I would that it were possible"—so Anthony Trollope, in the opening pages of *Is He Popenjoy?* —"so to tell a story that a reader should beforehand know every detail of it up to a certain point, or be so circumstanced that he might be supposed to know…The story must be made intelligible from the beginning, or the real novel readers will not like it." Trollope's proposal to free the character from the concealments compositionally practised by the novelist for effect seems to chime with a habit of Miss Spark's in some of her novels, where revelation of coming ends of particular stories or the particular fortunes of particular characters is an important technical feature. But Trollope's aim is to free the character and the reader from an unnecessary naïveté, so that the story can be more densely and substantially told and the screw of exposition and plot need not be so tightly turned. That is not Muriel Spark's aim, and it is a dubious freedom she confers on her characters, and her readers; for one thing, it puts her as a novelist in a flamboyantly strong position, and for another it produces elegant perspectives on the chronological present which make the told substance seem not more solid but rather less so. She is very like Mauriac's novelist of intervention. And she has something else to say, which is that plot is destiny. In her more recent work, it is that perspectivism which has come to interest her more; and this has produced a curious paring down or partialization of that original world. Over her last three books one wants to discern a distinct aesthetic phase, not unlike the phases of certain modern painters who have localized aspects of an originally somewhat eclectic endeavour and made them objects of recurrent formal attention.

II

Over these books certain common things occur: the length reduces to novella size; the expository material diminishes sharply in quantity; a good part of the substance is established through a pointed and economical dialogue; the time-span shortens, to one or two days; the length of the particular scene, or what Henry James would call the "discriminated occasion" of the telling, increases; and a self-aware abstemiousness, coupled with skilled and attentive use of prime variables like point-of-view and time-pointing, establishes high authority with the reader. A psychological centre in or sympathy with a given character is avoided as part of the general economy. There is exposition through small, contingent, material things. But what specially distinguishes these stories is that they are all novels of ending, are, indeed, all endings; the luminous scene begins on the edge of finality, avoiding any bulk of early exposition, and completes it. Frank Kermode has told us that one of the dilemmas of life and fiction alike is the relation of the time of a life and the time of the world, but death and apocalypse are logical termini[2]; and death

---

[2]Frank Kermode, *The Sense of an Ending: Studies in the Theory of Fiction* (New York/ London, 1967). One might say that the closeness between an important novelist and an important critic one senses here has itself an exciting cul-

is very much Miss Spark's present subject. In *The Public Image,*
the death of Frederick, the husband of the English tiger-lady
film-actress Annabel Christopher, by suicide is an effort to expose,
dramatically, the public wealth and private squalor of her life.
That is Frederick's plot; but the perspectives of the novel are
managed through Annabel, who manages to assimilate the plot
into her own capacity for survival, include it in her public image.
In *The Driver's Seat,* the most economically perfect and precise
of the three works, the action moves straight—how straight it
takes us time to discover—to the mortal terminus; that is the book
to which, in a moment, I want to return. In *Not to Disturb* we
have again a story told at a distance and through techniques of
ominous prefiguration. In many novels of the past (and reading
this novel, which is perhaps a little too much pastiche, we think
of many novels of the past) the story, the plot, happens to the
middle-classes and is told by the servants; so Nelly Dean in
Wuthering Heights, and so the bulk of the exposition in traditional up-at-the-Grange, big-house detective stories. It is these
traditional fiction makers and reporters of the crimes of high
passion, of the corpse in the drawing room and the shouts in the
night, these non-participant observers, who in *Not to Disturb*
have learned to ape the manners of their betters, acquiring press-
agents, and aspirations to film-script writing, and also that gift of
forward plotting of which Miss Spark herself is an exponent. They
also serve who only stand and wait: having worked out the ending
before the event, these avant garde servants have a fiction to
preserve. Indeed they have no small interest in discouraging
callers, encouraging appropriate developments, and in all ways
ensuring that the ending, when by anti-climax it comes, is in
accord with their prior or prefigurative fictions. Technically
innocent, morally implicated, they aid death's business; it is their
business too. As for the mode of telling, the sense of dark necessity, of programming and prefiguring, the process of making the
story of the event which can then shape and contain the great
terminal event itself, are all of the substance. It need hardly be
added that these situational and procedural ironies, while they

tural significance; certainly Kermode's reviews of Miss Spark's novels—see
Modern Essays (London, 1971), for most of them—are sympathetically very
inward comments upon her work, and represent the finest criticism she has
received.

have the air of dwelling on the essential things, do so at the level
of a deep moral impudence. The aesthetic sophistication compli-
cates our responses as well as makes them. *Not to Disturb*, indeed;
they do, and do so by the pure elegance of the joke, their status
as masterpieces of hard construction, to all appearances indifferent to their human content.

In all this, these novels seem the antithesis of that concern for
freedom which has been so much at stake in the modern novel
and which has generated so many of its paradoxes and problems.
We might recall what Henry James sought, according to his preface, to do in *The Portrait of a Lady* — he sought as a novelist to
do what he enacts Ralph Touchett doing as a character, which is
to set Isabel Archer, his heroine, "free," free from the specified
determinants of economics, or of her milieu, and of the tight
onerousness of "plot"; this he does by taking her as the "essence"
and placing her in the centre of his creative consciousness, the
onward run of his imagination and the incremental motion of the
language and structure, in order that she might find her own
"end." Nonetheless there *is* an ending, which we see as a rescind-
ing, a commitment; we take it with a sense of loss, not only because of what happens, but because endings *are* losses. In *The
Ambassadors* James tries again more purely; he sets the novel
close to the consciousness of his hero, Lambert Strether, who is
poised for impression, being newly dislocated from his American
past by a just completed act of transatlantic passage, and placed
in the position of "inquirer," so that he is forced to assimilate
contingencies and insights in free order until at the end the logic
coheres and he makes both the plot of the book and an essential
moral discovery. This has less of the onerous overtone; but we
still sense the powers of ends, even in works of high formal purity,
though here too we see how a book might be mostly contingent
and only finally *necessary*. The problems recur in John Fowles's
The French Lieutenant's Woman, where Fowles offers us two
equal endings — and indeed a third, but unequal, one — to
choose from in the interests of establishing the freedom of his
characters and the potential evolution of their wants as they
conflict: "The only way I can take no part in the fight is to show
two versions of it." Intruding his own surrogate in his second
ending, Fowles shows him as an egoist: "the kind of man who
travels first class or not at all, for whom the first is the only pro-

noun, who in short has first things on the brain…" Miss Spark has last things on the brain; where Fowles's novels are beginning directed, have a guilty-looking author and move uneasily to endings, spawning much complex and creative substance on the way, hers are end-directed and no author could be surer. From her works the beginning, which creates expectation and freedom, and the middle, which substantiates and qualifies it, have gone. Her characters arise at the last, and *from* the last; and what has withered away is substantially a world of motive and purpose and aspiration. The curious inescapability of plot is her subject, and in some real sense her satisfaction. In this respect her purism is, when compared with James's in *The Ambassadors,* a good deal less humane; she has nothing to offer us about the significance of impressions, the taking in of experience, the value of the vaunted scene, and there is no substantial self to be made from apprehending the contingencies of experience. In that way her work conveys significant absences, a feeling of omission, and in this respect it has considerable resemblances to a good deal of contemporary art, including the *nouveau roman.* In the end, it seems finally to deny the notion of personal authenticity out of which humanists, gently, and existentialists, assertively, make character.

This may press the point too far; needless to say, though, the essence of the art is its hardness. One of the reasons for the substantial economy of these novels is that the psychological centre virtually disappears from them. On the one hand there is a substantive material world, contingent and solid and given in high specificity, as the detail of Lise's apartment, or the plastic horrors of the airplane meal, are in *The Driver's Seat;* on the other there are Miss Spark's people, who have will and style but no psychologically established motives, or real history, or conditioning milieu. No pathetic fallacy links the two; things are inert in their quiddity and very present in their presentness, and people move among objects, as if they themselves are object-like, in a present shading into a future (*The Driver's Seat* is a present-tense novel, and the "she was to…" tense is structural to *The Public Image*). This hard world appears to be part of the high aesthetic clarity of the books, but it has also an historical — by which I mean a contemporary — reference or relevance; this is why Miss Spark's technics have, like some of those in the contemporary cinema, a pointed immediate importance. For her people, in their instantaneousness, their very want of psychology and history, populate a random world. Socially, they take their places in the decidedly trendy milieux of a highly modernized Europe which is expanding materially, intensifying its inner communications and sharing its institutions, at once converging, and throwing off the past. These are milieux which have become very much hers and which, since her move to Rome, she has had the better opportunity to observe. The filmstar Rome of *The Public Image,* the northern and southern cities of *The Driver's Seat,* the *dolce vita* of the modern aristocracy in *Not to Disturb,* seem to have common roots in a Euromart, trendy, polyclass bohemian scene which is taking shape for her as a stylized society, not unlike that of, say, Antonioni's films. This modernised scenario — to use an analogy that decidedly interests Miss Spark — consorts appropriately with her sense of the human stage of behaviour; her characters are a-historical figures exposedly playing their modern parts in the modern comedy of history as fashion, in that large group-theatre that has come to pass for us as a fit condition of life, and in which any practice that is stageable is apparently tolerable. It would be hard to say of Miss Spark that she loved any world, but especially hard to say that she loves this one; the overtones of decadence are compelling, even if they are to her cool eyes no more than might be expected. But it is in this universe of moral psychic contingency that Miss Spark's sense of an ending is so decidedly telling; she forces us to read contingency for significance. Only at the simplest level is her strategy designed not to disturb, in short; and we should take her preoccupations with plots and grids and fictions as more than a part of a current speculative rage for aesthetic order, but also as a distinct urgency about truth — a desire to rouse through the model of the writer's action the eschatological question. Of that particular obsession there are many instances, but of these three books it is *The Driver's Seat* that bears the brunt of it: to it I want to turn.

III

The Driver's Seat is the narrative of a few brief, continuous hours in the life of Lise, a middle-aged, inelegant, shrill woman with a "final and judging mouth," a not untypical Muriel Spark heroine. She is on holiday from the normal run of her life; she leaves her job in an accountant's office somewhere in an unnamed northern city, buys new clothes, including a dress that will stain, makes arrangements to leave the key of her flat, and takes a plane-flight to a southern city, where, it appears, she expects some kind of encounter to occur. Indeed throughout the journey she seems about to meet someone; she behaves flamboyantly, drawing considerable attention to herself, and is attentive to all the people she encounters. Muriel Spark, who recounts this in a present tense with a future element, ominously promises significance in all this, and details about it in the forthcoming issues of the newspapers. On arrival in the unspecified city, she shops in a modern department store, encounters a modern student demonstration, acquires a car, and in the last lines of the novella meets her death by murder. Of this ending Muriel Spark and increasingly we as readers have acquired foreknowledge; we learn before the end what the terminus of the story is to be. The altogether exceptional feature of the telling is that we come to understand that Lise knows too. Indeed, she is actively seeking it, and her flamboyance, her stainable dress, her steady selectivity among acquaintance and experience, is a devotion to this end. This culminates in a complicity with her own murderer, and hence in a sharp moral issue about responsibility. But there are further guilty parties implicated; further threads to unravel; there is a very decided complicity between Lise, who prefigures and predicts or seeks out the ending, and the novelist, Miss Spark herself, the virtuoso who plants and plays with the plot and the telling, displays and preens its elements, insists, indeed, on its elegant delight. Lise takes over the driver's seat from the pathological figure she finds to murder her. But she also takes it over from the novelist, offering herself as the alternative plot-maker, and generating the substance of her own fiction. Like Annabel, Lise indeed has a public image to consider; she knows herself to be ripe for a story in the newspapers; she acts in the world of communal fictions. And since she does have more to lay on the line than the novelist, namely her own mortality, her defeat of her author is pretty well complete. "I intend to stand aside and see if the novel has any real form apart from this artificial plot. I happen to be a Christian," says Caroline in *The Comforters;* there is no standing aside for Lise, whose independence from her creator is constituted by her own mastery over the plot that contains her, not by any stepping away from it.

In all of this Lise overwhelms or outwits contingency; and that of course is the staple of her victory. *The Driver's Seat* is at first sight a very contingent book indeed, in manner not unlike the *nouveau roman* hardness of some of Miss Spark's French contemporaries. The fact that Lise is shown as taking a journey to a new and unknown place, so that she moves through a sequence of fresh and apparently unrelated associations, is one reason for this. Another is the kind of relationship presumed between the matter of the world and its human occupants; so the description of Lise's flat, at the start of the novel. Then, too, the book has a tight and unified timespan, with a detailed precision to matters which do very little more — or so it seems — than fill the clock of hours. The telling of the story in the present increases instantaneousness at the expense of connectedness. And finally, though Lise's will to movement is given, her motives are not; the omniscient narrator, the narrator above, retains her hard complexion. But the telling *is* future-directed, which means that expositionally it works like a detective story, implying motives that we will one day come to comprehend, coherences that we will grasp if only we can wait. We push towards hypotheses; it is Miss Spark's great gift for being appalling that makes for suspense, and only with the ending does it all come clear. But clear it does become; read from conclusion backward — as Fielding, once a plot is done, implies we might — we have another sensation; the sequence was a movement in prime logic, complicated by a series of elegant aesthetic perspectives. But that is to simplify; for both character and novelist are awarded their own victories, which are victories having to do with the value both attach to plot and above all to the fact that plot is, indeed, destiny. The character's victory, Lise's victory, is that in the chaotic run of the present she has always known a future. The casual relationships with strangers, the hints of sexual complicity, the passing claims of politics, the truth or otherwise of revolutionary promise and of the substantial world of economic or material temptations; these are the things that make up the main substance of the story, diverse alternatives which are then put in their place by her own discounting of the contingent by the morally, philosophically and theologically artful use of her own mortality. Lise has a soul to consider, and she makes the subtlest use of it she can, the most dangerous flirtation with suicide she might; she has all the casuistry of the higher Sparkian heroine, and in this partakes of her narrator to high degree. For the novelist's victory — happily derived at lesser cost, though the language, in its precision, shows that it is not at little cost — is also casuistical, a kind of outwitting of the *nouveau roman* by showing that if the world is all present and disconnected there is always the claim of a future; plot can be won from a plotless world.

Not only is it far from being a humanist novel; its elegant and macabre wit and its moral and theological sophistication make it decidedly fancy as a religious one. For of course in the end Lise may not outwit or excel her author; her mastery is of course complete, and smaller fictions lie within bigger, the one who commands the language of the telling commanding everything. Still, in establishing the power of plot both Lise and Miss Spark establish what they want to show; by, so to speak, natural deduction destiny or purpose does exist. This is a point, and in many respects a comic point, located very close to the heart of the fiction-making process; it is partly because it is so close that the sheer purity of the novel delights so very much. But the matter does not end there. One elegant result of the book is that the reader witnesses how out of contingency comes a fiction, in all its paradox; and, as a practised devotee of novels he is granted an extraordinary professional joy, as the sequence unfolds and his own tactics of hypothesizing and cohering fictional matter are played with, as he watches the way in which a character who, at the start, seems the subordinated victim of writerly manipulation in a pre-ordained world suddenly become, by virtue of the maximation of the greatest risks she can take, a consort of the writer herself and hence an ironically free agent, doing willingly what the lesser novelist would compel. But in case this sounds like a book for critics only, then let me add that the creative energy of it is dense, vigorous, and in some ways most erotic, and that there is an avid precision of rendering which makes the substantive world of Miss Spark's consciously fictional world sit in illuminating relationship with the real one. In fact it is precisely this capacity Muriel Spark reveals to turn our familiar world into an exceptional, even a surreal, milieu that makes the book work so well. In this universe of strangenesses—this universe where the very act of shopping becomes a strange and terrifying human performance among things and choices — Lise's own mania or oddity becomes itself a kind of sanity. She appears before us first as a victim of this vivid but somewhat onerous milieu of objects and events; she concludes her time before us as an instigator in its grim comedies and grotesqueries. Muriel Spark has got effects somewhat like this before, in *Memento Mori*, for example; but it is in this case a very pure endeavour indeed. The phrase "black humour" fits this side of things; but one then has to add that there is a very distinctive quality in her particular version of it whereby the follies of this world are threatened from the next, and that the sense of the deathly reminder, the skull beneath the skin, is very much part of the point. In this respect Miss Spark's aesthetics are a kind of religious or rather metaphysical wit; and a very *modern* kind. There is a very pure elegance here then, and we read backwards and forwards, for *integritas, consonantia, claritas;* there is also a decided comic pleasure to be had of it. But, given the extremities it reaches to, its movement not only to the aesthetic but also to the moral extreme of its own substance, its neatness is hardly designed not to disturb.

Delta Wedding as Region
and Symbol

by John Edward Hardy

The reputation of Eudora Welty is beginning to outrun criticism of her work. We need something comprehensive in the way of a study, something less hasty than the review and something at once more objective and not so essentially condescending as the *bon voyage* essay. Wherever it was she was going, I think it will be generally agreed that Miss Welty has by now arrived—perhaps for the second or third time—and it would be no longer very discerning to treat the seasoned traveler as if she were the young Isabel Archer.

But such is the nature of her work itself, a study that is to be really comprehensive must be most particular. We will have to take one thing—or one thing at a time, anyway. The Welty reader too should be lessoned with the characterizing refrain-phrase of E. M. Forster's little essay on Virginia Woolf—"one thing—one." And the one thing I want to consider here is *Delta Wedding*. A great many critics seem to think that Miss Welty is at her best in the shorter forms; and perhaps she feels so too, to judge from the continued emphasis of her work. But this novel, it seems to me, is not only still the biggest thing, but still the most rigidly restricted, disciplined. It has most characteristically developed that sense of the symbolic particularity of things, of a place and a time and people, which can make the good regionalist the most universal of artists—or of novelists, at any rate. It is the most "one"—whole.

I mean to suggest, then, that the most important thing about the novel is its formal structure. But if the nature of its design has, perhaps, escaped many readers, the reasons are not hard to find.

There is considerable prejudice against a "serious" novelist's treating material of this kind with such an attitude of sympathy as Miss Welty assumes. Certainly it was obvious from the start, to a reader with any sensitivity at all, that *Delta Wedding* was not simply another Mississippi plantation, "historical" novel, designed for a bosom-and-columns dust jacket. But, if the author's irony is felt from the first sentence, its essence is very subtle. And the patience of a good many of the liberal reviewers a few years ago was pretty short.

If Miss Welty wasn't starry-eyed in quite the usual way about "the South," she wasn't indignant either, or even decently tough and realistic now and again. She had distinctly her own version of what Wyndham Lewis called Faulkner's "whippoorwill tank"; but it might have seemed only unfortunately less manageable than his. The novel *was,* after all, historical—that its time was only about twenty and not seventy-five or a hundred years past was calculated to allay suspicion only slightly. Few eyebrows were raised particularly over the treatment of the Negroes in the novel; but they might well have been. The darkies were sometimes just a little too charmingly typical. And where the attitude went beyond one of placid acceptance—this remains, I think, one of the most genuinely distressing flaws of the novel—it often became only half-heartedly apologetic, with a rather strong suggestion of the old "well, at least they had *status*" routine. What Miss Welty could do with Negroes at her best in some of the short stories seemed rather sadly absent here. And one could go only so far in justifying it on grounds of dramatic propriety, that the author was bound to the point-of-view of the white characters of the story; simply for purposes of realism, it might easily have been made a little *more* apparent how severely restricted that outlook was in this regard.

And yet the immediate inferences from all this are, clearly, not correct. And perhaps the best way of getting at *why* they are not correct is simply to allow the novel to establish for itself the perspective in which we are to look at its features.

One has first to see that Miss Welty is not taking *any* attitude toward "the South." The story is about the Delta, at the most— not the South, not even Mississippi. Yankees, of course, are unthinkable; but Ellen, the Virginian, is acutely conscious all her life of *her* difference from the Delta family she mothers. And the circle is drawn even closer; Troy Flavin, who is largely responsible for the significance of the wedding as a symbol of threatened disruption, is alien by virtue of being a *hill-country* Mississippian. And (disregarding for the moment Laura McRaven, whose case is rather special), Robbie Reid, whom the family wisely regard as a far greater threat to the insularity of their world even than Troy, is foreign as a native of the ~~town~~ of Fairchilds, as distinguished from the plantation.

The psychological basis of the relationship of the characters one to another here is simple enough, of course. The barrier between Robbie Reid and the Fairchilds is greatest for several reasons—simply that she is a woman, that she is the unworthy wife of the darling of the family, but most important of all, that she *is* a lifelong near neighbor. In any society, of course, class distinctions are always, though ironically, most keenly appreciated by native members of the immediate community. Troy Flavin, not so much out of mere stupidity as simply because his origins are more remote, finds nothing so terribly formidable in the family he is "marrying into"—as he puts it with a confidence which dismays and amuses those who know the Fairchilds. And in the face of his naïve assurance, the family are fairly constrained to be gentle with him, though they make little effort to hide their feelings from Dabney. But the point I want to make just now is that this narrowing of the circle is carried so far that it finally excludes emphasis upon the kind of typicality, the true provincialism, in character and situation, which is characteristic of the commonplace regional novel. The Fairchilds are finally most typical, if at all, in their very singularity. And it is at this point that the principle of exclusiveness almost ceases, or for the reader's purposes in understanding the novel ought almost to cease, to be a social principle at all. It becomes, rather, the *formal* principle, and the principle of sensibility, in a version of pastoral which has been before only vaguely hinted at in the Southern novel.

Miss Welty's awareness of the classic elements of pastoral in the situation she is dealing with is quite evident. One may take as an initial statement of the conventional "paradox" of pastoral, the familiar principle of inversion of values, one of Laura's early reflections—"Jackson was a big town, with twenty-five thousand people, and Fairchilds was just a store and a gin and a bridge and one big house, yet she was the one who felt like a little country cousin when she arrived...."

But it is just the awareness it reveals which is most important about a passage like this. What it says, the statement of the pastoral "formula" in these terms, is only a starting point. The tradition of the Southern novel has been all but exclusively pastoral from the start, of course—and in a great many different ways, both naturalistic and romantic. But there has been before no such fully *conscious* exploring of the implications of the mode as Miss Welty's, an insight which finally carries beyond the significance of the form for the *mores* of the society which produced it.

(Something of this sort—its wit, its merging of realism and magic, its delicacy, its formal and elegiac ironies, its universal mythiness, and basic to all the rest its struggle between anonymity and self-consciousness—is inevitable toward the *end* of any cycle of pastoral. And the reader might well have to go back to the Sixteenth and Seventeenth centuries of English literature for instructive parallels.)

Miss Welty's depiction of the Delta society and its structure, of the family as the typical unit of that society, is studiedly accurate, right, always in substance and, with the exception of a few distressing lapses into an over-precious style, nearly always in tone. The rightness of it meets the test of communication certainly even to the reader unfamiliar with the actuality. And the structure of the society, in the pattern of the novel as well as in fact, clearly produces and supports the kind of hyper-developed individuality which the characters severally manifest. But it is one of the basic paradoxes of the novel—one of which several of the characters are keenly aware—that the strength of the society to support is entirely the dynamic of the personality's constant and tireless struggle with it. And the center of interest, finally, is in the exercise of entirely private sensibilities—not so much in the relationships abstractly as such among the various people, as in the way in which each person privately *sees* those relationships.

Indeed, at the beginning of the novel, and again qualifiedly at the end, it is not even people and their relationships which are *seen*—but *things,* rather. Laura comes into the Delta country with the bemused aloneness of the adventurer into an enchanted forest. Other people, as people, are secondary realities—the signs of their existence, to the extent that she is aware of them at all, becoming talismans of a significance entirely private to her, the ticket she had stuck in her hat band, "in imitation of the drummer across the aisle." It is things that are most alive—the fields, the train itself becoming a creature of the fields. And then the train "seemed to be racing with a butterfly."

The vision is not quite ecstatic. The sun which in its sinking momentarily obliterates the most basic distinction—"all that had been bright or dark was now one color"—is a real sun. It sinks, and Laura arrives, and is met by the Fairchild cousins, real, other people. The last word on Laura before the conductor cries "Fairchilds!" is simply that she "felt what an arriver in a land feels." And though there has been fair warning that the land is to be much more than *a* land—"the clouds were large...larger than anything except the fields the Fairchilds planted"; "the Delta buzzards...seemed to wheel as high and wide as the sun"; "the west was a milk-white edge, like the foam of the sea"—it is only a warning so far. There is no immediate plunge to that depth of the private consciousness in which the particular becomes the universal. If the reader constructs a cloud-cuckoo land here, it is his own doing. Miss Welty has no unrealistic intention of giving away her story in one lyric offering. Certain pertinent, practical facts stick in Laura's mind. She knows where she came from and where she is going and why. She is conscious of time— and her reality in it—she has been here before. (The fact that the visit, to "nature," out of the life of the city, is a *return,* functions similarly to the same fact in Wordsworth's *Tintern Abbey,* for example). Even in her vision of the immensity of the clouds it is not just the fields that they are compared to, but the fields "that the Fairchilds planted." The fields belong to them, and not simply as a matter of economics either, we are soon to discover. The myth is theirs too. The train was a legendary creature, it had its name of the Yellow Dog, in *their* consciousness before hers. Their baffling otherness, their exclusive possessiveness, threatens both to invade and to shut her out at every level of her sensibility.

But what we do get in this opening passage is just enough of the ecstatic to reassure us that Laura's personal emotional problem doesn't *matter* a great deal. (The reader is never permitted actually to "feel sorry" for Laura; the "poor Laura, little mother- less girl" greeting which she anticipates has only a ritualistic solemnity, no real sadness). And, conversely, we are assured that the personal "problems" of the others aren't going to matter a great deal either—which, in turn, is further assurance on Laura's account. We get, in other words, the symbolic sense—we begin to see things with a great, though not quite a whole, measure of aesthetic distance. (This, by the way, accounts I think for the time-setting of the novel. Aside from the fact that the early Twenties actually were a period of significant social and economic transition—the slight, but only slight, removal in time makes it easier for the author to put the emphasis just where she wants it, upon probability rather than upon the kind of mere possibility which our generation demands not only of the immediately contemporary novel but of the usual historical one as well.) The action takes on from the beginning, and never quite loses, even at the highest pitch of visual excitement, the somewhat cool, formal tone of the conscious pastoral.

One feels from the beginning that it is not actions, but reactions, which are to count. A few things do manage to happen in the course of the novel—Dabney and Troy do marry, Robbie comes back to George, it is decided that Laura will stay at Shellmound, at least for a time. But this is not a great deal, after all. And—the marriage is the most obvious example—it is perfectly clear that none of these things is of great moment in itself. The word "wedding" in the title is important. It is in a sense with the wedding, the ritual, not the marriage, that Miss Welty is concerned. The ritual sense is private, of course; the ceremony itself is passed over in a few words—"Mr. Rondo married Dabney and Troy." Mr. Rondo's status, the status of the church in the Fairchild world, perfectly defines the more than baronial self-sufficiency of the family, their superiority to any larger public, institutional significance of their affairs. But, private both in the sense that the family has its peculiar rituals and even more in the sense that each individual has his own in which the others do not participate, it is ritual nonetheless. There are no raw emotions in the novel—and little of a structure of personal involvements, conflicts, as we have observed, about the center of a "problem" which is carried through to some resolution in action. Nor is it that the story is action-less simply in the sense of being introspective—with much private examination of motives, intentions, much logical self-analysis. No one has time for much introspection in this usual sense. There is, in fact, a great deal *going on* all the time. But the incidents are important mainly as points of refraction, from which light is cast back upon various moments of symbolic perception in the minds of the several characters.

This is where Miss Welty is at her best, and where one has to

start looking for the "meaning" of the novel, in the whole particularity of the moment, the single, illuminating, still act of
private *perception*. It is where one has to look for the truth about
the characters, severally. They don't communicate much of themselves to one another, however much they are in a sense involved
with one another, and mutually dependent.

The thing is stated over and over again, this impregnable, at
times reassuring, at times to one or another hopelessly baffling,
privacy of the consciousness of every person, of the being of
every thing which the consciousness entertains, even of every
separate *moment* of consciousness. There are the various lights,
with the obvious significance of light, especially of light *inside*
something. The lamp which the aunts give to Dabney, a *night*-
light, notably, itself an object of family tradition but, given to
Dabney, becoming the prime symbol of her independence, her
private rebellion of indifference when she carelessly breaks it,
carrying out the theme of general disaster which the very flame
itself, the intended source of light and comfort, draws out upon
the shade—"The picture on it was a little town. Next, in the
translucence, over the little town with trees, towers, people,
windowed houses, and a bridge, over the clouds and stars and
moon and sun, you saw a redness glow and the little town was all
on fire, even to the motion of fire, which came from the candle
flame drawing." The same lamp in India's perception, precious
and cherished, but in infinite secrecy, and so again a symbol of
impenetrable isolation, the magic circle of her privacy—"India
made a circle with her fingers, imagining she held the little
lamp"—the vessel of light filled, paradoxically, "with the mysterious and flowing air of night." The light on the back porch,
when Shelley comes in alone for a moment away from the dancers,
and "the moths spread upon the screens, the hard beetles knocked
upon the radius of light like an adamant door," as she falls into
musing; the light in her room, as she sits writing in her diary,
with the beetle again clawing at the screen.

The various places of hiding and retreat. The seemingly in-
numerable rooms of the house itself. The wood in which Ellen
walks, with its mysteriously ageless, directionless paths. The
privilege, if it is a privilege altogether, is denied not even to
the Negroes. Partheny, in the chinaberry-hidden fastness of her
house in Brunswicktown, retiring into the undisturbed, unques-
tioned and unanswerable, mystery of her "mindlessness." Aunt

Studney, with her jealously guarded sack that is to the children perhaps the source of life itself, the place where babies come from—her very existence hardly more, as the reader is permitted to perceive it, than a legendary creation of the family's very love of the eternal secret, than the name which puns her one, uncommunicative phrase—"Ain't studyin' you."

Or simply the sudden, isolated moments of private illumination. Dabney's ride in the morning, when she sees Marmion, sees it first *reflected* in the river, "and then the house itself reared delicate and vast, with a strict tower, up from its reflection," sees it defiantly and exultantly alone, "while they never guessed, she had seen Marmion...all had been before her eyes when she was all by herself." The loneliness of Laura, abandoned during the game of hide-and-seek, in which she perceives the necessity of George's isolation. "Then she saw Uncle George walk out of the house and stare out into the late day. She wanted to call out to him, but...something told her...that it was right for him to stand apart, and that when he opened an envelope in a room no one should enter. Now she felt matter-of-factly intimate with it, with his stand and his predicament."

Or, more definitive still, the sound of Mary Lamar Mackey's piano—the constant music which is a figure of the author's omnipresence, proceeding from an all but invisible source (we get only one brief close-up of Mary Lamar), only now and again distinctly heard at some chance pause in the activity, but always there. At a moment of tense silence during the first hours of Robbie's visit, Mary Lamar "was playing a nocturne—like the dropping of rain or the calling of a bird the notes came from another room, effortless and endless, isolated from them, yet near, and sweet like the guessed existence of mystery. It made the house like a nameless forest, wherein many little lives lived privately, each to its lyric pursuit and shy protection...." The momentary perfection of the pastoral vision.

And it is this sort of thing, of course, that gives the novel its first appearance of disorder. The characters seem hopelessly unpredictable, their actions unmotivated and obscure, without intelligible issue; the transitions, from one scene to another, from the reflections of one character to another, appear entirely capricious. It would seem at first glance that Miss Welty has sacrificed an order of the whole entirely in the interest of an illusion of life in the details. But it ought to be apparent from the very symbols,

and symbolic instances, of the privacy of consciousness given
here, that there is order of a kind. The lives, the thoughts, of all
the characters are intensely private—but because they are ritualistic too, and ritual is always inevitable, they fall into patterns
which transcend the privacy, with or without the consciousness of
the particular character. And, if the characters themselves are
not often conscious of the pattern, the author is clearly conscious
of it. It emerges, beyond its inevitability, as a principle of deliberate and controlled artistry, in an order of *recurrence* which
informs the whole action of the novel. The order of the novel is a
poetic order—of recurrent themes, symbols, and motives of
symbolic metaphor. And it must be close-read, as a poem.

Perhaps the thread nearest the center of the design is that of
the story, told and re-told, again and again reflected upon and
alluded to, of George and Maureen on the railroad trestle. Certain reasons for the importance of the story to the Fairchilds are
immediately apparent. It was just after the incident on the trestle
that Troy and Dabney had "gone on up the railroad track and got
engaged"—thus beginning the latest threat to the solidarity of
the Fairchild world. It was then that Robbie Reid, providing the
climax to the story with her accusation, "George Fairchild, you
didn't do this for *me*!," brought into the open the whole complex
of bitter feelings which the Fairchilds entertain for this earlier,
and even more significant than Dabney's, "bad match"—their
resentment at the love of poor, common little Robbie for George,
George who is the universally acknowledged, living embodiment of their ideal of Fairchild man, their infuriated amusement
at her daring to intrude the voice of her "rights" even against his
defense of what is even more holy to the Fairchilds than George
or any *living* thing, the memory of the dead Denis. Robbie's
thinking of herself at that moment, her indignation at George's
willingness to sacrifice himself for the semi-idiotic Maureen,
defines perfectly for the Fairchild *women* especially her hopeless failure to understand their vision of themselves—and their
investment of that vision in Denis, of whom nothing remains but
his daughter Maureen, the crazy Virgie Lee, a few vague stories
and a little pathetic "poetry," but who in their minds is the more
dignified by the "tragedy" of indignities, and who finally is beyond reproach (as even George cannot be) simply by virtue of
being dead, who as the symbol of the holy past is worthy of *any*
sacrifice. Robbie's behavior at the trestle is all of a piece with the

absurdity, the hopeless childishness, of her taunt that the Fair-childs are "not even rich!"—her failure to comprehend the myth of their aristocracy.

This much, then—beyond what is simply their love, aristo-cratically both pious and hilariously irreverent, for a *story,* any story, which involves the family—all the Fairchilds understand, in one way or another. They understand also something of how important it is that the train was the familiar Yellow Dog, the train that is almost itself their property—so that it *could not* actually have killed George (thus the whole thing became absurd enough for amusement), and yet, faithful servitor, provides enough of the thrill of danger, of death, for the purposes of their ritual.

Ellen, who retains enough of the attitude of an outsider always to see (or to have to see, to figure out consciously) a little more than the others, understands also what it meant for Robbie—she is a little daunted, even, seeing that Robbie has had a vision, a vision of *fact,* that makes the Fairchilds' prattling over their legend a little ridiculous. She understands that a train on that track *can* kill, that it has killed the astonishingly beautiful girl she met in the woods, and that if her daughters are spared it is only perhaps because they are *not* that beautiful, not beautiful enough to be heroines of a genuine tragedy. And she understands, finally, George's role in all of it. In a way that no one else can be, because no one else knows about the lost girl, she is at once both grateful and ashamed at the implications of George's constant sacrifice. She comprehends the simple fact that George is a man, that he has reacted simply as a man to the beauty of the girl when he "took her over to the old Argyle gin and slept with her." She understands that it is with his possession and his knowledge of such facts, literally the facts of life, that he defends the Fairchilds *against* the intrusion of fact, against all that comes, like the train, bearing down upon them. She suspects, perhaps, that the Fair-child women are vaguely aware of the condescension in his nobil-ity, aware that he can *afford* to indulge them in their disparagement and ignorance of fact, the fact of the outside world which begins at Memphis, simply because he does know it so well and because the knowledge is supremely self-sufficient. She suspects that it is out of chagrin at this element of his attitude, at their own half-realized envy of his knowledge, his knowledge of life present and real, that they continue to shade his glory under the image of the

dead Denis. She knows that he has worked the device of disparagement on her, in telling her what he has done with the girl,
protecting *her* from too sudden a vision of what beauty it is (not
the garnet pin!) that is lost in the wood, that she has lost and the
world knows; but she knows also that George's act has *not* degraded the girl's beauty, that if anything it has enhanced it. In
short, she knows George—George the unknowable.

But beyond all of this even, beyond Ellen's or all the characters' conscious experience of it together, the legend serves as
a unifying force. Basically, the train and the bridge (trestle) are
communication symbols. In Ellen's case, the relationships she discovers in the light of the incident result in the one most nearly
perfect personal communication of the story. The separate incidents of the trestle episode itself and of her meeting with the
girl in the wood are brought together in her mind, after the
photographer has told the wedding party of the girl his train
has killed on the way down from Memphis, in a single, comprehensive vision which opens the way to her wordless communication with George at the dance. But the most important
significance of her experience in the whole purposes of the novel
is not for our interest in her, her effort to know George personally;
her insight is important, rather, simply as an example of the kind
of structural relationships that are to be seen. We have to go on
to see that the Yellow Dog is also the train that has brought Laura
to Shellmound—still another visitant from the outside world,
and a permanent one, since she is heiress to Marmion. It brings
even the shepherd crooks, ironically, and other furnishings for
the wedding, from Memphis. We have to see, further, that the
symbols, characteristically, work both ways. That is, the legend
for some means the failure of communication—for Robbie with
the family, as we have seen, and for Shelley with Dabney, the en-
gagement to Troy having closed a door upon Shelley's understanding of her sister, perhaps even upon her sympathy with the
entire family.

Or, another way of putting it is that Ellen's "knowing" George
is, after all, only a final understanding of the fact of his independence, the fact that he *is* unknowable. The legend makes
George himself a symbol. Ellen specifically repudiates her "young
girl's love of symbols" in her final attitude toward George—that
is, the sort of thing that the Fairchilds make of him. Hers is a
vision of the unmanageable *fact* of him. But Ellen's, perhaps, is

a schoolgirl's understanding of the term. And in the larger purposes of the novel he remains a symbol; not entirely the Fairchilds' symbol—but his very factuality itself becomes symbolic. It is notable that none of the *men* in the novel admit the reader very often to their minds. Such is the Fairchild women's notion of their men, which the author accepts as a technical principle, that they are a kind of serviceable gods—infinitely capable, having access to wonderful powers of the outer world, and always *decently* keeping their own counsel. And if one uneasily suspects, with Ellen, that George is actually godlike in his manhood, that his stalwart impenetrability is not a matter of decency, but of *having* some counsel to keep, an unsearchable purpose—still this is only the excess of heroic typicality. As the reader has to know him, as he functions in the novel, the legend has made him—with the final qualification only that it has made all the Fairchilds too, and not, as they sometimes suppose, they the legend. (This is the point, of course, of Shelley's realization, when she runs the car across the tracks in front of the Yellow Dog, that it won't do to try "contriving" it).

As an example of George's symbolic function, we may consider again Laura's experience. Ellen's, in fact, is not quite so exclusive an understanding of George as it might at first appear. At her childish level, Laura has entertained the same vision—of his necessary isolation, we will remember, and felt "matter-of-factly intimate" with the fact of the isolation, with him. And potentially this experience is a basis of sympathy between Laura and Ellen in the little girl's effort to make herself a part of the family. But George has "brought them together" without any conscious intention, without any rational understanding even of what is happening in the situation, either on his part or theirs. There is no willed, in the usual sense *personal*, communication anywhere in the relationship. George functions here, then, precisely in the way that the various symbolic *objects* function to establish, and to illuminate, certain relationships. George is, in fact, the ultimate embodiment of the author's subtle conception of the subject-object relationship which is symbol—the object *informed* by, inseparable from, an always quickening, always manifest, but always inscrutable intelligence.

The people, then, as well as things, are carried out of themselves by the legend. And, finally, the significance of the particular story carries outside itself to other stories; every legend is all legend. The way in which we have seen the thread of the trestle incident becoming involved with Ellen's reflections upon the fate of the girl she met wandering in the woods—the girl and the meeting figure in the statement of what might be followed out as a distinct, major theme in itself, the theme of loss—is but one illustration of the complexity of the structure. The symbols of the trestle story are actually parts of certain larger, extended motives. The train is one of several means of transportation which have a symbolic function, more or less explicit, wherever they appear. The horses—Troy's horse, the horse which George gives to Dabney (having thought of it, significantly, when Robbie took his car to run away in), the horse which Dabney rides on her visit to her aunts (carrying a "wedding-present home on horseback"); the cars too—George's car which Robbie has wrecked, the new Pierce Arrow (all cars are still comparatively new), the darkened car which Dabney and Troy ride away in after the wedding, the lighted car in which the mayor and his family arrive for the reception. And so on. The trestle, over Dry Creek, is closely related to what may be loosely defined as the *water* motif—the bridge over the bayou "whose rackety rhythm Laura remembered," the old stories of the whirlpool, Laura's trip to Marmion with Roy when in a kind of baptismal ceremony she is pushed into the Yazoo and loses Ellen's garnet pin.

And any one of dozens of incidents, observations, unspoken perceptions, can become the "central" nexus in the whole complexity of interconnection. One need not start with the trestle episode or with any of the more obviously prominent incidents. One such observation as Shelley's at the reception—of the contrast between the darkened car of the newlyweds and the lighted car bringing the mayor, that "had come up alight like a *boat* in the night" (italics mine)—is enough. The simile has associations —we might assume at this level even somewhat consciously felt by Shelley—as remote as the comparison, early in the story, of a certain lamp in the living room at Shellmound to "a lighted shoe-box toy, a 'choo-choo boat' with its colored paper windows." Here, with the recollection of the dear and familiar object of their childhood play, the lamp itself having the radiance of its associations too already mingled with the light of the toy, is much of the pathos of Shelley's ironic realization that the public gaiety of the wedding party, the extraneous and trivial display of the "occasion" which the visit of so inconsequential and alien a personage as the mayor epitomizes, is a mockery of that darkness of marriage which has closed between her and Dabney. (The darkness which is the inevitable privacy of any marriage, the darkness which for Shelley is especially associated with Troy Flavin, of his hateful "overseer's soul," of the blood of Negroes on the floor of the office.) But beyond any possibility of Shelley's consciousness of the significance of her thought, the *boat* suggests all boats—the boat in which Laura rode with Roy when *she* saw Marmion, the house which is to be hers eventually, not Dabney's, and when she was admitted to the mystery of the Yazoo, the river that measures the time or the timelessness of the Fairchild world. (The prophecy of Shelley's fear for her sister's marriage is not, perhaps, altogether dark.) Or, reinforcing the first effect, the light, the lamp, is all the lamps—the heirloom night-light which Dabney broke.

One can follow a single object through the significance of its reappearances. The garnet pin—first as Battle's gift, and then through Ellen's use of her dream about it as a lullaby-story to Bluet, associated with her motherhood, the symbol both of loss and of gain; figuring in a re-statement of the same theme in her meeting with the girl in the wood; in her effort to get Partheny's assistance in finding it, becoming the symbol of the old Negress's second sight; appearing finally as the central symbol in an incident which embraces all these themes, the womb-return descent of Laura into the waters of the Yazoo. "As though Aunt Studney's sack had opened after all, like a whale's mouth, Laura opening her eyes head down saw its insides all around her—dark water and fearful fishes." And the pin, lost in the water, becomes the image of a relationship between Laura and her new mother Ellen, between her and the Fairchilds a union in the untold *secret* of the loss, which is more enduring even than what she had hoped for as a reward for her finding and returning the jewel.

One could, and would, go on. Devious ways are open from any point. But perhaps with this much of detail, we can hazard a few conclusive generalizations.

To return to the question of Miss Welty's attitude toward the society which she depicts, it should be apparent by now that in terms of approval or disapproval the evidence is mixed. In Ellen's vision of the hero, George, what appears to be a devastating criticism is implicit—the Fairchilds' "myth of happiness" would seem to be myth clearly in the worst sense, a childish retreat from reality. And it is possible to infer that the "wedding" of Dabney

and Troy is a mockery of the failure of true marriage everywhere
—even the marriage of Battle and Ellen; the marriage of the
Fairchilds with the past, or with the future, whichever way one
wants to approach it; the marriage of minds among all the
characters.

But perhaps the crucial point of the problem is the status of
the Negroes. If it must be admitted that Miss Welty does, as we
have already suggested, "accept" the Fairchilds' typical attitude
here—I think that acceptance is finally, though not perhaps quite
so clearly, like her acceptance of the women's attitude toward the
men. It is an acceptance as a technical principle only, and one
which comes in at a deeper level for some very heavy qualification. For the purposes of that double attitude of pastoral which
William Empson has defined, as well as in a more practical sense
for people like the Fairchilds, the Negroes are a great convenience.
It is at the expense of these "*rude* swains" that the Fairchilds can
be the "*gentle* swains" (to use Milton's phrases for it) that they
are—so that we can at once look down upon the narrow com-
placency, and envy the imaginative and moral richness, of their
country simplicity. But Miss Welty implicitly recognizes the
"convenience" for what it is. And the recognition is, in fact, very
closely tied in with that problem of the women's attitude toward
the men.

Dabney's preparations for her marriage are, significantly,
associated with her riding forth into the fields. Troy Flavin
emerges partially as a kind of "field god," similar to Floyd in
At the Landing, or Cash in *Livvie.* And the mystery of his virility
is in the present situation very closely connected, of course, with
his intimate knowledge of the Negroes. It is this of which Shelley
is at once so afraid and so contemptuous when she finds Troy
settling a fight among the Negroes in the overseer's office. And
the phrase of her reflection on her way back to the house, her
wondering if "all *men*" are like him, makes the connection with
George's role. George too, about whom Dabney is thinking on
her ride to visit her aunts, is marked with the *blood* of the Negroes
—he with the blood of compassion when he caught the knife and
bound up the wounds of the little Negro boy, Troy with the blood
of his knowledge of the Negroes in their labor. But, the significance of such distinctions as the latter aside, they are *men*—
George coming naked from the water to catch the knife, Troy the
dark figure on a horse that Dabney catches sight of on her way to

her aunts' house; and their tolerance for the blood of Negroes is an essential part of their maleness. And Dabney senses something of this, the part that a new knowledge of the lives of the Negroes, of their intimacy with the earth, must play in the rebellion from her family which her marriage represents.

But this is the crucial point also in the sense that Dabney's discovery of the male mystery is clearly hopeful for the society as well as critical of it. Troy *is* the field god, and as such he is a principle of rejuvenation. The marriage promises ultimately, perhaps, not disruption but renewal, or renewal out of the disruption. And while Troy's is in a sense an influence from outside, it is defined, as we have seen, and complemented, partially by the role of George—and that, paradoxically, as an essential part of his status as the family hero. It can hardly be denied that Miss Welty does see the strength for rejuvenation as in part the family's own strength, the strength of their own myth as they themselves understand it, though she sees with equal clarity the limitations of that understanding.

Or, if the argument requires further elaboration, one must not forget that central to the old aunts' family sense is the *reverence* for disaster. Primrose insisted that people keep "their kinfolks and their tragedies straight." And there is reason to believe that they can accommodate Dabney's breaking the lamp too, that her breaking it is one with her keeping it ultimately, the "present" is given and must be kept whether she will or no, whether the "little old piece of glass" is kept intact or not. The themes of protection and disaster are inextricably bound up together from the first, in the family legend as in the design of the lamp and its shade, and their unity is unbreakable. Accepting the implicit pun on *present*—perhaps the marriage of past and present is not broken; perhaps that quality of the Fairchilds which is at first so baffling to Laura, their being so intensely "of the moment," is simply the result of their feeling supremely confident of their footing in the past. And, finally, Laura herself—who comes closer than anyone else to being Miss Welty's stand-in in the novel—remains to live with the family on terms which are, though again qualifiedly, both sympathetic and hopeful.

And yet I would insist that the question of approval or disapproval, of a prophecy of hope or disaster, is still not the key to Miss Welty's final attitude. Her principal interest in the society, her sympathy with it, is for the *vision* which it supports. We need not trouble ourselves ultimately over the fate of the society as such, or its worth in itself, or even the problem of whether it ever existed or could exist, actually, quite as it is pictured. The picture is *right* enough, in every sense, to provide the vision. And that is unquestionable—the novel itself, its living form, the constant order and quickness of its sensibility, is the essential proof of the vision. In fact, the novel *is* the vision. And I do not see, from the evidence of the novel itself, that Miss Welty is especially either disturbed or elated by the prospects of the actual Fairchild world. She is simply, like Laura with George, for the all-important moment "matter-of-factly intimate" with the dual paradox of the pastoral outlook—that all human society being ultimately suspect, the vision *must* to some extent condemn the society which produces it, and yet that the particular society which makes this truth most apparent is the "best" society.

This is the essential *realism* of Miss Welty's art. This is how her intensely narrow view—the concentration of her narrative which requires more than two hundred pages for the treatment of the events of a few days in the life of a hopelessly provincial family— becomes precisely at its most restricted a world-view.

But the last scene of the novel sums up the situation. We come back to the mind with which we began—Laura McRaven's mind. And Laura achieves her sense of "belonging" at last. She has been told that she is to stay, that Marmion is to be hers some day. The picnic, for her, is a celebration of her reception as a member of the family. But she accepts the decisions from the first with the secret thought that sometime she may go back to Jackson, to her father. The reservation does not diminish her present joy. But it is there. And the moment at which she feels most overwhelmingly at one with the family is when she can hardly see any of them, but sees *with* them the falling star. The "star" *is* a star—single, remote and inaccessibly indifferent. And if it is not quite indifferent, if it does belong to the family in their common seeing, then it is *falling*. And yet, for the moment of its falling, it brings them together. Laura, and the Fairchilds, and the star, are one in the light of the star—and turning again with a gesture of embracing them, she embraces the firmament, "both arms held out to the radiant night." That one moment of pure vision, the people themselves in darkness, unseen, the star unseeing, becomes the sufficient thing in itself—the one thing.

Eudora's Web

by Joyce Carol Oates

Eudora Welty's eighth book [*Losing Battles*], a novel about domestic love, opens with this exquisite passage:

> When the rooster crowed, the moon had still not left the world but was going down on flushed cheek, one day short of the full. A long thin cloud crossed it slowly, drawing itself out like a name being called. The air changed, as if a mile or so away a wooden door had swung open, and a smell, more of warmth than wet, from a river at low stage, moved upward into the clay hills that stood in darkness.
>
> Then a house appeared on its ridge, like an old man's silver watch pulled once more out of its pocket. A dog leaped up from where he'd lain like a stone and began barking for today as if he meant never to stop.
>
> Then a baby bolted naked out of the house. She monkey-climbed down the steps and ran open-armed into the yard, knocking at the walls of flowers still colorless as faces....

Losing Battles is as musical throughout as these first passages suggest. Its world is natural, and yet a world heavily dependent upon metaphor, upon the seeing of one thing in terms of another: the "natural" seen in terms of something more natural, because it is more human. Everything is brought back to its most humble origins; there is a wonderful gravitation backward, downward, inward, to the deepest and most simple and most soothing area of the imagination.

It is the hill country of north-eastern Mississippi, a summer in the 1930s. The idyllic hills are subjected, however, to two kinds of time. For many chapters we are entangled in a past that must be lyrically analyzed, repeated, defined, distorted, and finally

cherished by the many voices of the novel, which belong mainly
to the descendants of one Elvira Jordan Vaughn, "Granny," who
is celebrating her ninetieth birthday. In the opening chapters,
as in the opening of a musical composition, a chorus takes over
the main "action" of the novel, preparing us for the two or three
simple confrontations that are to take place soon. We hear about
the young hero, Jack; we hear about his exploits, his courage, his
foolishness, his falling in love with the young girl who is his
teacher; we hear about the bride herself and about her infant girl;
gradually, as if we were strangers somehow invited to the Renfro
home for this celebration, we begin to make sense of all the gossip,
setting things in place, understanding how the hero and his bride
came to be separated and how they will be joined again. How can
we move into the future until the past is explained?

On this Sunday more than fifty people are gathering at the
Renfros'. It is a family reunion to celebrate Granny Vaughn's
birthday, in the hills outside a small town called Banner. At
first we hear only voices with sketchy bodies attached, the common din of family life—confusing, elliptical, coy—as it centers
on the problems of domesticity, particularly the preparation of
food. But then, as in an old-fashioned romantic comedy, the
images of unserious "battle" are presented, and we wait impatient-
ly for the young hero, Jack Renfro, to appear. Unfortunately he
is in the state prison, but no one doubts that he will escape in time
for his grandmother's birthday celebration, and to be reunited
with his beautiful red-haired wife, Gloria, and to greet his infant
daughter, Lady May Renfro, whom he has never seen. The chorus
of hill people—Renfros, Beechams, Vaughns, and others—defines the young hero for us long before he actually appears, and
he turns out to be the hero of summery comedy, nineteen years
old and totally innocent, hotheaded, proud, muscular, loving,
and fiercely loyal to his family. Though he is about to be paroled,
he doesn't hesitate to break out of prison a day earlier, in order
to arrive well in time for his grandmother's party.

When Jack appears, time begins again; we are removed from
some of the concerns of the past and can contemplate the future.
The judge who sentenced Jack so harshly (having misunderstood
the circumstances of his "stealing" a safe) turns up, with his wife,
and is taken in by the Renfros; the day will not be complete until
he is "forgiven" for his deed. In fact, everyone will be forgiven.
Then there is the more serious matter of the death and funeral of

an aged schoolteacher who has taught everyone in Banner at one time or another, and whose protégée Jack's wife has been. The novel begins with a birthday celebration and ends with the lowering of a coffin into a grave. So the young people pay homage to the mysteries of their idyllic world, and time opens into the future. In the end Jack declares fiercely that though he has lost certain battles,

> They can't take away what no human can take away. My family.... My wife and baby girl and all of 'em at home. And I've got my strength. I may not have all the time I used to have—but I can provide.

It is a very human and very convincing little victory.

Losing Battles, like Miss Welty's earlier *Delta Wedding*, is a novel filled with voices. It is sweetly musical, and its sour chords (the extreme poverty of these proud people, who will be forced onto welfare before long) are sounded discreetly; one feels, strangely enough, that these fundamental economic problems really are not important. What is important is love—the bonds of blood and memory that hold people together, eccentric and argumentative and ignorant though these people are. The basic unit of humanity is the *family*, the expanded family and not the selfish little family of modern days. What real people the Renfros are, we think as we read this novel. How exact the tone of their teasing, their scolding, the clashing and harmonizing of their memories!

And yet they are very nearly extinct.

In 1970 the concerns of *Losing Battles* are extinct. The large, happy family and its outdoor feast are extinct; the loyalty to a postage-stamp corner of the world is extinct; the unquestioning Christian faith, the complex and yet very simple web of relationships that give these people their identities, binding them to a particular past and promising for them a particular, inescapable future: all extinct. This is a world that has vanished from literature, and yet one which will remain, most beautifully and paradoxically, only in literature. To know our own origins, or to know alternate possibilities for our own lives, we must study Miss Welty's fiction, for we will not get this kind of knowledge from life. Its time is past; it is extinct. The simple social ceremonies of these Americans, these birthdays, weddings, and funerals, provide a dizzying motion that turns and turns upon itself, tying everyone together, telescoping years. All is in motion, yes, yet is is stilled, silent, fossilized. The art of *Losing Battles* lies in its perfection, its symmetry, its irrelevance to all that concerns our troubled contemporary America.

Last spring, the literary quarterly *Shenandoah* devoted an entire, excellent, issue to Eudora Welty. One of the most interesting contributions was a brief appreciative essay on Jane Austen by Miss Welty herself. Her obvious admiration for this novelist, and certain comments she makes about her novels, help to illuminate the delicate, and occasionally bewildering, art Miss Welty has given us.

Jane Austen, she says, is perhaps in danger of seeming remote to us, or to future readers, for soon she will be "closer in calendar time to Shakespeare" than to us. Much in Austen is taken for granted; much is assumed and is never explained. And this is essential for a certain kind of comedy.

> Is there not some good connection between this confidence [of Jane Austen in her society] and the flow of comedy? Comedy is sociable and positive, and exacting: its methods, its boundaries, its *point*, all belong to the familiar.

The "familiar" may not be commonplace, but it must seem commonplace and it must be presented without hesitation or cynicism; a world so real, so matter-of-fact, that it is absorbed into the novelist's vision and is the effortless background of his art. Miss Welty's South is familiar in this way, and yet she brings to it an occasional wry, teasing note that alarms us; is she not, in her own way, a far more skillful writer than Jane Austen? If not more "skillful," then more honest, more believable, a more trustworthy guide to the densities of ordinary life? Genteel as she is, Eudora Welty is still mercilessly just. Nothing happens in her world that does not deserve to happen. Good fortune eludes her people, and catastrophe usually eludes them as well; but nearby, perhaps only a few miles away, the world may be coming tragically unhinged.

She is an original, though she is also a "Southern" writer. If her world comes to seem familiar to us, we must remember that it has been made familiar, even predictable, by her graceful art; in reality, the community of Banner and its fundamentalist Christianity is as remote to most of us as an African nation. Their typical acquiescence to fate is equally remote. The domesticity of their preoccupations puzzles us. And the complicated family connections! Their everlasting concern with one another and with anecdotes from their common past! We find ourselves charmed by all this, gradually, and so it is something of a shock to discover that the beautiful Mrs. Renfro, the ex-schoolteacher, Gloria, feels an almost desperate impatience with this web of love, a desire to break free, to be—perhaps—as free as the rest of us.

Eudora Welty is only partly informed by the kind of intelligent, satirical graciousness we associate with Jane Austen. In many of her short stories—the famous "Petrified Man" or "Why I Live at the P.O." or "A Curtain of Green"—she reveals a sense of terror that is sharpened by humor, the kind of abrupt, comic-strip juxtaposing of pain and farce that so influenced Flannery O'Connor. And, in an amiable, chatty, domestic novel like *Delta Wedding,* she is not to be trusted; she shares certain preoccupations with such ungenteel writers as Faulkner and Kafka, but the terror in Miss Welty is perhaps more bitter because it is so sweetly absorbed by the constant bustle of females in their production of food and love. In *Delta Wedding,* a beautiful, headstrong young girl (rather like Gloria of *Losing Battles*) prepares for her wedding, is fussed over, bullied, and loved; another girl, a stranger, an outsider who never appears in the novel but is simply mentioned (she is killed by a train) does not count at all. Why is one human being valued so highly, and another human being valued not at all? Why does society protect one and exclude the other, loving one and destroying the other? Eudora Welty does not answer these questions, nor does she ask them; she causes them to be asked.

There is nothing simple about her vision of life. It is many-faceted, it cannot be reduced to any helpful, minimal statement. So far as I can judge, she has no "ideas" whatsoever. She has no political or spiritual arguments. She has no social arguments. She is aware of, but does not insist upon, the injustices of the economic establishment. And what of her philosophical tone? The tone of "The Petrified Man" and that of "The Bride of the Innisfallen" are quite different; the tone of *Losing Battles* and that of a recent, marvelous story, "The Demonstrators" (anthologized as the winner of the 1968 O. Henry Prize), are quite different. And yet, one knows immediately that these works are by Eudora Welty.

How to assess this new novel? Well, it is not a work that will appeal to everyone. It does not seem to me as successful a novel as *Delta Wedding*, nor is it as warmly comic and appealing as *The Ponder Heart*. Its serious social and psychological concerns are muted, and so it must depend a great deal upon interludes of comedy and charm (there is, perhaps, too much made of the innocent prettiness of starched dresses and the ubiquitous baby, Lady May Renfro, and the casual give-and-take of family life). Miss Welty has taken on a difficult task, to narrow so deliberately her range of vision, to strain her talent for dialogue to its utmost, to put so much dramatic weight upon characters that are appealing, but do not emerge as especially memorable or even very eccentric. Yet the novel mystifies, it insists upon its own integrity—the absolute value of these simpleminded Renfros and their problems. We come to believe in them. They convince us of their existence.

What Eudora Welty has said of Jane Austen is true for her own art:

> ...the more original the work of imagination, the greater the danger of its succumbing to the violence of transportation. Insomuch as it is alive, it must remain fixed in its own time and place, whole and intact, inviolable as a diamond. It abides in its own element, and this of course is the mind....Jane Austen cannot follow readers into any other time....It is not her world or her time, but her art, that is approachable. The novels in their radiance are a destination.

Chronology of Important Dates

1894, Aug. 24	Jean Rhys born (Welsh father, Creole mother) in Roseau, Dominica, West Indies.
1909, April 13	Eudora Welty born in Jackson, Miss.
1910	Rhys moves to England.
1911, Oct. 12	Ann Petry born (Ann Lane) in Old Saybrook, Conn.
1912, June 21	Mary McCarthy born in Seattle, Wash.
1918	Muriel Spark born.
1919, July 15	Iris Murdoch born in Dublin, Ireland.
1919, Oct. 22	Doris Lessing born in Persia.
1927	*The Left Bank and Other Stories* (Rhys; preface by Ford Madox Ford).
1928	*Postures* (Rhys; U.S. title, *Quartet*).
1929	Welty receives B.A., University of Wisconsin.
1930	*After Leaving Mr. Mackenzie* (Rhys).
1930-31	Welty attends Columbia School of Advertising.
1931	Petry receives Ph.G., University of Connecticut; practices as pharmacist, 1931-38.
1933	McCarthy receives Vassar B.A., marries Harold Johnsrud, actor and playwright; later divorced. Lessing leaves Girls' High School in Salisbury, Southern Rhodesia.

1934   *Voyage in the Dark* (Rhys).

1938   Petry marries George D. Petry, by whom she has one daughter; works for next six years as advertising saleswoman and newspaper reporter.

McCarthy marries Edmund Wilson, by whom she has one son; later divorced.

Spark marries, has one son; later divorced.

1939   Lessing marries Frank Wisdom, by whom she has two children; later divorced.

1939   *Good Morning, Midnight* (Rhys).

May 6. Margaret Drabble born in Sheffield, England.

1941   *A Curtain of Green* (Welty, stories).

1942   *The Robber Bridegroom* (Welty); *The Company She Keeps* (McCarthy).

Murdoch receives degree in philosophy, Somerville College, Oxford; works in political administrative positions until 1947, when she takes a studentship in philosophy at Cambridge University.

1945   Lessing marries Gottfried Lessing, has one son; later divorced.

1946   *The Street* (Petry).

1947   Rhys marries Max Hamer, Dutch poet, now deceased; has one daughter.

Country Place (Petry).

1948   Murdoch made fellow, St. Anne's College, Oxford.

1949   *The Golden Apples* (Welty); *The Oasis* (McCarthy).

1950   *The Grass Is Singing* (Lessing); *Cast A Cold Eye* (McCarthy).

1952   *The Groves of Academe* (McCarthy); *Martha Quest* (Lessing; Part I, *Children of Violence*).

1953   *The Narrows* (Petry, who also published four children's books between 1949 and 1970); *Sartre, Romantic Rationalist* (Murdoch).

1954   *The Ponder Heart* (Welty); *Under the Net* (Murdoch); *A Proper Marriage* (Lessing; *Children of Violence*, II); *The*

Comforters (Spark, who became a convert to Roman Catholicism at this time and began writing novels, having previously published poetry and critical prose).

1955   *The Bride of the Innisfallen and Other Stories* (Welty); *A Charmed Life* (McCarthy).

1956   *The Flight from the Enchanter* (Murdoch); Murdoch marries John Oliver Bayley, novelist, poet, critic.

1957   *The Sandcastle* (Murdoch); *Memories of a Catholic Girlhood* (McCarthy); *Place in Fiction* (Welty, lectures).

1958   *A Ripple from the Storm* (Lessing, *Children of Violence*, III); *Robinson, Memento Mori* (Spark); *The Bell* (Murdoch).

1960   *The Ballad of Peckham Rye, The Bachelors* (Spark); Drabble receives B.A., Newnham College, Cambridge; marries Clive Walter Swift, actor with Royal Shakespeare Company, by whom she has four children.

1961   *The Prime of Miss Jean Brodie* (Spark).

1962   *The Golden Notebook* (Lessing).

1963   *A Man and Two Women* (Lessing, stories); *A Summer Bird-Cage* (Drabble); *The Group* (McCarthy); *The Unicorn* (Murdoch); Murdoch becomes lecturer at Royal College of Art (through 1967).

1965   *The Millstone* (Drabble); *The Mandelbaum Gate* (Spark); *The Red and the Green* (Murdoch).

1966   *Wordsworth* (Drabble, criticism); *Wide Sargasso Sea* (Rhys).

1967   *Jerusalem the Golden* (Drabble).

1968   *Tigers Are Better-Looking* (Rhys, stories).

1969   *The Waterfall* (Drabble); *Landlocked* (Lessing, *Children of Violence*, IV), *The Four-Gated City* (*Children of Violence*, V).

1970   *The Driver's Seat* (Spark); *Losing Battles* (Welty).

1971   *Not to Disturb* (Spark); *Miss Muriel and Other Stories* (Petry); *Birds of America* (McCarthy); *An Accidental Man* (Murdoch); *Briefing for a Descent into Hell* (Lessing).

1972   *The Needle's Eye* (Drabble); *The Optimist's Daughter* (Welty).

1973   *The Summer Before the Dark* (Lessing).

1974   *Memoirs of a Survivor* (Lessing); *The Abbess of Crewe* (Spark);
          The Sacred and Profane Love Machine (Murdoch); *The Mask
          of State: Watergate Portraits* (McCarthy); *Arnold Bennett*
          (Drabble; biography).

1975   *The Realms of Gold* (Drabble); *A Word Child* (Murdoch).

Notes on the Editor and Contributors

PATRICIA MEYER SPACKS, Professor of English at Wellesley College, has written extensively about autobiographies and fiction by women.

DAGMAR BARNOUW is Associate Professor of German Literature at Purdue University.

VIRGINIA K. BEARDS teaches English at the Delaware County Campus of Pennsylvania State University.

MALCOLM BRADBURY, Professor of American Studies at the University of East Anglia, has written several books of fiction and criticism, including *Possibilities: Essays on the State of the Novel.*

JOHN EDWARD HARDY, Head of the English Department, University of Southern Alabama, writes often on modern fiction; his books include *Man in the Modern Novel.*

FREDERICK R. KARL is Director of Graduate Studies in English at City College, CUNY, and author of several studies of nineteenth- and twentieth-century fiction, including *The Contemporary English Novel.*

LINDA V. KUEHL, who teaches writing at the New School, is the author of a biography of Billie Holiday to be published in spring, 1977.

NORMAN MAILER, novelist, short story writer, and social critic, has written about many aspects of contemporary life.

ELGIN W. MELLOWN (Professor of English, Duke University) has published studies of Edwin Muir and of the twentieth-century novel.

JOYCE CAROL OATES, a prolific writer of fiction, poetry, and criticism, teaches English at the University of Windsor, Ontario.

THELMA J. SHINN teaches English at Westfield State College, Westfield, Mass.; she is author of a study of Henry James.

Selected Bibliography

Margaret Drabble

Hardin, N. S. "Drabble's *The Millstone:* A Fable for Our Times." *Critique* 15 (1973): 22-34. Interprets the novel as a latter-day moral tale, engaging existential issues and exploring possibilities of freedom.

Libby, M. V. "Fate and Feminism in the Novels of Margaret Drabble." *Contemporary Literature* 16 (1975): 175-92. Perceiving Drabble as possessed by an "almost seventeenth-century version of fatalism," the critic dwells particularly on *The Needle's Eye,* with its dramatized tension between circumstance and individual will, a peculiarly female dilemma at its center.

Rose, E. C. "Margaret Drabble: Surviving the Future." *Critique* 15 (1973): 5-21. Drabble's novels investigate the relation of illusion and reality, specifically with regard to protagonists' dreams of future possibility.

Doris Lessing

Brewster, Dorothy. *Doris Lessing* (New York: Twayne, 1965). A biographical and critical introduction, with stress on the importance of ideas in Lessing's fiction.

Burkom, Selma R. *Doris Lessing: A Checklist of Primary and Secondary Sources.* Troy, N.Y.: Whitston Publishing Co., 1973.

― ― ―. "'Only Connect': Form and Content in the Works of Doris Lessing," *Critique* 11 (1968): 51-68. Concentrates on the relation of the individual to society in Lessing's work.

Contemporary Literature 15 (1973): 418-97. Issue devoted to Lessing, including essays on the novels, an interview with the author, and a bibliographical checklist. Republished as L. S. Dembo and A. Pratt, eds., *Doris Lessing: Critical Essays,* Madison, Wisc.: University of Wisconsin Press, 1974.

Lessing, Doris. "On *The Golden Notebook.*" *Partisan Review* 40 (Winter, 1973): 14-30. Author claims that this novel did not issue from Women's Liberation movement, but was written to explore problems of fragmentation and freedom; its form contains its meaning.

Markow, Alice. "The Pathology of Feminine Failure in the Fiction of Doris Lessing." *Critique* 16 (1974): 88-100. Understands novels as arguing that women must surmount their nostalgia for dependence.

Ryf, Robert S. "Beyond Ideology: Doris Lessing's Mature Vision." *Modern Fiction Studies* 21 (1975): 193-202. Sees an "evolution beyond ideology toward existence" in Lessing's late novels, with increasing distrust of abstractions.

Schlueter, Paul. *The Novels of Doris Lessing.* Carbondale: Southern Illinois University Press, 1973. A study of themes in Lessing's fiction.

Spilka, Mark, "Lessing and Lawrence: The Battle of the Sexes." *Contemporary Literature* 16 (1975): 218-40. Discovers a continuity of concern between the Lawrence of *Women in Love* and Lessing in *The Golden Notebook,* finding Lessing better at rendering female experience. Defines nature of Lessing's "modern sensibility."

Thorpe, Michael. *Doris Lessing.* Harlow, Essex: published for the British Council by Longman Group, 1973. Brief general introduction with selected bibliography.

Mary McCarthy

Chamberlain, John. "The Novels of Mary McCarthy." *The Creative Present,* Edited by Nona Balakian and Charles Simmons, pp. 241-55. New York: Doubleday, 1963. Sees McCarthy as an essentially conservative satirist, partaking of the tradition of Jane Austen, who has not yet found an adequate subject.

Goldman, Sherll E. *Mary McCarthy: A Bibliography.* New York: Harcourt, Brace and World, 1968.

Grumbach, Doris. *The Company She Kept.* New York: Coward-McCann, 1967. Primarily biographical, with some rather sketchy criticism.

Niebuhr, E. "Mary McCarthy." *Writers At Work,* 2nd ser., pp. 283-315. New York: Viking, 1963. An interview about McCarthy's life and work.

Podhoretz, Norman. "John O'Hara and Mary McCarthy." *Doings and Undoings,* pp. 76-93. New York: Farrar, Straus, 1964. On *A Charmed Life* and *The Group,* praising the former for its dramatization of the conflict between reason and impulse, damning the latter for triviality.

180   *Mary McCarthy*

Schlueter, Paul. "The Dissections of Mary McCarthy." *Contemporary American Novelists.* Edited by Harry T. Moore, pp. 54-64. Carbondale, Ill.: Southern Illinois University Press, 1964. Dissection of social pretense and hypocrisy is central to McCarthy's work, but her novels are "ultimately sterile and animalistic."

Stock, Irvin. *Mary McCarthy.* Minneapolis: University of Minnesota Press, 1968. Brief critical introduction contains selected bibliography.

Iris Murdoch

Byatt, A. S. *Degrees of Freedom: The Novels of Iris Murdoch.* New York: Barnes and Noble, 1965. Detailed critical study of the novels in relation to Murdoch's articulated philosophic positions.

Gindin, James. "Images of Illusion in the Work of Iris Murdoch." *Postwar British Fiction,* pp. 178-95. Berkeley: University of California Press, 1962. The novelist dwells on the human attempt to live by structures of illusion in a fragmented world, analyzing the tendency toward "ratiocinative pretense."

Hall, James. "Blurring the Will: Iris Murdoch." *The Lunatic Giant in the Drawing Room,* pp. 181-212. Bloomington: Indiana University Press, 1968. Sees in Murdoch a "mind determined to find imaginative equivalents for a changing view of reality and wish," — a mind whose novels of conflicting forces are dominated by "confidence in the play of intelligence."

Kermode, Frank. "House of Fiction: Interviews with Seven English Novelists." *Partisan Review* 30 (1963). Includes comments by Murdoch (pp. 62-65) and by Muriel Spark (pp. 79-82) about their theories of fiction-writing.

Modern Fiction Studies 15 (1969): 335-457. Entire issue on fiction by Murdoch, including checklist of critical studies.

Rabinovitz, Rubin. *Iris Murdoch.* New York: Columbia University Press, 1968. Introductory critical essay; contains selected bibliography.

Scholes, Robert. *The Fabulators,* pp. 106-34. New York: Oxford University Press, 1967. Full examination of the structure and meaning of *The Unicorn,* which Scholes sees as modern allegory.

Wolfe, Peter. *The Disciplined Heart: Iris Murdoch and Her Novels.* Columbia, Mo.: University of Missouri Press, 1966. Critical study of Murdoch's first eight novels, emphasizing her role as philosopher and social critic.

Ann Petry

Bone, Robert A. *The Negro Novel in America,* pp. 180-85. New Haven: Yale University Press, 1958. Brief biographical sketch; critical analysis concentrating on *Country Place,* understood to focus on theme of lost illusion.

Ivy, James. "Ann Petry Talks About Her First Novel." *Crisis* 53 (1946): 48-49. Popularized interview.

Rosenblatt, Roger. *Black Fiction,* pp. 137-42. Cambridge: Harvard University Press, 1974. Sees *Country Place* as confronting the problem, "How does a people needing and seeking a past find one in a country which denies the value of the past?"

Jean Rhys

Allen, Walter. Review of *Wide Sargasso Sea, New York Times Book Review,* June 18, 1967, p. 5. Rhys has received almost no critical attention except in reviews. This representative example comments on the typical Rhys heroine as a passive figure doomed to destruction by men.

Miles, Rosalind. *The Fiction of Sex: Themes and Functions of Sex Difference in the Modern Novel,* pp. 96-106. New York: Barnes and Noble, 1974. The central theme of Rhys's fiction is "that women are permanent and perpetual victims of masculine society."

Wyndham, Francis. Introduction to *Wide Sargasso Sea,* pp. 5-13. New York: Norton, 1967. Although brief, the most important critical appreciation of Rhys, arguing that she was not adequately valued in the twenties because she was ahead of her time. The central figure in her fiction is always "a victim of men's incomprehension of women, a symptom of women's mistrust of men."

Muriel Spark

Berthoff, Warner. "Fortunes of the Novel: Muriel Spark and Iris Murdoch." *Massachusetts Review* 8 (1967): 301-32. Detailed comparison of Spark and Murdoch, centering on *The Mandelbaum Gate* and *The Red and the Green,* as exemplifying the contemporary willingness not to attempt the creation of asterpieces; finds Spark empty "at the center," Murdoch more seriously engaged with real issues.

Greene, George. "A Reading of Muriel Spark." *Thought* 43 (1968): 393-407. The formal strategies of Spark's novels reflect her metaphysical convictions.

Hoyt, Charles Alva. "Muriel Spark: The Surrealist Jane Austen." *Contemporary British Novelists*. Edited by Charles Shapiro, pp. 125-43. Carbondale: Southern Illinois University Press, 1965. "Mischief" is Spark's key quality; her "meticulous ironic intelligence" presides over a surrealist world.

Kemp, Peter. *Muriel Spark*. New York: Barnes and Noble, 1975. Detailed and enthusiastic analyses of the novels in sequence through 1973.

Malkoff, Karl. *Muriel Spark*. New York: Columbia University Press, 1968. Introductory critical essay; contains selected bibliography.

Ohmann, Carol. "Muriel Spark's *Robinson.*" *Critique* 8 (1965): 70-85. Detailed reading of the novel as a pattern of formal discipline suggesting Spark's later technical development.

Richmond, V. B. "The Darkening Vision of Muriel Spark." *Critique* 15 (1973): 71-85. Spark's later novels increasingly stress the crassness, mindlessness, and evil of the contemporary world.

Stubbs, Patricia. *Muriel Spark*. Harlow, Essex: published for the British Council by Longman Group, 1973. General critical introduction; selected bibliography.

Eudora Welty

Appel, Alfred. *A Season of Dreams: The Fiction of Eudora Welty*. Baton Rouge: Louisiana State University Press, 1965. Emphasizes the special world evoked by Welty's fiction, offering detailed analyses of individual works.

Bryant, J. A., Jr. *Eudora Welty*. Minneapolis: University of Minnesota Press, 1968. Brief general introduction, with selected bibliography.

Bryant, J. A., Jr. "Seeing Double in *The Golden Apples.*" *Sewanee Review* 82 (1974): 300-15. A significant force for unity in this curious work of Welty's is "a special way of seeing, or perceiving, which conditions in some degree the total vision of most of the principal characters."

Howell, Elmo. "Eudora Welty's Comedy of Manners." *South Atlantic Quarterly* 69 (1970): 469-70. Welty's concern with tradition expresses itself, in *Delta Wedding*, through detailed attention to family history and the complexities of relationship.

McMillen, William E. "Conflict and Resolution in Welty's *Losing Battles.*" *Critique* 15 (1973): 110-24. Central conflicts of novel involve clashing life-styles and the struggle of husband and wife.

Rubin, Louis. "The Golden Apples of the Sun." *Writers of the Modern South: The Faraway Country,* pp. 131-54. Seattle: University of Washington Press, 1963. Argues that in scope and insight, *Delta Wedding* and *The Golden Apples* merit comparison with Faulkner.

Shenandoah 20 (Spring, 1969). Entire issue on Welty, concentrating on short fiction but including essay by author.

Vande Kieft, Ruth M. *Eudora Welty.* New York: Twayne, 1962. A demonstration of the variety of Welty's art, focused mainly on short stories which establish writer's dominant themes and techniques.